Investigating Change
Web-based Analyses of US Census and American Community Survey Data

THIRD EDITION

William H. Frey
University of Michigan

Written in collaboration with

**Stephanie Somerman, John P. DeWitt, and
Associates of the Social Science Data Analysis Network**

WADSWORTH
CENGAGE Learning™

Australia • Brazil • Japan • Korea • Mexico • Singapore • Spain • United Kingdom • United States

For product information and technology assistance, contact us at **Cengage Learning Customer & Sales Support, 1-800-354-9706**

For permission to use material from this text or product, submit all requests online at **www.cengage.com/permissions** Further permissions questions can be emailed to **permissionrequest@cengage.com**

ISBN-13: 978-0-8400-3253-9
ISBN-10: 0-8400-3253-6

Wadsworth
20 Davis Drive
Belmont, CA 94002-3098
USA

Cengage Learning is a leading provider of customized learning solutions with office locations around the globe, including Singapore, the United Kingdom, Australia, Mexico, Brazil, and Japan. Locate your local office at: **www.cengage.com/global**

Cengage Learning products are represented in Canada by Nelson Education, Ltd.

To learn more about Wadsworth, visit **www.cengage.com/wadsworth**

Purchase any of our products at your local college store or at our preferred online store **www.cengagebrain.com**

Printed in the United States of America
1 2 3 4 5 6 7 14 13 12 11 10

CONTENTS

PREFACE

This book's approach is based on the premise that engaging, hands-on data analysis cannot be introduced early enough into the social science curriculum. Or, to borrow the motto of a well-known athletic shoe company, "Just do it!" The investigations in this book were intentionally developed to be accessible, relevant, and user-friendly enough (that is, both student-friendly and teacher-friendly) for use in a wide range of substantive courses in sociology and related disciplines.

How to Use This Book in Your Course

The subjects covered in this book can be integrated into courses on a variety of topics, including introductory sociology, social problems, the family, social stratification, racial/ethnic studies, gender studies, demography, research methods, and American society. To incorporate the topics included in this book into your course, you can mix and match the chapters so that they follow the logic of your syllabus. For example, a course on the family might use Chapter Five: Marriage, Divorce, and Cohabitation; Chapter Seven: Households and Families; Chapter Eight: Poverty; and Chapter Nine: Children, while a course in social stratification might use Chapter Two: Racial/Ethnic Inequality; Chapter Three: Immigrant Assimilation; Chapter Four: Labor Force; Chapter Six: Gender Inequality; and Chapter Eight: Poverty. You can choose the chapters you will use according to the goals you have for your course, and you can present them in whatever order most successfully achieves these goals. Furthermore, the subjects covered in each chapter are presented in a manner that makes them flexible enough to be used with a variety of texts and readings on the same subject.

The subject matter within each chapter follows a sequence consistent with the way in which the topic at hand is typically covered in existing courses. For example, Chapter Two: Racial/Ethnic Inequality and Chapter Six: Gender Inequality follow the classic status attainment model that relates gender and race differences in earnings to differences in education and occupation. The inequalities in both are first explored with respect to educational attainment, then occupation, then earnings. Students will develop the skills they need to test and prove theories by going through the exercises in this order.

At the end of each chapter there are Think Tank questions, which are less structured than the discussion sections that follow each section and can be the basis for class dialogue or team-based reports. Please feel free to design your own questions with the datasets that are provided for use with this book. The possibilities are nearly unlimited! The last section of the book, titled "Guide to Datasets," contains a complete list of all the datasets and variables used in this book. Also at the back of the book, you will find a list of useful web sites with brief descriptions of the resources they offer. These materials are also available on the textbook website, http://www.cengage.com/sociology/frey.

Unique Features

One distinguishing feature of this book is its use of trend data from 1950 through present day, with data from US decennial censuses and the American Community Survey. These data have been carefully compiled to examine significant societal trends, and are organized into datasets that focus on the chapter topics and related issues. This book takes special advantage of rich American Community Survey (ACS) data to investigate current issues and social differences. After the 2000 Census, the US Census Bureau decided to put most of its detailed questions on this annual survey, allowing us to update our datasets more frequently. Thus all current data in this workbook are drawn from recently compiled ACS data.

Different broad topics are covered in separate chapters. In Chapter Three, students are able to compare the relationship between duration in the US and immigrant assimilation with respect to occupation, earnings, and English language proficiency for specific Latin American- and Asian-origin groups. In Chapter Six, they can assess gender inequality in earnings for men and women in specific occupations such as full-time year-round physicians. Because census concepts are nearly universally recognized and stay fairly constant over time, we are able to introduce a Key Concepts section in each Chapter that defines in simple terms how concepts like poverty, the family, and labor force are utilized by social scientists.

A word about the computer software: because of my interest in making these investigations readily accessible, the choice of software was an important concern when designing this book. With the idea that the programs used should be as easy as possible for students to "get into," I have chosen to use the data analysis program WebCHIP—a web-based counterpart to the popular StudentCHIP program. Most students will be able to learn the basic features of the WebCHIP software in a single class session. The simple interface of WebCHIP makes it especially suited to our exercises based on the analysis of tables, with one or more control variables. For a beginner, this approach is more than sufficient to grasp the logic of analyzing data without encountering the burdens of "higher level" statistics. To further aid to the student's understanding of the data analysis process, most of the exercises are centered on graphing, asking students to translate their tables into line graphs, bar charts or pie charts that facilitate interpretation. The whole system is so intuitive that a little practice and an hour spent with our web-based tutorials are all that is needed to get going.

Expanded Online Capabilities

An important feature with this edition of the book allows students to conduct their analysis directly on the web. The internet-based WebCHIP version of the traditional StudentCHIP software permits students to access datasets and create tables on any computer that has an Internet connection. Moreover, the textbook homepage at http://www.cengage.com/sociology/frey lets the student access all of the data simply and directly. In addition, this site also offers a number of tutorials, references, aids, and analysis tools that will come in handy for you and your students.

SSDAN Faculty Network

In the early 1990s, with help from grants from the Department of Education FIPSE and the NSF Department of Undergraduate Education, I began to establish a network of faculty interested in sharing experiences and trading exercises using the quantitative approach embodied in this book. Today, the Social Science Data Analysis Network (SSDAN) includes hundreds of faculty members in all fifty states and several foreign countries. The SSDAN office at the University of Michigan produces a wide variety of demographic media, including user guides, websites, and hands-on computer classroom materials, all designed to make U.S. Census data and similar information accessible to students and teachers alike. On the SSDAN website, http://www.ssdan.net, you can connect with other faculty using this book to trade exercises and download additional WebCHIP datasets. You can also request to receive an email newsletter a few times a year, updating you on SSDAN programs and projects.

"Just Do It!"

This brings me back to my "just do it" philosophy. Based on more than two decades of firsthand experience here at Michigan and that related to me by dozens of other faculty, I can tell you that it works to introduce data analysis exercises into introductory courses, and substantive courses taken by freshmen, sophomores, and juniors. By marrying data analysis to engaging substantive questions and issues, students at all levels come to appreciate why empirical evidence is important and can actually have fun doing it. I invite your comments, criticisms, and shared experiences about your use of these materials in your class.

ACKNOWLEDGMENTS

By one way of reckoning, this book has been in the works for over two decades. In 1987, the University's Provost office awarded me an Undergraduate Initiatives grant to develop a then-innovative course to introduce data analysis to sociology undergraduates at an early stage. Sociology 231, "Investigating Social and Demographic Change in America," became a regular course offering thanks to the support of the Department of Sociology and the Population Studies Center at the Institute for Social Research.

Along the way, we have been able to disseminate computer materials consistent with this approach to other campuses, first with a grant from the Alfred P. Sloan Foundation. Later, with a grant from the US Department of Education FIPSE, a formal tie-in was established with the Great Lakes Colleges Association (GLCA) and a more broad-based national distribution was facilitated by grants from the National Science Foundation, Division of Undergraduate Education. Together, these dissemination activities have helped to create the Social Science Data Analysis Network (www.ssdan.net) discussed in the Preface.

Front Row: John DeWitt, Joel Ruhter, Zach Martin, Clark Frye, Lauren Johns, Olivia Lopez, and Sarah Parsons
Back Row: Jane Shim, Jessica Malouf, and Christina Zajicek
Not Pictured: Stephanie Somerman

With subsequent NSF support, we joined forces with the American Sociological Association to integrate our approach into undergraduate curricula on a department-wide basis. And more recently, in partnership with the Interuniversity Consortium for Political and Social Research, we received support in the form of NSF Course, Curriculum, and Laboratory Improvement grant NSF-0816517, which allows us to update this book with recent data from the

US Census Bureau's American Community Survey and provide ancillary instructional activities.

This book could not have been written without the support of our editors at Wadsworth/Cengage Learning, including Erin Mitchell, who guided the current edition, and Eve Howard and Bob Jucha for earlier editions. Ruth Bogart, founding president of Zeta Data, Inc. has been wonderfully cooperative in helping us link WebCHIP with our datasets.

The production of this book's third edition, like those before it, was a local team effort involving University of Michigan students and associates of the Social Science Data Analysis Network (SSDAN). Assisting me in team coordination for this edition were Stephanie Somerman and John Paul DeWitt whose leadership and efforts were essential toward introducing current American Community Survey data into the website and analysis exercises. This work builds on that of Cheryl First-Bornstein, team coordinator of the first edition who helped to turn the initial concept of this book into a reality; and Tarek Anandan and Megan Cook, team coordinators of the second edition, who guided the transition to web-based data access.

SSDAN Programmers: Aidan Feldman, Aravindh Baskaran, and Sui Yan

Stephanie and John spent long hours in coordinating the tasks of our team in efforts to both extend our US Census data time series from 1950 to 2000 to incorporate recent American Community Survey data, and update the content as well as the "look and feel" of the text. Assisting with updating the text and figures were Lauren Johns, Jessica Malouf, Olivia Lopez, Sarah Parsons, Jane Shim, Zach Martin, Clark Frye, Christina Zajicek, and Joel Ruhter.

I am especially grateful to Cathy Sun, senior computer scientist at the Population Studies Center, and an expert in census concepts and data, who assembled the data sets for our exercises, from microfiles of decennial censuses from 1950 through 2000 and the recent American Community Survey. Finally, I am indebted to all the students who have taken Sociology 231 since its first offering in 1987, as their ideas, feedback and comments are reflected in the Investigations and chapters that follow.

William H. Frey
Population Studies Center | Institute for Social Research
Department of Sociology | University of Michigan
Director, Social Science Data Analysis Network (www.SSDAN.net)

SECTION I
Overview and Getting Started

TIMELINE
WWII through the 1950s

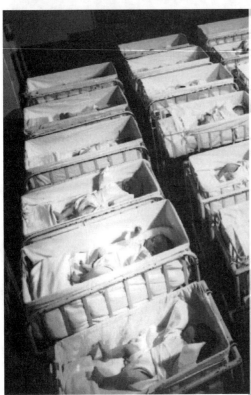

1945 — Germany surrenders, ending the war in Europe.

1945 — Japan surrenders four months later, end of World War II.

1946 — The Baby Boom begins.

1946 — Dr. Benjamin Spock's *The Common Sense Book of Baby and Child Care* is published.

1947 — Jackie Robinson signs with the Brooklyn Dodgers.

1947 — *Howdy Doody* premieres on TV.

1948 — The McDonald brothers open their first restaurant in San Bernardino, California.

1950 — Korean War begins.

1951 — *I Love Lucy* premieres on TV.

1952 — *The Adventures of Ozzie and Harriet* debuts.

1952 — Dwight D. Eisenhower elected President.

1952 — Passage of the McCarran-Walter Act, which delineates the Asia-Pacific Triangle and establishes a quota system for countries within this triangle.

1953 — Refugee Relief Act passed, admitting 214,000 more refugees into the U.S.

1953 — Congress creates the Department of Health, Education and Welfare.

1953 — Korean War ends.

1954 — In *Brown vs. Board of Education of Topeka, Kansas*, the Supreme Court declares segregation in public schools unconstitutional.

1954 — C.A. Swanson and Son introduce frozen dinners.

1954 — Elvis Presley's first professional record released.

1955 — Rosa Parks begins Montgomery, Alabama bus boycott.

1955 — Disneyland opens outside Los Angeles.

1955 — The song "Rock Around the Clock" begins the rock era.

1955 — *The Mickey Mouse Club Show* begins on afternoon TV.

1957 — Dr. Seuss publishes *The Cat in the Hat*.

1957 — *Leave It to Beaver* debuts on TV.

1957 — Vietnam War begins.

1957 — President Eisenhower orders federal troops to Little Rock, Arkansas to prevent interference with school integration at Central High School.

1959 — Mattel Inc. introduces Barbie doll.

TIMELINE

1960s

1960s — Motown music becomes popular.

1960 — John F. Kennedy elected President.

1960 — The first oral contraceptive pill sold in the U.S.

1962 — James Meredith escorted by federal marshals to the University of Mississippi campus.

1963 — 250,000 march in D.C. for civil rights; Martin L. King, Jr. gives "I have a Dream" speech.

1963 — John F. Kennedy assassinated; Lyndon B. Johnson sworn in as President.

1963 — *The Feminine Mystique* published.

1964 — Baby Boom ends.

1964 — Civil Rights Act of 1964 prohibits discrimination in public places based on race, color, religion, national origin and gender, and creates the Equal Employment and Opportunity Commission.

1964 — The Beatles' first visit to the U.S.

1964 — Ford Mustang introduced at the World's Fair.

1965 — President Johnson sends U.S. Marines to Da Nang, Vietnam.

1965 — Voting Rights Act of 1965 makes literacy tests for voter registration illegal.

1965 — Immigration and Naturalization Act eliminates restrictive racial and ethnic quotas.

1965 — Medicaid, Medicare and Head Start programs begin as a part of the Great Society's War on Poverty.

1965 — Riots in Watts, L.A., and other cities leave fifty-five dead and cause 200 million dollars in damages.

1966 — Psychedelic music by artists like Janis Joplin and Jimi Hendrix becomes popular.

1967 — *The Graduate*, starring Dustan Hoffman, is released.

1967 — 17,000 Americans have died in Vietnam since 1961.

1967 — President Lyndon Johnson appoints Thurgood Marshall to the Supreme Court.

1967 — Martin L. King, Jr. assassinated.

1968 — Richard M. Nixon elected President.

1969 — Neil A. Armstrong becomes first person to walk on moon.

1969 — The Woodstock festival draws upwards of 300,000 young people to upstate New York.

1969 — *The Brady Bunch* and *Sesame Street* debut on TV.

TIMELINE

1970s

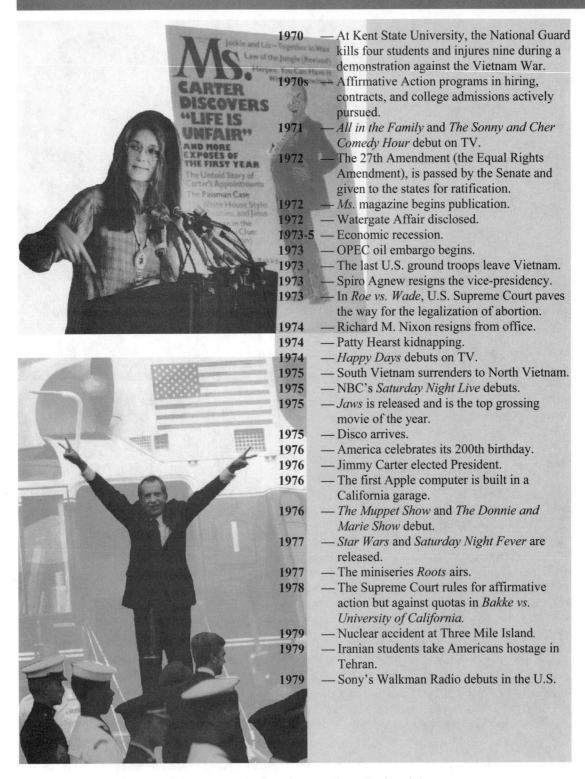

1970	— At Kent State University, the National Guard kills four students and injures nine during a demonstration against the Vietnam War.
1970s	— Affirmative Action programs in hiring, contracts, and college admissions actively pursued.
1971	— *All in the Family* and *The Sonny and Cher Comedy Hour* debut on TV.
1972	— The 27th Amendment (the Equal Rights Amendment), is passed by the Senate and given to the states for ratification.
1972	— *Ms.* magazine begins publication.
1972	— Watergate Affair disclosed.
1973-5	— Economic recession.
1973	— OPEC oil embargo begins.
1973	— The last U.S. ground troops leave Vietnam.
1973	— Spiro Agnew resigns the vice-presidency.
1973	— In *Roe vs. Wade*, U.S. Supreme Court paves the way for the legalization of abortion.
1974	— Richard M. Nixon resigns from office.
1974	— Patty Hearst kidnapping.
1974	— *Happy Days* debuts on TV.
1975	— South Vietnam surrenders to North Vietnam.
1975	— NBC's *Saturday Night Live* debuts.
1975	— *Jaws* is released and is the top grossing movie of the year.
1975	— Disco arrives.
1976	— America celebrates its 200th birthday.
1976	— Jimmy Carter elected President.
1976	— The first Apple computer is built in a California garage.
1976	— *The Muppet Show* and *The Donnie and Marie Show* debut.
1977	— *Star Wars* and *Saturday Night Fever* are released.
1977	— The miniseries *Roots* airs.
1978	— The Supreme Court rules for affirmative action but against quotas in *Bakke vs. University of California.*
1979	— Nuclear accident at Three Mile Island.
1979	— Iranian students take Americans hostage in Tehran.
1979	— Sony's Walkman Radio debuts in the U.S.

TIMELINE

1980s

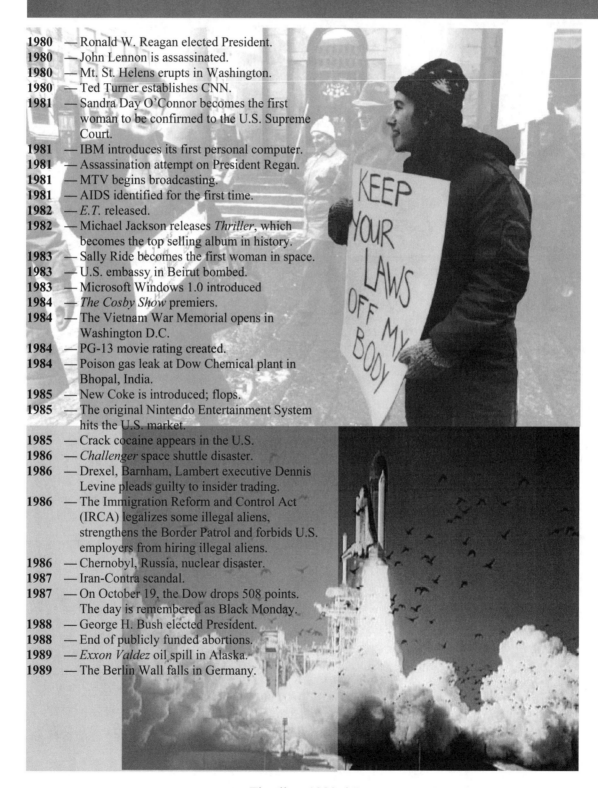

1980 — Ronald W. Reagan elected President.
1980 — John Lennon is assassinated.
1980 — Mt. St. Helens erupts in Washington.
1980 — Ted Turner establishes CNN.
1981 — Sandra Day O'Connor becomes the first woman to be confirmed to the U.S. Supreme Court.
1981 — IBM introduces its first personal computer.
1981 — Assassination attempt on President Regan.
1981 — MTV begins broadcasting.
1981 — AIDS identified for the first time.
1982 — *E.T.* released.
1982 — Michael Jackson releases *Thriller*, which becomes the top selling album in history.
1983 — Sally Ride becomes the first woman in space.
1983 — U.S. embassy in Beirut bombed.
1983 — Microsoft Windows 1.0 introduced
1984 — *The Cosby Show* premiers.
1984 — The Vietnam War Memorial opens in Washington D.C.
1984 — PG-13 movie rating created.
1984 — Poison gas leak at Dow Chemical plant in Bhopal, India.
1985 — New Coke is introduced; flops.
1985 — The original Nintendo Entertainment System hits the U.S. market.
1985 — Crack cocaine appears in the U.S.
1986 — *Challenger* space shuttle disaster.
1986 — Drexel, Barnham, Lambert executive Dennis Levine pleads guilty to insider trading.
1986 — The Immigration Reform and Control Act (IRCA) legalizes some illegal aliens, strengthens the Border Patrol and forbids U.S. employers from hiring illegal aliens.
1986 — Chernobyl, Russia, nuclear disaster.
1987 — Iran-Contra scandal.
1987 — On October 19, the Dow drops 508 points. The day is remembered as Black Monday.
1988 — George H. Bush elected President.
1988 — End of publicly funded abortions.
1989 — *Exxon Valdez* oil spill in Alaska.
1989 — The Berlin Wall falls in Germany.

TIMELINE

1990s

1989-93	— Recession
1990	— The Hubble Telescope launched into space.
1990	— Iraqi troops invade Kuwait.
1990	— *Seinfeld* debuts on TV.
1991	— Soviet Union collapses.
1991	— War begins in former Yugoslavia.
1991	— Iraqis accept a cease-fire agreement and the Persian Gulf War ends.
1992	— Bill Clinton elected President.
1992	— The Rodney King trial verdict sparks riots in L.A. and other cities.
1993	— Family Leave Act of 1993.
1993	— Raid on the Branch Davidian compound in Waco, Texas.
1994	— The Proposition 187 initiative, which denies illegal aliens public health, education and social services, is approved in California.
1994	— Whitewater scandal.
1994	— Major League Baseball players strike.
1995	— O.J. Simpson trial.
1995	— Oklahoma federal building bombed.
1995	— Violence Against Women Act passed.
1996	— First Baby Boomer turns 50.
1996	— Oakland, CA schools recognize "Ebonics" as a separate language.
1996	— Unabomber Ted Kaczynski arrested.
1996	— Welfare system overhauled under the Personal Responsibility and Work Opportunity Reconciliation Act
1998	— 2 American embassies in Africa bombed.
1998	— India and Pakistan test nuclear weapons.
1998	— Viagra hits the market.
1998	— President Clinton impeached.
1998	— *Titanic* becomes the top-grossing film of all time.
1999	— Columbine High School shootings in Littleton, Colorado.
1999	— Dot-com bubble bursts.
1999	— The Euro becomes the new European currency.

TIMELINE

2000 — George W. Bush elected president amid Florida vote-counting controversy

2001 — Terrorist-hijacked planes hit the Pentagon and Word Trade Center.

2002 — War in Afghanistan.

2003 — Second U.S.-led war in Iraq.

2003 — Space shuttle *Columbia* explodes.

2003 — The U.S. Supreme Court upholds affirmative action in higher education.

2003 — Saddam Hussein is found and captured by U.S. troops.

2004 — Former Enron CFO Andrew Fastow pleads guilty to defrauding Enron.

2004 — Massachusetts becomes first state to legalize gay marriage.

2004 — Tsunami, triggered by 2nd largest recorded earthquake, hits 11 Asian countries.

2005 — Pope John Paul II dies, Benedict XVI replaces him.

2005 — Hurricane Katrina hits the Gulf Coast.

2005 — Africa's first female head of state, Ellen Johnson Sirleaf elected.

2006 — Pluto is reclassified as a dwarf planet.

2006 — U.S. population officially reaches 300 million.

2006 — Saddam Hussein is executed in Iraq.

2007 — Nancy Pelosi becomes first female U.S. Speaker of the House of Representatives.

2007 — Virginia Tech shootings.

2007 — U.S. minimum wage increases from $5.15 to $5.85.

2007 — Al Gore wins Nobel Peace Prize for his effort increasing awareness of climate change.

2008 — Fidel Castro resigns as President of Cuba, replaced by his brother, Raul.

2008 — Earthquake kills thousands in China months before the Summer Olympics

2008 — California's Proposition 8 passes, outlawing same-sex marriage.

2008 — Barack Obama elected first African-American U.S. President.

2009 — Bernard Madoff sentenced to life in prison for Ponzi scheme.

2009 — Michael Jackson dies.

2009 — Nidal Malik Hasan, an army psychiatrist, opens fire at Ford Hood, TX, killing 13.

2009 — Minimum wage increased from $5.85 to $7.25.

2009 — President Barak Obama wins the Noble Peace Prize.

2010 — Earthquake of catastrophic magnitude hits Haiti kills hundreds of thousands.

INVESTIGATING CHANGE

American society has undergone remarkable transformation in the past sixty years. At each step throughout this transformation, a distinctive generation was born. Each generation has left its unique mark on American society, visible in the policies, attitudes, movements, creative expression, and ideals that characterize the decades. The relationship between social transformation and distinctive generations may be reciprocal: the times changed the people, and the people changed the times.

Today, we reflect upon the 1950s with nostalgia. It was a decade of abundance and complacency, characterized by a booming economy, "Leave it to Beaver" families flourishing in suburbia, and complacent youth enjoying the 'simplicity' of the Eisenhower years. But the children of the so-called "Greatest Generation" were also restless, looking up to rebels like James Dean and Jack Kerouac and listening to a new kind of music called rock-n-roll that foreshadowed the more socially rebellious times to come.

Indeed, it seems appropriate to characterize the Baby Boomers who came of age in the 1960s as rebellious. The Supreme Court decision in Brown vs. Board of Education and the Montgomery Bus Boycott launched the Civil Rights Movement and provided a new foundation with which the generation shaped its social consciousness. As the Boomer generation became an economic and political force in American society, the American Dream as a collective, self-centered pursuit was replaced by a largely generation-wide mobilization toward social justice and action. Throughout America, African Americans organized for enforcement of civil rights and the right to vote, college students mobilized in opposition to the Vietnam War, and new issues ranging from the environment to women's rights made their way onto the political agenda. The attention focused on these and other social issues led, in turn, to new legislation and increased federal spending on public welfare programs.

While much of the fervently optimistic, revolutionary idealism faded after the 1960s, the call for social justice and action did not. In contrast, it proliferated, forming the core of modern American liberalism. With the fading of optimism in the 1970s came a period of political pessimism and a harsher economic reality. The Watergate scandal that led to the resignation of President Richard Nixon broke American faith in government leadership, and the Ford and Carter administrations that followed were marked by rapidly rising inflation and unemployment that led to large-scale disappointment and stress as large numbers of baby-boomers, minorities and women entered the labor force. Fertility rates dropped, divorce rates rose, and unmarried singles put off the commitment of marriage.

With the 1980s, conservative leaders and religious groups ascended to national prominence amid economic recession and calls for a return to traditional morality. In this period, many Americans engaged in fierce moral debates, such as abortion rights, and watched in anticipation as the stock market rose to new heights. Minorities and the poor seemed to be left behind, and the wealthy didn't mind. Social and economic divisions between the 'haves' and 'have-nots' widened, benefitting the affluent minority while handicapping the poorer majority. As in the "affluent society" of the 1950s, few noticed the rising poverty rate and shrinking middle class, or predicted what would happen as a result.

In many ways, the 1990s were a period of political and social moderation that avoided the extremes of earlier years. The labor force experienced an influx of young adults from Generation X who tended to rely heavily on technological skills and to be more pragmatic about personal and professional goals. In 1992, the first Baby Boomer elected to the White House became President Bill Clinton. The Clinton Administration held to the middle of the political spectrum as both major parties attempted to capture independent voters. Presidential candidate Senator Robert Dole failed to convince Americans they should return to the "golden age" of the 1950s, and in 1996, voters elected Clinton to a second term. During his eight years in office, Clinton weathered a surprising number of scandals, indicating the degree to which the nation's expectations of its leaders had changed between the 1950s and the mid-1990s.

Though economic conditions were rosy for most Americans during the last half of the 1990s, African Americans and immigrants from Mexico, Latin America, and parts of Asia continued to lag behind the nation as a whole. The economy stumbled in the late 1990s as the dot-com bubble burst, a situation exacerbated by repercussions from the terrorist attacks on the World Trade Center on September 11th 2001 and the subsequent wars in Afghanistan and Iraq. These changes impacted all Americans, but tended to affect the poor and minorities most of all.

In the late 2000s, a wave of pessimism and disappointment once again swallowed America. President George W. Bush's popularity fell significantly due to his unpopular handling of the wars in Iraq and Afghanistan, the Abu-Ghraib scandal, both domestic and international policy, and the economy. In 2005, Hurricane Katrina devastated the Gulf Coast and government response proved to be neither timely nor well managed. Beginning in 2007, America became the source of the worst global economic recession since the Great Depression. The collapse of the global housing bubble led to significant decline in the stock trade. Economies worldwide suffered as credit tightened, international trade declined, unemployment rose and commodity prices slumped. Governments and central banks responded with unprecedented stimulus packages, institutional bailouts and monetary policy expansion. In 2009, the economy began showing small signs of improvement, but the U.S. has yet to regain financial standing. However, the pessimism resulting from the recession was countered, to some extent, by the 2008 election of Barack Obama, the first African-American president.

Today, many Americans look forward to the future with cautious optimism. If birth rates, an aging population, changing roles of women and families, where people live, and race have an impact on everyday life, then, as many have said, "demography is destiny." The lessons contained in this book may help you to better understand the shape of that future, and your own place within it.

PURPOSE OF THIS BOOK

As we've just seen, the late twentieth century was in many ways a period of remarkable change, which continues to reverberate through society today. To appreciate the divisions that currently exists between men and women, across racial and ethnic groups, among generations, and between social classes, we must first look at how they came into being and how they evolved over time. Understanding when and how the events and attitudes that shape contemporary American society occurred can help us connect them to important social, economic and political events.

Take, for example, the long-term impact of 1960s civil rights legislation. That legislation helped to narrow the gap between blacks and whites in education, employment, and income, but did not have an immediate impact on society. Rather, its effect could only be observed gradually, both over time and across successive generations. If we examine these changes over time, we find that the blacks in the Baby Boom generation, who were children and teenagers during the 1960s, were the first to take full advantage of the movement in terms of social advancement, a trend that has continued with the younger members of Generation X. When we examine the total population today, we see that while socio-economic differences between blacks and whites still exist, they are much narrower among those under the age 50, a phenomenon that can be explained in large part by this generational effect.

This book will allow you to conduct a hands-on investigation of data and to develop your own understanding of trends like the one described above. Over the course of this book you will explore a wide range of issues associated with recent changes in America's population, from the aging of the Baby Boomers to the young and growing multiracial population.

HANDS-ON EXPLORATIONS WITH U. S. CENSUS BUREAU DATA

For years, comprehensive data on American demographics has been available from the United States Census Bureau (see "The Census and the American Community Survey" section in the back of this book). The US Decennial Census and American Community Survey are widely regarded to be the best and most complete of their kind. However, they are published in raw form, so social scientists must spend hours working sifting through these valuable statistics. In this workbook, you will see this work is already done. You will be given access to an enormous amount of census data tailored to highlight specific concepts in each exercise. By making the data available online, this book allows novice students to easily explore the data through the exercises, and investigate trends further using the wide range of variables.

For data analysis, you will use WebCHIP, a user-friendly, web-based version of the popular StudentCHIP software. Students, even those with little to no experience with computers or statistics, can learn how to use the program in an hour or less. For guidance familiarizing yourself with the program, see the tutorial on the textbook website. Exploring the census data used in this book is at least straightforward, if not even fun.

HAPPY INVESTIGATING!

This book will be your guide as you explore the wide range of social and economic disparities that exist in society. You will learn about topics such as racial inequality, immigrant assimilation, gender inequality, marriage trends, and differences in poverty levels among children and the elderly. By guiding you through some basic work with quantitative data, this text will provide you with all the necessary tools to begin exploring demographic data on your own.

After working through the exercises and gaining a taste for demographic data, you may choose to return to the data sets and pursue the areas of inquiry that interest you. Near the beginning of each chapter, you will find a section called "Key Concepts." These sections provide simple definitions of the most important social or economic concepts (i.e., poverty status or cohabiter) introduced in that chapter. Another important resource is the textbook website. Here you will find a guide to all the WebCHIP datasets used with this book, links to additional resources in-print and online, and a WebCHIP tutorial. While this book provides class assignments, the website goes beyond this to give you all the tools necessary to work with the datasets on your own and expand your knowledge of the issues discussed in the text.

It may be that even after you've finished the course, you will continue to be interested in exploring questions about social trends and differences. Even if you don't, we hope that this book will arouse your curiosity, teach you something about American society, and give you a feel for the way social scientists do their work. Happy exploring!

ACCESSING THE DATA
and Making Tables

All of the exercises in this book require the use of census data found in custom-designed datasets for use with the StudentCHIP data analysis software, and its web based counterpart, WebCHIP.

TWO WAYS TO ACCESS DATA

To begin, you will need to visit the textbook website. Here you will find a variety of resources to help you use this book, but most importantly, you will find the following options for accessing datasets:

1. **By Exercise**

   On the main page of the textbook website, you will find a link labeled "Datasets by Chapter and Exercise." Clicking here will take you to a list of chapters. Simply follow the appropriate links to find your exercise. As in the book, the name and directory of the dataset to be used in conjunction with the exercise will appear after the text. In the example below, the dataset to be used with Exercise 1 is called "POPSTRUC.TREND".

   ## EXAMPLE:

   Exercise 1 The size of the U.S. population between the ages of 0-4 reflects the recent fertility levels in the United States. Look at the number of people 0-4 years old at successive 10-year intervals, from 1930 to present. Do these patterns suggest high levels of fertility during years the Baby Boom cohorts were born?

   ▶ *Dataset*: POPSTRUC.TREND

   Clicking on the name of the dataset will automatically open the dataset for use in WebCHIP.

2. **By Dataset Name**

   If you already know the name of the dataset you would like to use, you can access it directly using the WebCHIP Launcher located on the left-hand side of the main page of the textbook website.

   To use the launcher, you will need to find your dataset in the directory. The ".TREND" datasets contains data from multiple decades, while the ".DAT" datasets contain up-to-date data from the most recent American Community Survey. (Note: The last section of this book, "Guide to Datasets," also provides a complete list of the datasets in each directory).

The launcher uses a pull-down menu. After you have chosen a dataset, click the "Select Dataset" button. The chosen dataset will open using the analysis software, WebCHIP.

NOW, ON TO THE ANALYSIS...

Now that you have opened a dataset using WebCHIP software, you need to learn how to use the software to perform data analysis. Before proceeding, we strongly suggest you read the online tutorial about making tables with WebCHIP software (there is a separate guide available for StudentCHIP). The tutorial covers all of the basic skills you will need to complete the exercises in this book, including:

▸ Making cross-tabulations
▸ Percentaging a table
▸ Controlling for additional variables

Knowing how to perform these functions is essential to successful data analysis. Once you've read and understood the tutorial, you are ready to begin using this book.

ACCESSING THE WEBSITE

Access to the datasets required for this book and its exercises is now easier than ever and available online.

Go to the website at **http://www.cengage.com/sociology/frey**

GRAPHING OVERVIEW

Over the course of this book, you will be asked to complete a number of graphs using demographic data from the included datasets. Before beginning, it is useful to have a good understanding of the sort of graphs that you will be asked to make. Graphs and other visual representations of data are useful for highlighting trends and making comparisons.

This overview will familiarize you with the four types of graphs used in this book: the line graph, the bar chart, the pie chart, and the stacked bar chart. Additionally, this section will offer you examples and suggestions for transferring data from the tables you generate using StudentCHIP or WebCHIP onto the graphs in the workbook.

LINE GRAPHS

Line graphs are often used to examine change over time. Plotting more than one line on the same set of axes allows you to compare the trends for two or more categories on the same graph.

Example: Use the data below to create a line graph showing the percentage of blacks and non-blacks who were never married, from 1950 to the most recent year (2008 in this example).

1950

	Currently Married	Widowed	Divorced	Separated	Never Married	Total
Black	57.6	10.5	2.3	7.8	21.7	100%
Non-Black	67.5	8.0	2.2	1.2	21.0	100%
All	66.6	8.2	2.2	1.9	21.1	100%

1960

	Currently Married	Widowed	Divorced	Separated	Never Married	Total
Black	56.0	10.0	3.2	7.7	23.2	100%
Non-Black	68.7	7.8	2.5	1.2	19.8	100%
All	67.5	8.0	2.6	1.8	20.1	100%

1970

	Currently Married	Widowed	Divorced	Separated	Never Married	Total
Black	49.1	9.8	4.3	7.6	29.1	100%
Non-Black	64.8	8.0	3.3	1.3	22.6	100%
All	63.2	8.2	3.4	1.9	23.3	100%

1980

	Currently Married	Widowed	Divorced	Separated	Never Married	Total
Black	39.4	8.6	7.7	7.3	**37.0**	100%
Non-Black	60.2	7.5	6.0	1.6	**24.6**	100%
All	58.0	7.6	6.2	2.2	26.0	100%

1990

	Currently Married	Widowed	Divorced	Separated	Never Married	Total
Black	35.2	8.0	10.1	6.6	**40.1**	100%
Non-Black	58.1	7.3	8.1	1.7	**24.7**	100%
All	55.6	7.4	8.3	2.3	26.4	100%

2000

	Currently Married	Widowed	Divorced	Separated	Never Married	Total
Black	36.1	7.0	11.1	5.2	**40.7**	100%
Non-Black	56.7	6.6	9.6	1.8	**25.3**	100%
All	54.4	6.6	9.7	2.2	27.1	100%

2008

	Currently Married	Widowed	Divorced	Separated	Never Married	Total
Black	30.4	6.3	11.6	4.7	**47.0**	100%
Non-Black	52.4	6.1	10.2	2.0	**29.3**	100%
All	50.2	6.3	10.6	2.2	30.8	100%

Source: American Community Survey 2008, 3-Year Estimates Data

The answer can be plotted as follows:

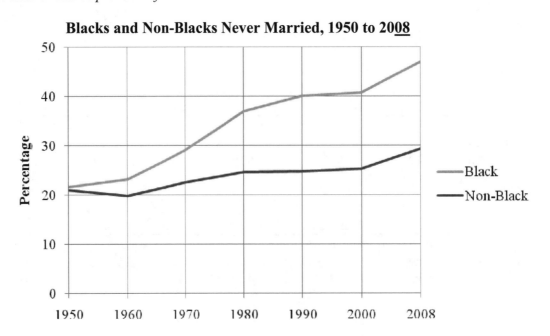

Blacks and Non-Blacks Never Married, 1950 to 2008

By placing both lines on the same axis you can effectively illustrate the trends over time for each group and view the differences in trends between the two groups.

BAR CHARTS

A bar chart is an effective way of showing how a particular characteristic varies across many groups. Bar charts are effective because they allow you to more precisely illustrate the exact values of the statistic you are investigating.

Example: Using the data in the table below, create a bar graph that illustrates the current percentage of people in each race/ethnicity (excluding Non-Hispanic Other) that had never been married.

	Currently Married	*Widowed*	*Divorced*	*Separated*	*Never Married*	*Total*
Non-Hispanic White	53.9%	7.0%	11.2%	1.5%	**26.4%**	100%
Black	30.4%	6.3%	11.6%	4.7%	**47.0%**	100%
Asian	59.6%	4.6%	5.0%	1.3%	**29.4%**	100%
Hispanic	47.2%	3.5%	8.0%	3.7%	**37.6%**	100%
AmIndian	38.8%	5.3%	12.8%	3.3%	**39.8%**	100%
Non-Hispanic Other	44.2%	3.1%	8.2%	3.7%	**40.8%**	100%
All	50.2%	6.3%	10.6%	2.2%	30.8%	100%

Source: American Community Survey 2008, 3-Year Estimates Data

The answer can be plotted as follows:

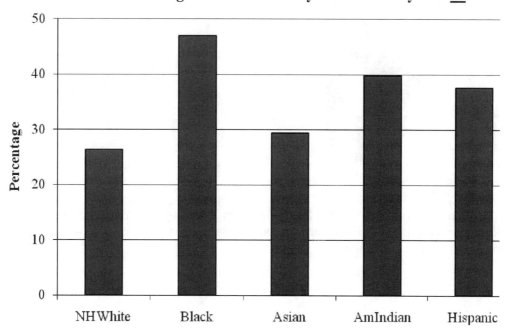

Percentage Never Married by Race/Ethnicity in 2008

By taking this data and placing it in the form of a bar chart, you can illustrate the specific values for each group while at the same time comparing differences among groups.

PIE CHARTS

The purpose of a pie chart is to show the distribution of a set of characteristics among a population, rather than showing just a single statistic from the group. Each slice represents a category and the size of the slice is the percentage share of the group. Pie charts allow you to visualize the entire distribution of a variable.

Example: Using the data from the most recent year, chart the marital status distribution of the entire population. (Note: distributions of this sort can be obtained in WebCHIP using the "marginals" command.)

	Currently Married	Widowed	Divorced	Separated	Never Married	Total
Total U.S. Population	50.2%	6.3%	10.6%	2.2%	30.8%	100%

Source: American Community Survey 2008 3-Year Data

The answer can be graphed as follows:

Marital Status Distribution, 2008

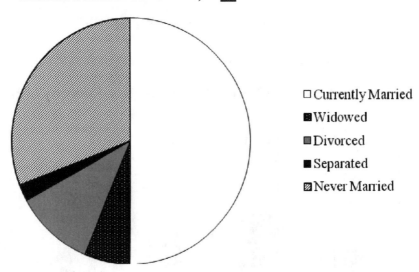

Taking this data and presenting it in the form of a pie chart helps you to visualize how certain subgroups of a population compare in size and percentage to the population as a whole, and to other groups within that population.

STACKED BAR CHARTS

A stacked bar chart is used to compare distributions across groups and provides an efficient alternative to using several bar or pie charts. Each bar in a stacked bar chart represents 100% of a group's population, and all the divisions of the bars represent categories of the variable, much like the slices of a pie chart represent portions of the whole.

Example: Use the following data to create a stacked bar chart showing the marital status distribution of Non-Hispanic Whites, Blacks, Asians, American Indians, and Hispanics.

	Currently Married	Widowed	Divorced	Separated	Never Married	Total
Non-Hispanic White	53.9%	7.0%	11.2%	1.5%	26.4%	100%
Black	30.4%	6.3%	11.6%	4.7%	47.0%	100%
Asian	59.6%	4.6%	5.0%	1.3%	29.4%	100%
Hispanic	47.2%	3.5%	8.0%	3.7%	37.6%	100%
AmIndian	38.8%	5.3%	12.8%	3.3%	39.8%	100%
Non-Hispanic Other	44.2%	3.1%	8.2%	3.7%	40.8%	100%
All	50.2%	6.3%	10.6%	2.2%	30.8%	100%

Source: American Community Survey 2008 3-Year Data

The answer can be graphed as follows:

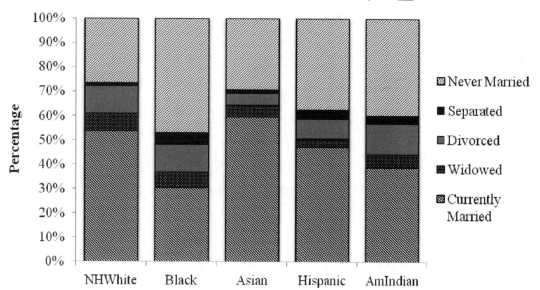

By taking the data and organizing it in the form of a stacked bar chart, you can illustrate the distribution within each group while simultaneously looking at how the distributions vary across groups.

SECTION II

Investigation Topics

1 POPULATION STRUCTURE: COHORTS, AGES, AND CHANGE

chapter

In a very general way, the population structure of the United States is this book's major theme. A population's structure includes its racial/ethnic distribution, its labor force characteristics, and the size and type of its families and households. The most fundamental aspects of a population's structure, however, are its age and gender distribution. These two factors determine many other characteristics of a population and how those characteristics change over time.

In this chapter, you will first familiarize yourself with the age structure of the U.S. population and how it has changed over the past 50 years. Birth cohorts are an important "engine" of change in America's age structure. Different cohorts living in a population at the same time can be of vastly different size, and as these cohorts age, the proportion of different age groups in the population changes. The best examples of this are the Baby Boom cohorts; huge cohorts that resulted from the large number of births that occurred from 1946 up through 1964. As these cohorts age over time, they tend to swell the sizes of the age categories they occupy. For example, by the year 2030, the size of the elderly population will be large because all of the Baby Boomers will be over the age of sixty-five.

Immigration has also affected the age structure of the U.S. population. Typically, immigrants come to the United States in early adulthood, increasing the population in their age group. Past immigration can also affect the population sizes of older age groups. For example, the large immigration waves in the early twentieth century now constitute a part of America's elderly population.

Mortality is another factor that affects the nation's age structure. In the United States, high levels of mortality do not occur in age groups under 65. This means that groups in the population under the age of 65 are unlikely to decrease remarkably in size due to deaths.

Live Births in the United States, 1930-2001

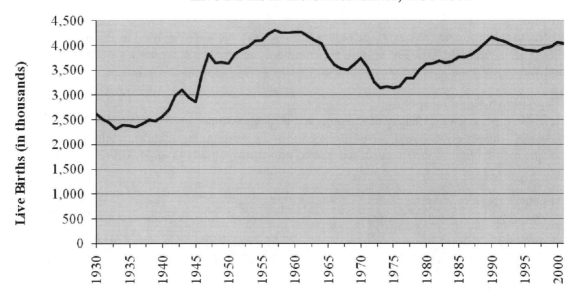

KEY

concepts

Age
The age of the person in complete years according to the person filling out the census. Ages are usually grouped into 5 or 10 year age groups for analysis purposes.

Gender
Male or Female.

Year
Years in which data were collected or future years for projected populations.

Cohort
A group of individuals born in the same period, usually in the same decade, sharing a common set of historical experiences. The cohorts of the twentieth century will be categorized here as the following:

Roaring Twenties Cohort (born 1916-1924)   *Late Baby Boomers Cohort* (born 1956-1965)
Depression Cohort (born 1925-1934)   *Generation X Cohort* (born 1966-1975)
World War II Cohort (born 1935-1945)   *Early Millennial Cohort* (born 1976-1985)
Baby Boomers Cohort (born 1946-1955)   *Late Millennial Cohort* (born 1986-1995)

NOTE: In the datasets, there is no separate "cohort" variable. Instead, you can identify a cohort from an age group in a given year (See Figure A on pg. 22). For example, the 25-34 year-old age group in 2000 belongs to the "Generation X Cohort".

State
Refers to each of the 50 U.S. states and the District of Columbia (Washington D.C.).

Region
Refers to the groupings of states (see Figure B on pg. 34) that are often used in studies of regional differences within the U.S. The regions are commonly referred to as Northeast, Midwest, South, and West.

City-Suburb-Nonmetropolitan
Refers to the population density of a geographic area where a person lives. People who live in a metropolitan area either live in the central city or in the surrounding suburbs, while persons living outside metropolitan areas are classified here as non-metropolitan (variable GEO 3 in datasets).

OTHER concepts

Education (Chapter Two)   **Marital Status** (Chapter Five)
Immigration Status (Chapter Three)   **Race/Ethnicity** (Chapter Two)

More than age distinguishes cohorts from one another—almost all other aspects of a population vary by cohort. For example, cohorts born before 1945 do not have the same educational attainment as those born in the 1950s and 1960s. The racial/ethnic composition of the U.S. population also differs by age. Recent immigration from Latin America and Asia has helped increase the number of Hispanics and Asians in the young adult cohorts, and higher fertility rates among Hispanics have led to a large number of Hispanics in the child population.

Finally, although most of this chapter focuses on the nation as a whole, it is useful to look at the population structure of smaller geographic areas like census regions, states, and city-suburb breakdowns. The population structure of these smaller geographic areas is affected by migration within the United States as well as cohort aging (a topic that will be explored in greater depth in Chapter 10) and immigration from abroad (which we will examine more closely in Chapter 3).

A. Cohorts and Changing Age Structure

A cohort refers to the number of people born in a specified period. Typically, this period is about ten years in length, though the number of births that occurred between 1946 and 1964 was so large that the birth cohorts for all of these years have been given the blanket term "Baby Boom cohorts". Still, at times it can be useful to distinguish between "early Baby Boom cohorts" (born between 1946 and 1955) and "late Baby Boom cohorts" (born between 1956 and 1964). The names of other cohorts are either related to their size or the historical period in which they were born. In this section, you will explore how the size of the birth cohort in any given period later affects the age structure of the population.

Exercise 1 The size of the U.S. population between the ages of 0-4 reflects the recent fertility levels in the United States. Look at the number of people 0-4 years old at successive 10-year intervals, from 1930 to the present. Do these patterns suggest high levels of fertility during years the Baby Boom cohorts were born?

▸ *Dataset*: PopStruc.trend

▸ Create a line graph that shows the number of children ages 0-4 in each census year from 1930 through the present. (Hint: The numbers in this dataset are in thousands.)

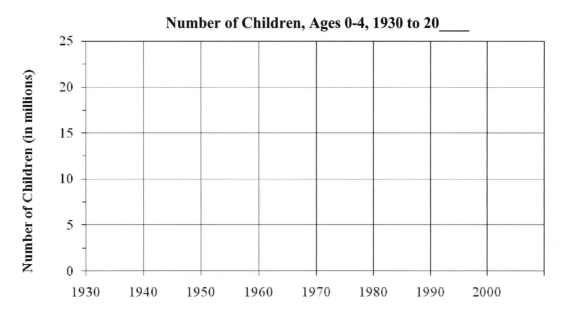

Number of Children, Ages 0-4, 1930 to 20____

Exercise 2 Refer to Figure A and notice that for any given year, each age group can be matched with the cohort currently occupying that age category. For example, in 1990, the Early Baby Boom cohorts (those born between 1946 and 1955) were 35-44. Determine the age group distribution of the current U.S. population. What does this tell you about the relative size of each cohort?

▸ *Dataset*: POPSTRUC.TREND

Figure A:

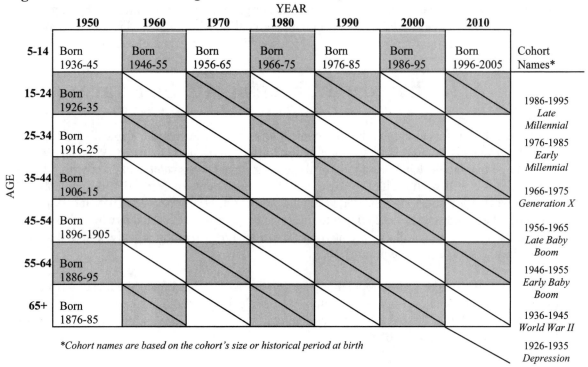

Cohort names are based on the cohort's size or historical period at birth

▸ Create a bar chart showing the percentage of the current U.S. population in each age group.

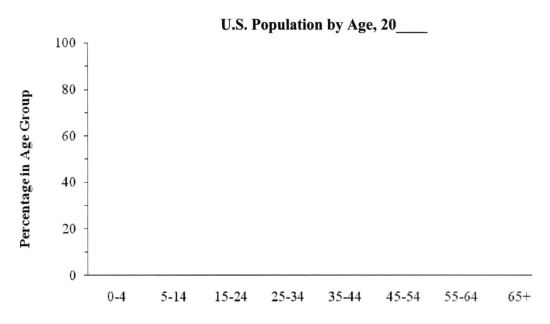

Exercise 3 Determine the age group distribution of the 1980 U.S. population. Which age groups are the largest? Which are the smallest? Are these results consistent with the distribution you found for the current year?

▸ *Dataset*: POPSTRUC.TREND

▸ Create a bar chart showing the percentage of the 1980 U.S. population in each age group.

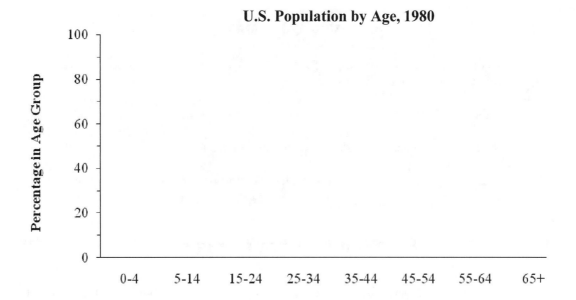

U.S. Population by Age, 1980

Exercise 4 Most Americans enter the labor force between the ages of 15 and 24. How did the aggregate size of this new-to-the-labor-force age group change between 1950 and the present? What impact did the early Baby Boom cohorts have on this population? The late Baby Boom cohorts? Finally, what has been the impact of the smaller "Generation X" cohorts?

▸ *Dataset*: POPSTRUC.TREND

▸ Create a line graph showing the number of persons ages 15-24 for each census year between 1950 and the present.

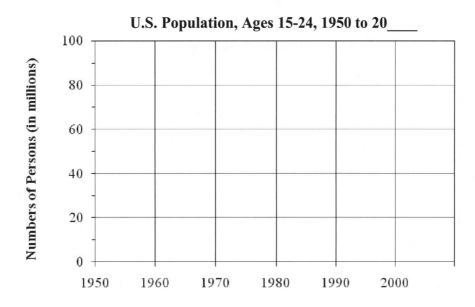

U.S. Population, Ages 15-24, 1950 to 20____

Exercise 5 The years between the ages 25 and 34 are often the prime years for entering the housing market. On your own, repeat Exercise 4 for the 25-34 age group. What does this say about the way the number of first-time homebuyers in the American population has changed over time? How would you interpret these changes in terms of different cohort sizes?

▶ *Dataset*: POPSTRUC.TREND

Discussion Questions

1. How does fluctuating cohort size impact age-related social institutions like public school systems or nursing homes?

2. After the year 2010, what effect will the retirement of the Baby Boom cohorts have on the United States Social Security system? Do you expect that your own cohort will be able to reap the benefits of this program after retirement? Why or why not?

3. Do you think it is better to be born into a large cohort or a small cohort? Explain.

B. Women Live Longer

An almost equal number of boys and girls are born into a given cohort, and, for most of a cohort's life span, the relative proportion of women to men does not change. Men, however, have lower life expectancies than women, and in the oldest age categories, women continue to outnumber men even as the average life expectancy for both genders rises.

Exercise 6 Calculate the size of the current female population in each age group. For which age groups do women make up more than 50 percent of the population?

▶ *Dataset*: POPUSA.DAT

▶ Create a bar chart with bars for each age group showing the current percentage of females within each age group.

Exercise 7 Has the percentage of females in the 65+ age group increased or decreased since 1950? What does this say about successive cohorts of elderly?

▸ *Dataset*: PopStruc.trend

▸ Create a line graph showing the percent of the 65+ age group made up of females in each census year from 1950 to the present.

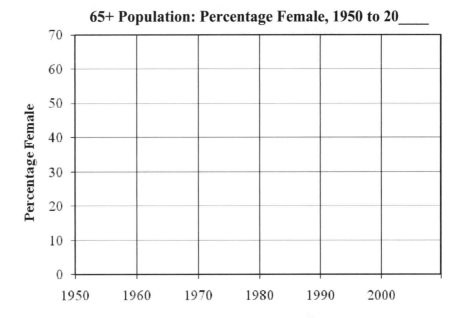

65+ Population: Percentage Female, 1950 to 20____

Discussion Questions

1. What are some of the social and economic consequences of having a much larger female than male elderly population? What are the implications of this for the large Baby Boom cohorts as they near the landmark age of 65?

2. If women tend to marry men a few years older, how is the marriage market affected by a situation where large cohorts are immediately followed by small cohorts? (This was the case when the late Baby Boom cohorts were followed by the smaller "Baby Bust cohorts.") Does this make the marriage market "better" or "worse" for women? Why?

C. Baby Boomers, Xers, and Diplomas

Some social forecasters make the assumption that as today's younger cohorts get older, they will take on the same social and economic attributes that older people in today's population have. One social attribute that clearly does not follow this assumption is educational attainment. Due in large part to nationwide improvements in public education during the 1950s and 60s, all of today's oldest age groups have lower education levels than the younger cohorts.

Exercise 8 Looking at the current population, determine the percentage of people in each age group who have graduated from college. Which age groups have the highest and lowest percentage of college graduates? What cohorts do they represent?

▶ *Dataset*: EDUC.TREND

▶ Create a bar chart with bars for each age group showing the percentage who have graduated from college.

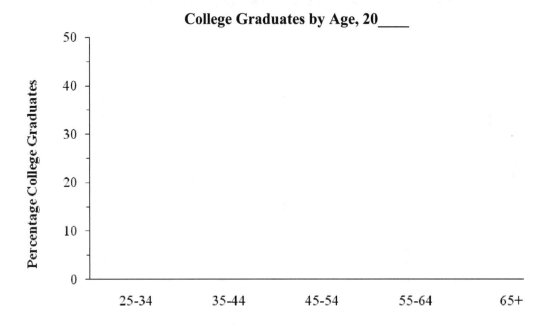

Exercise 9 Contrast the educational attainment of 25-34 year-olds in 1950 with those in the present year. What are the main differences? What might account for these changes?

▶ *Dataset*: EDUC.TREND

▶ Create two pie charts, one for 1950 and one for the present year. In each chart, indicate the educational attainment distribution of 25-34 year-olds.

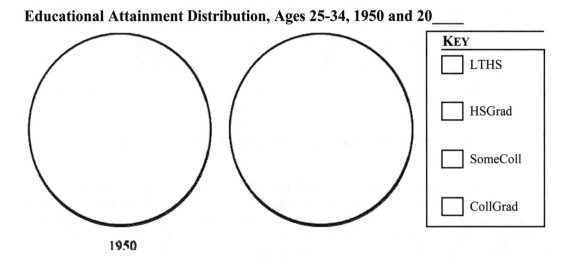

D. Cohort Differences in Marital Status

The 1950s were a period when couples married early and tended to stay together until "death do us part." Permanent marriage at a young age is much less common today. Similar to the education comparisons above, we cannot look at the marital status experiences of our older population as the path most likely to be taken by today's younger cohorts.

Exercise 10 Were young adults in the 1950s and 60s really more likely to be married than current young people? Looking at persons ages 25-34, calculate the percentage "currently married" in each census year from 1950 to the present.

▸ *Dataset*: MARITAL.TREND

▸ Create a line chart showing the percentage of 25-34 year-olds "currently married" in each census year from 1950 to the present.

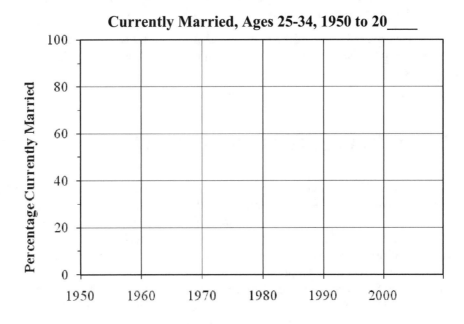

Exercise 11 Looking just at 1950 and present, compare the percentage of people in each age group who were "currently married." Has the trend away from marriage affected all groups equally? In which cohorts is the trend away from marriage most clearly evident?

‣ *Dataset*: MARITAL.TREND

‣ Create a bar chart with side by side bars for 1950 and present. For each age group, show the percent currently married.

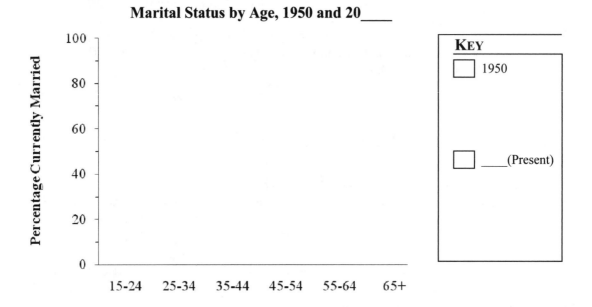

Marital Status by Age, 1950 and 20____

Discussion Questions

1. Why do you think young adult cohorts since the mid-60s have been less inclined to marry and remain married for long periods of time? Do you think that in the future there may be a return to more stable and long-lasting marriages?

2. What does the overall aging of the population, along with lower life expectancy for men, suggest to you about the marital status and living arrangements of older women?

E. Recent Immigration and Population Structure

Immigration to the United States also plays an important role in determining the nation's age structure. This role has been especially prominent in the years since the passage of the 1965 Immigration Act, which led to both a rise in the number of immigrants and a change in regions of origin. Today, the majority of new immigrants come from Latin America, with Asia as the second most common region of origin. Though immigrants to the United States tend to settle in specific areas of the country, they affect the total population's racial/ethnic composition. However, not all immigrants to the United States arrived since 1965. Some of our immigrant population arrived prior to 1930 and now comprises a part of our nation's elderly population. A much smaller number of immigrants arrived between 1930 and 1965 as a result of restrictive immigration laws, the Great Depression, and disruptions due to World War II. Nonetheless, these citizens also have had an impact on their respective cohorts.

Exercise 12 Show, for each age group in the present year, the percentage of the foreign-born population in that age group who arrived prior to 1980, and the percentage that arrived after 1980.

> ▸ *Dataset*: POPUSA.DAT

> ▸ Create a stacked bar chart with bars for each age group; stack by the percentage of native-born people, immigrants who came before 1980 and those who arrived between 1980 and the present. (Hint: You will need to add the numbers from the foreign-born categories 1980-89 and 1990-present to get the total for 1980-present.)

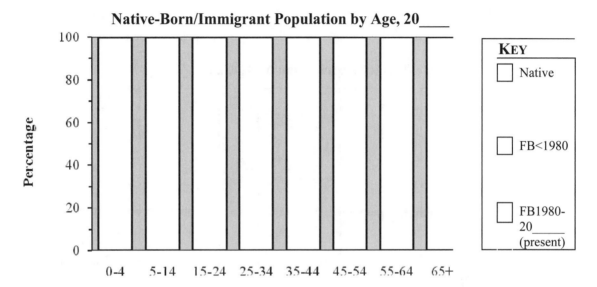

Exercise 13 On your own, compare the number of foreign-born Americans across age groups (rather than their percentage of the population). Again, look separately at those who arrived before 1980 and those who came between 1980 and the present. What do these numbers indicate about the age distribution of recent immigrants to the United States?

> ▸ *Dataset*: POPUSA.DAT

Discussion Questions

1. Consider the impact of post-1980 immigration on the nation's age structure. What are the possible benefits of increasing the size of the younger population at a time when the larger Baby Boom cohorts are growing older?

2. The percent of persons in the 0-4 age group that are native-born is much higher than in any other age group. Why do you think this is the case?

F. Immigration, Age, and Race/Ethnicity

The 2000 and 2010 Censuses allowed respondents to self-identify with a number of racial categories including Black, Asian, American Indian (including Eskimos and Aleuts), White, Pacific Islander or Native Hawaiian, and multiracial. Every respondent was also asked if he or she identified as Hispanic or Latino. (For more discussion of these categories, see "Key Concepts" in

Chapter 2.) While all of these groups have long histories of residence in the U.S., the number of Asians and Hispanics living in the U.S. has risen in recent years as a result of immigration. Because of the age at which individuals tend to immigrate, recent arrivals from both of these groups are most heavily represented among younger adult and child age groups.

Exercise 14 Contrast the racial/ethnic composition of the following four age groups in the current year: 5-14, 25-34, 45-54, and 65+. What differences in race/ethnicity do you find among the age groups? How would you account for these differences?

> ▸ *Dataset*: POPUSA.DAT

> ▸ Create a stacked bar chart with bars for each age group; stack by race/ethnicity.

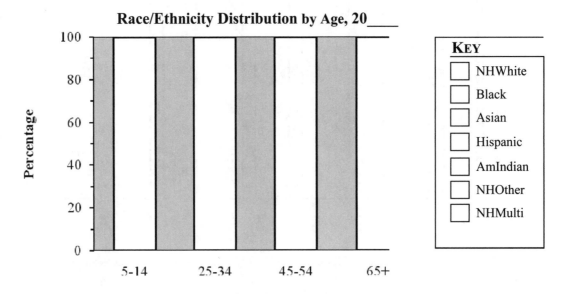

Race/Ethnicity Distribution by Age, 20____

Exercise 15 What percentage of the large Hispanic and Asian populations in the 25-34 age group is foreign-born? Compare the present racial/ethnic distribution for the foreign-born population, ages 25-34, to that of the native-born population in the same age group.

> ▸ *Dataset*: POPUSA.DAT

> ▸ Create two pie charts, one for the combined foreign-born population, ages 25-34, and one for the native-born population of the same age. In each pie, show the race/ethnicity distribution.

Race/Ethnicity Distribution of 25-34 Year-Olds by Immigration Status, 20____

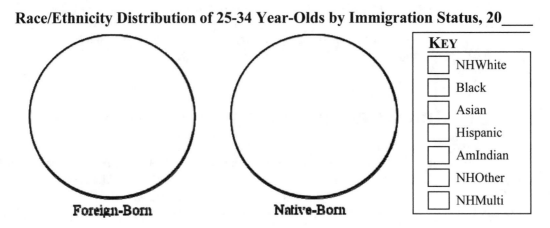

Exercise 16 On your own, compare the age distributions of whites, blacks, Hispanics, and Asians in the present year. To what extent do you think recent immigration may contribute to the differences in the age distributions of these groups?

▸ *Dataset*: POPUSA.DAT

Discussion Questions

1. In 2000, the elderly population had a lower percentage of racial and ethnic minorities than most of the younger age groups. Do you think this situation will change by the year 2020? Explain.

2. What role do you think the different fertility patterns of blacks, whites, Hispanics, and Asians play in determining the racial and ethnic composition of future cohorts? How will the future racial and ethnic composition of the U.S. be affected by marriages between individuals of different racial and ethnic backgrounds?

G. The Multiracial Population

The 2000 Census marked the first time that respondents were allowed to select two or more racial groups when answering the race question. Prior to the 2000 Census, individuals from a multiracial background had to identify with a single race or write in their race as "biracial," "multiracial," or "multiethnic," in which case their race was recorded as "other." The 2000 Census was the first U.S. census to included detailed information on Americans whose ancestry includes two or more racial groups, and provides valuable insight into the growing diversity of America's racial makeup. Many of the people who selected two or more races represented what many Americans think of as "typical" multiracial combinations: white and black, white and American Indian, or white and Asian.

In 2008, people who identify with two or more racial groups made up 2.2% of the U.S. population. More than forty-eight percent of the multiracial population was under the age of eighteen, suggesting the growing role that this population will play in American society in the twenty-first century.

Exercise 17 How does the racial distribution of America's youngest cohorts compare to the distribution of those just a few years older? Compare racial distributions across age groups, giving special attention to the size of the multiracial population. Does anything about your findings surprise you?

▸ *Dataset*: POPGEO.DAT

▸ Create a bar chart with bars for each age group in the present year. For each age group, indicate the percentage multiracial.

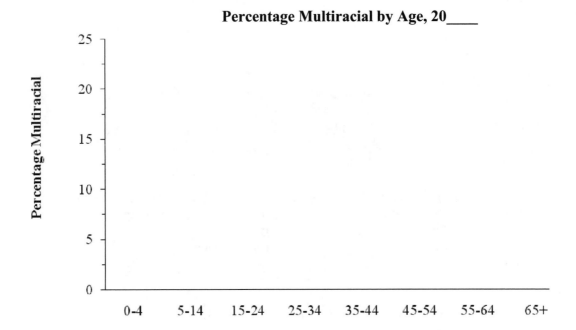

Percentage Multiracial by Age, 20____

Exercise 18 Consider the same factors you examined in the previous exercise from a different angle: how does the age distribution of the multiracial population compare to the age distribution for the population as a whole? What does this suggest about the future of the multiracial population in the U.S.?

▸ *Dataset*: PopGeo.dat

▸ Create two stacked bar charts, one for the multiracial population and one for the U.S. population as a whole. In each chart, stack by the age distribution.

Age Distribution for Multiracial and Total Population, 20____

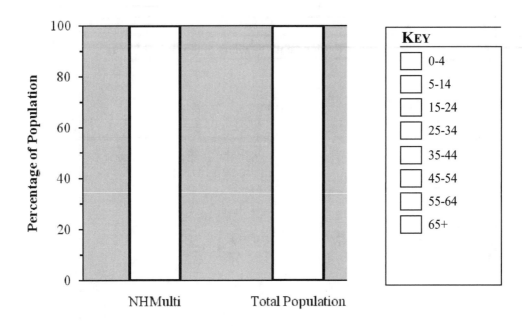

H. **Geography**

Until now we have concentrated on the entire U.S. population. However, it is often useful to focus on particular areas of the country, such as the 50 states and District of Columbia, or the four regions the Census Bureau uses to categorize the country — Northeast, South, Midwest, and West (see Figure B). Another useful way to classify the population is by the type of area people live in. Most of the U.S. population lives in one of more than 300 metropolitan areas. Within these areas, they either live inside the central city or in the suburbs. In total, three categories can be used to classify the types of areas people live in: central city, suburbs, and non-metropolitan, or rural, areas. Besides these categories, there are many other ways to look at geographic distinctions within the national population, from relatively large areas like counties down to small areas like city blocks. The exercises below are based on examining states, regions, cities, suburbs, and non-metropolitan (rural) areas.

Figure B: *Map of the U.S. Showing Census Regions*

Exercise 19 The age structure of a region often reflects its recent growth patterns. Growing regions tend to have higher percentages of young adults and children, a result of the higher mobility of younger populations in the U.S., while the average age of the population tends to rise in areas that are experiencing periods of stagnation or population loss. What can you tell about the recent growth patterns of the four census regions by examining their current age distributions?

▸ *Dataset*: POPGEO.DAT

▸ Using present-year data, create a stacked bar chart with bars for each census region (Northeast, Midwest, South, and West); stack by age group.

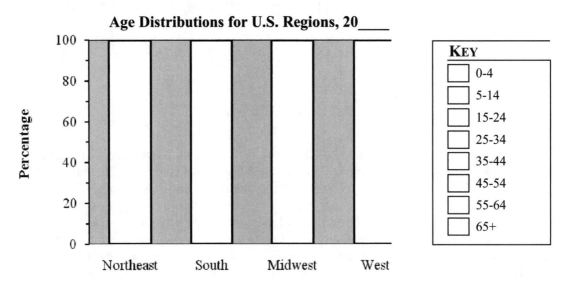

Exercise 20 Now compare the racial/ethnic distributions of the four census regions. Based on your results, which regions do you think have received a large number of recent immigrants to the U.S.? In which region is the percentage of blacks highest?

▶ *Dataset*: POPGEO.DAT

▶ Create a stacked bar chart with bars for each census region in the present year; stack by the racial/ethnic group.

Race/Ethnicity Distributions for U.S. Regions, 20____

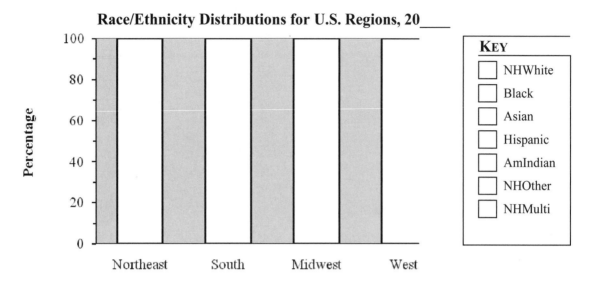

Exercise 21 In the past few decades, the bulk of new immigrants have settled in a handful of states (more information to come in Chapter 3). Consequently, these states have higher percentages of Hispanic and Asian populations than most of the country. To explore how recent immigration might impact future state populations, compare the projected year 2020 racial/ethnic distribution in the total U.S. population to that of California, Florida, New York and Texas.

▶ *Dataset*: POPPROJ.DAT

▶ Create a stacked bar chart with bars for the total U.S. population, California, Texas, Florida and New York; stack by the current year racial/ethnic distribution.

2020 Race/Ethnicity Distribution

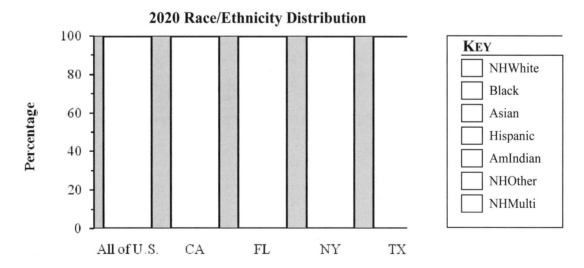

Exercise 22 Central cities and suburbs are generally considered to appeal to different age groups: "young singles" often want to live in the central city, while many older adults with children choose to live in the suburbs. Find out if this conventional wisdom is true by examining the

percentage of children (ages under 15) and the percentage of young adults (ages 15-24) in each type of area.

▸ *Dataset*: POPGEO.DAT

▸ Create a bar chart with side-by-side bars for central cities and suburbs showing the percent living in that area for each age group (under 15 and 15-24).

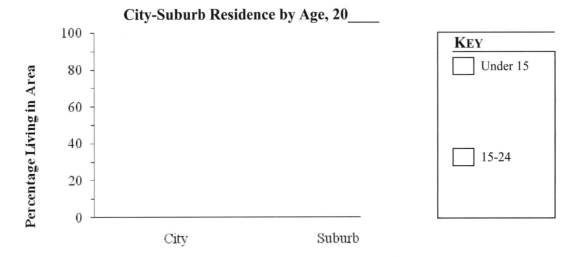

City-Suburb Residence by Age, 20____

Exercise 23 Non-metropolitan areas are generally assumed to have a higher percentage of elderly residents than other areas. Some of these areas attract the elderly due to their amenities and other attractions for new retirees, while other non-metropolitan areas have a high percentage of elderly because they have lost a disproportionate share of their younger populations. For the U.S. as a whole, do non-metropolitan areas have a higher proportion of elderly residents than metropolitan areas?

▸ *Dataset*: POPGEO.DAT

▸ Create two pie charts: one for metropolitan areas and one for non-metropolitan areas. In each chart, show the current age distribution. (Hint: Add or combine categories such as City and Suburb to create the Metropolitan Area category.)

Age Distribution by Residence Area, 20____

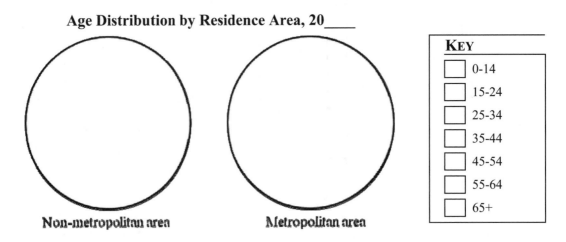

Exercise 24 Examine the racial/ethnic distribution of central cities, suburbs, and non-metropolitan areas in the present year. Are the distributions of these areas as different as you expected them to be? If not, what might account for the similarity?

▶ *Dataset*: PopGeo.dat

▶ Create a stacked bar chart with bars for city, suburb, and non-metropolitan areas; stack by current racial/ethnic distribution.

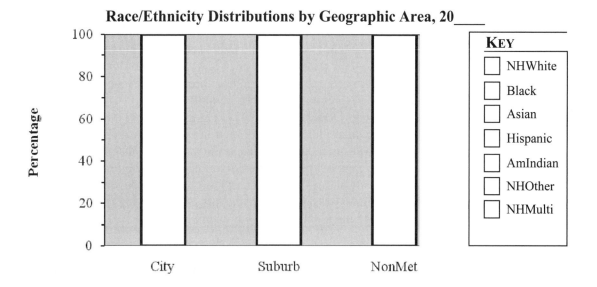

Race/Ethnicity Distributions by Geographic Area, 20____

KEY
☐ NHWhite
☐ Black
☐ Asian
☐ Hispanic
☐ AmIndian
☐ NHOther
☐ NHMulti

Discussion Questions

1. Why do national patterns of age structure and racial and ethnic composition not necessarily characterize individual states, regions, or cities?

2. Consider the following statement: It is easier to predict the future age structure of the U.S. population than it is to project the future age distribution of an individual state. Do you agree? Why or why not?

THINK
tank

1. The patterns of marriage, divorce, and family life followed by most of the pre-Baby Boom cohorts are not similar for the early or late Baby Boomers. Similarly, the educational levels of these early cohorts are generally lower than they are for people born since 1945. In light of these trends, and considering the data you looked at in this chapter, speculate on the future marital patterns, childbearing, and occupational choices of your own cohort. How might changing economic and social realities lead to different choices for your cohort than the pre-Baby Boom cohorts? The Baby Boom cohorts? Elaborate.

2. California, Texas, Illinois, New York, and Florida are all states with diverse populations, but which one will have the largest increase in the percentage of Hispanic children through 2020? Based on 2000 and current data, would you expect each Hispanic subgroup to show the same amount of increase in each state? Are some Hispanic subgroups likely to be more influential in some states than others? Explain your conclusions and support your answers with data.

Learning More With CensusScope.org

As you work through this textbook, you may be interested in learning how the facts and trends you study relate to your state, county, or city. Although the Census Bureau provides data for all of these geographies, navigating through large amounts of information in order to find what you are looking for can be quite difficult.

CensusScope.org (http://www.censusscope.org), a demographic tool developed by SSDAN, makes finding basic data on a state, county, or metropolitan area easy for even the novice data user. Combining decennial census data and the most up-to-date American Community Survey data, CensusScope.org presents demographic data in the form of simple and easy-to-read maps, charts and tables. With CensusScope.org, you can discover:

▶ How fast your local area grew (or shrank) over the last 20 years.
▶ How prevalent multiracial individuals are in your county.
▶ The degree of racial segregation in your town or city.
▶ Much More!

chapter 2 RACIAL/ETHNIC INEQUALITY

The growing diversity of the United States population has had an unparalleled impact on the cultural, political, and economic landscape of American life. Our schools, workplaces, legislatures, and national character are constantly evolving in the face of an increasingly heterogeneous population. Today, more than ever, racial/ethnic issues concern the entire nation.

Before examining the similarities and discrepancies among racial/ethnic groups, it is helpful to gain a historical perspective on events that contributed to the current state of racial/ethnic inequality in the United States. Oppression of African-American slaves and the implementation of Jim Crow laws is the foundation of racial inequality, but discrimination against minority groups continued long after these institutions were dismantled. In the mid-twentieth century, the unjust treatment of African-Americans was confronted head-on, sparking the Civil Rights Movement.

The Supreme Court decision in *Brown v. Board of Education* served as the starting point of this movement. The ruling determined separate facilities for blacks were inherently unequal and segregation was no longer constitutional. Although this was a significant victory for the supporters of the Civil Rights Movement, the struggle was not over. With the passage of the Civil Rights Act of 1964, the nation would no longer recognize legal distinctions based upon race, color, creed, or national origin in the workplace. Any employer who did not honor this newly established standard of equality would be in violation of the law.

Today, the ongoing struggle for equal opportunities among races is embodied in the creation and implementation of Affirmative Action programs, which apply to several ethnic groups. These programs have increased minority access to colleges and workplaces by enforcing specific and compulsory admittance and hiring guidelines. Although some people may feel Affirmative Action programs are unjust, few can deny that these programs have produced a great deal of diversity in the United States' workplaces and educational institutions.

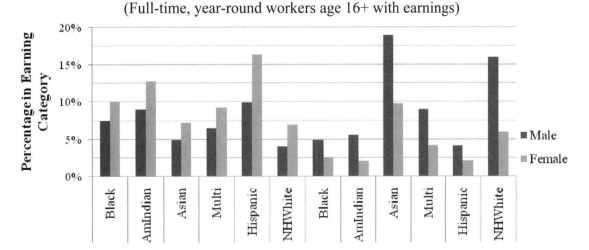

2008 Earnings by Race/Ethnicity
(Full-time, year-round workers age 16+ with earnings)

KEY

concepts

Race/Ethnicity

Identifies the major racial/ethnic groups, combining the race and Hispanic-origin categories used by the Census Bureau. A person's categorization in a racial/ethnic group is based on his or her self-identification on the Census form.

> **Non-Hispanic White (White)**—All persons who indicated their race as white and who also indicated that they were not of Hispanic origin.

> **Black**—All persons who indicated their race as black.

> **American Indian (American Indian, Eskimo, or Aleut)**—All persons who classified themselves as American Indian, Eskimo, or Aleut.

> **Hispanic**—Persons who identified themselves as white or "some other race" and who also identified themselves as Hispanic, or with a specific Hispanic group such as Mexican, Puerto Rican, Cuban, or Spanish. This category can refer to the ancestry, nationality group, lineage, or country of birth of the person, the person's parents, or the person's ancestors before their arrival in the United States.

> **Asian (Asian or Pacific Islander)**—Includes all persons who indicated their ethnicity or race as Asian Indian, Chinese, Korean, Filipino, Japanese, Vietnamese, or any other Asian group. Also includes persons who indicated their race as Hawaiian, Samoan, Guanamanian, or other Pacific Islander.

> **Non-Hispanic Other (Other Race)**—Includes persons who indicated "other" in the race classification and who are not of Hispanic origin. For Census years prior to 2000, this category also includes persons who identified themselves as interracial, multiracial, or multiethnic and not Hispanic.

> **Non-Hispanic Multiracial***—Includes persons who indicated a heritage that includes two or more of the races listed above or who identified themselves as interracial, multiracial, or multiethnic. For purposes of this book, individuals included in this category are of non-Hispanic origin. *Does not apply *prior* to the 2000 Census.

> **NOTE:** The RACE and RACEETH variables in the datasets often combine some of these categories. For example, RACEETH2 combines the category of American Indians with Other and Multiracial.

Education

The highest level of school completed or the highest degree received.

> **< 9 Years**—Persons who have completed less than 9 years of schooling.

> **9-12 Years**—Persons who have completed 9-12 years of schooling but have not graduated from high school.

> **High School Graduate**—Persons who have graduated from high school or who have received the equivalent of a high school diploma such as a GED.

Some College—Persons who have completed some years of college but have not graduated, or who have attained an Associate degree but not a Bachelor's degree.

College Graduate—Persons who have graduated from college and received a Bachelor's degree.

Master's Degree—Persons who have completed an MA, MS, Med, MSW, MBA, or other similar degree.

PhD or Professional Degree—Persons who have completed a terminal degree in their field (PhD, EdD) or a professional school degree (MD, DDS, DDM, LLB, JD).

NOTE: The education variables in the datasets sometimes combine these categories. For example, the category "CollGrad" in variable EDUC refers to all persons who have completed a college degree, regardless of additional graduate education.

Occupation

The classification system for this category has changed significantly over the years. It includes all employed workers, and in its simplest form divides them into white collar, blue collar, and service workers.

Top White Collar—Professional workers, executives, administrators, and managers.

Other White Collar—Administrative support, clerical and sales workers, technicians, and related support occupations.

Top Blue Collar—"Skilled blue collar" jobs such as precision production, craft, and repair workers.

Other Blue Collar—Workers in less skilled blue collar jobs.

Service Workers—Private household, protective service, and other service workers.

Farm Workers—Workers in farming, forestry, and fishery occupations.

Earnings

The amount of money a person makes in wages or salary before taxes and other deductions are taken, usually a yearly measure.

While keeping these historical events in mind, look at the similarities and discrepancies among different racial/ethnic groups in terms of educational attainment, occupational status, and earnings distribution. Over time, all racial/ethnic groups have experienced increased education levels, more occupational choices, and higher earnings. However, the rate of these gains varies among racial/ethnic groups, with historically disadvantaged minorities gaining at a slower rate than non-Hispanic whites. After seeing the gaps among racial/ethnic groups, you will consider why these discrepancies exist. As you work through the following exercises, consider whether we have made much progress towards racial/ethnic equality since the passage of the Civil Rights Act in 1964. What evidence of racial discrimination still remains in society today?

A. Education and Race/Ethnicity

Over the last few decades, the educational attainment of all racial/ethnic groups in the United States has increased steadily due to a variety of factors. The national mandate for compulsory education for children under the age of sixteen contributed to an increase in the percentage of high school graduates of all races, while the court ruling in *Brown v. Board of Education* increased access to public education for black children. Today, the Affirmative Action policies in place at many colleges and universities aim to provide higher education opportunities that were previously unavailable to most minority students. In addition to legal mandates, changes in the United States economy have influenced educational attainment across society. As the nation moves from an industrial economy into an age of technology, higher education has become the key to entry into stable, well-paying jobs, influencing many individuals to pursue additional schooling after finishing high school.

Despite growth in both access and demand, educational attainment has not increased at an equal rate for all racial/ethnic groups. As education is a necessary component of many kinds of social and economic advancement, the growing gap in educational attainment between non-Hispanic whites and other groups means that these other groups may continue to lag behind in other areas. In this section, you will examine trends in educational attainment since 1950 and the current discrepancies in educational attainment among racial/ethnic groups. As you work through the exercises, consider why the educational attainment of racial/ethnic groups has not increased at an equal rate.

Exercise 1 Using data from 1950 to the present, examine changes in the percentage of blacks and non-blacks, ages 25-34, with a high school education or more. Describe the overall trends as well as how differences between the two groups have changed over time. Do you think it is useful to focus on the 25-34 year-old age group for this trend? Why or why not?

▸ *Dataset*: EDUC.TREND

▸ Create a line graph with two lines, one for blacks and one for non-blacks, ages 25-34. For each year, indicate the percentage of each group with a high school education or more. (Hint: Add or combine into a single category: high school graduates, those with some college, and college graduates.)

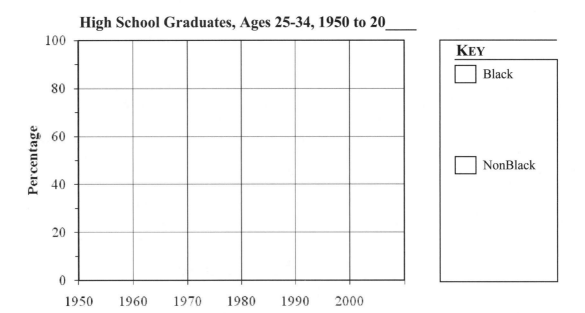

Exercise 2 Using data from 1950 to the present, examine changes in the percentage of blacks and non-blacks, ages 25-34, who have graduated from college. How are the trends similar and/or different to your findings for high school graduates? Give possible explanations for any gaps between the races that you might find.

▸ *Dataset*: EDUC.TREND

▸ Create a line graph with two lines, one for blacks and one for non-blacks, ages 25-34. For each year, indicate the percentage of college graduates in each group.

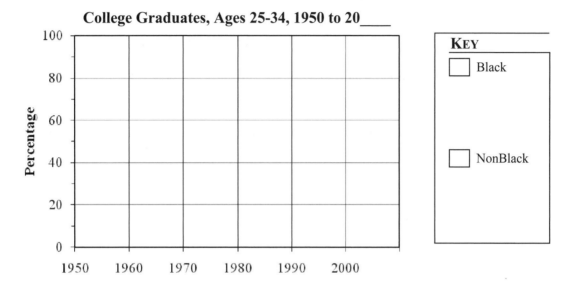

College Graduates, Ages 25-34, 1950 to 20____

KEY
☐ Black
☐ NonBlack

Exercise 3 Focusing on the present, look at the educational attainment of people ages 25-34 in each racial/ethnic group. Describe the differences among the groups and give a possible explanation.

▸ *Dataset*: EDUCIMM.DAT

▸ Create a stacked bar chart, stacking by education level that shows the distribution of educational attainment within each racial/ethnic group.

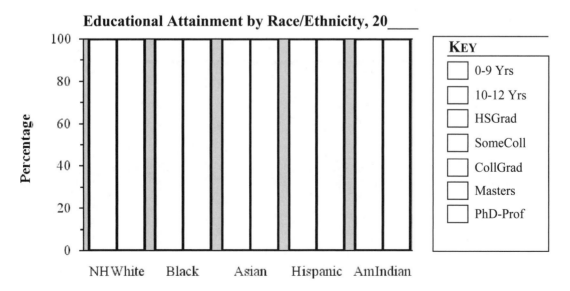

Educational Attainment by Race/Ethnicity, 20____

KEY
☐ 0-9 Yrs
☐ 10-12 Yrs
☐ HSGrad
☐ SomeColl
☐ CollGrad
☐ Masters
☐ PhD-Prof

Exercise 4 On your own, repeat Exercise 3 for people ages 45-54. Are the gaps among racial/ethnic groups wider in older cohorts? Offer possible explanations for your findings.

▶ *Dataset*: EDUCIMM.DAT

Exercise 5 Using current data, look at the educational attainment of 25-34 year-olds in each specific Asian ethnic category and describe any differences you find among the groups. Overall, how do Asians' educational levels compare to the attainment of the other racial/ethnic groups?

▶ *Dataset*: EARNASIANALL.DAT

▶ On your own, create a stacked bar chart showing the educational attainment distribution within each specific Asian group; stack by education level.

Exercise 6 On your own, repeat the previous exercise for specific Hispanic groups.

▶ *Dataset*: EDUC.TREND EDUCHISPALL.DAT

Exercise 7 Focusing on people ages 25-34, describe the race/ethnicity distribution of persons holding PhDs and other professional degrees in the present. Compare the representation of each racial/ethnic group to the representation of whites and other groups.

▶ *Dataset*: EDUCIMM.DAT

▶ Create a pie chart with divisions for each race/ethnicity.

PhD and Professional Degree Holders, 20____

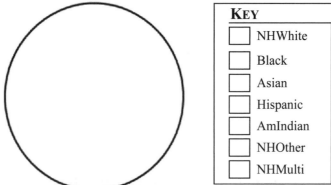

KEY	
☐	NHWhite
☐	Black
☐	Asian
☐	Hispanic
☐	AmIndian
☐	NHOther
☐	NHMulti

Discussion Questions

1. What do you think caused the gaps in educational attainment among racial/ethnic groups? What are the factors that affected the educational opportunities of certain racial/ethnic groups?

2. What might explain changes in educational attainment over time, overall, and within specific racial/ethnic groups?

3. Consider your findings regarding trends in the educational attainment of blacks and non-blacks since 1950 (Exercises 1 and 2). Does there appear to be a need for affirmative action programs and other policies designed to help improve educational opportunities for blacks? Why or why not?

B. Occupation and Race/Ethnicity

The last half of the twentieth century witnessed great changes in the racial/ethnic composition of the U.S. labor force. In recent years, many occupations traditionally held by white males have gradually become more representative of the population as a whole. Today, minorities are filling more managerial and professional positions than ever before.

Several factors have contributed to this shift. The Civil Rights Act of 1964 paved the way towards eliminating discrimination in hiring and promotion practices. Affirmative action programs in government jobs and in many large companies have continued the effort to open new job opportunities to minority groups. In addition, the influx of minority high school and college graduates into the workforce has improved the overall occupational status of minorities.

However, minorities are still faced with barriers to advancement. They are often clustered in lower-status occupations and face continued discrimination in hiring and promotions. Though from the shop floor to the executive office, doors seem to be opening for minorities, they often encounter closed doors farther along the career path. In many corporations, minority employees face a so-called "glass ceiling" where a qualified person is denied senior positions because of some sort of discrimination such as sexism, racism, or disability.

In the following exercises, you will examine the racial/ethnic composition of several occupational categories and determine how this distribution has changed since 1950. You will also look at the race/ethnicity of doctors and lawyers in 2000 in an effort to gauge how many minorities have gained entry into these prestigious occupations.

Exercise 8 Using data from 1950 to the present, look at the percentage of the labor force in each occupational category. What kind of trends do you see in the positions held by men versus those held by women?

▸ *Dataset*: EDUCOCCUP.TREND

▸ Create two stacked bar charts, one for men and one for women. In each chart, for each year, stack by occupational categories.

Women's Occupations, 1950 to 20____

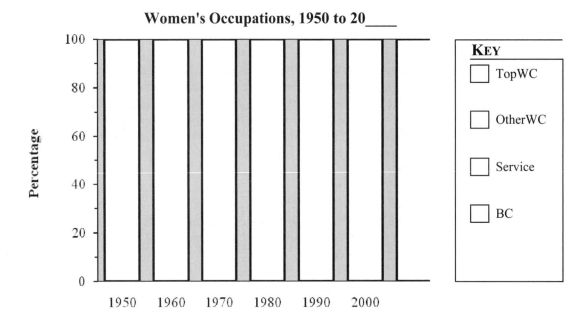

Exercise 9 Looking at data from 1950 through the present, examine the occupational distribution of black and non-black men aged 35 to 44. Compare the distribution of these two groups to each other and to the overall trends in occupational categories that you found in Exercise 8. Do you find it useful to look only at 35-44 year-olds when making occupational comparisons? Why or why not?

▶ *Dataset*: EDUCOCCUP.TREND

▶ Create four line graphs, one for each occupational category. Draw two lines in each chart, one for black men and one for non-black men between the ages of 35 and 44. For each year, indicate the percentage of each group employed in the specified occupational category.

Top White Collar: Black & Non-Black Men, 1950 to 20____

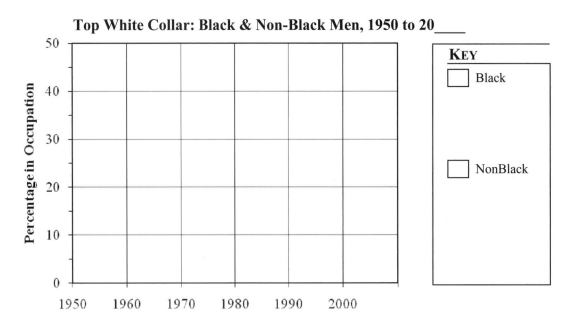

Other White Collar: Black & Non-Black Men, 1950 to 20____

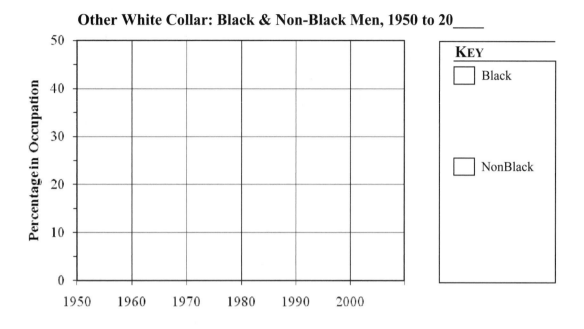

Service: Black and Non-Black Men, 1950 to 20____

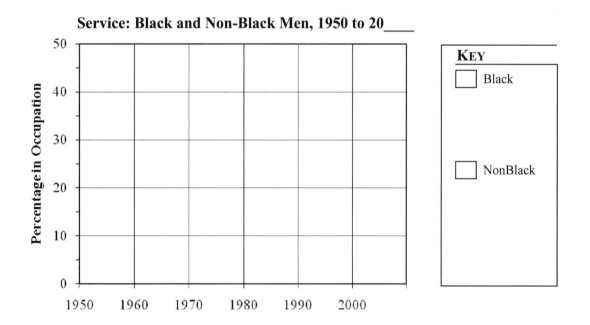

Blue Collar: Black and Non-Black Men, 1950 to 20____

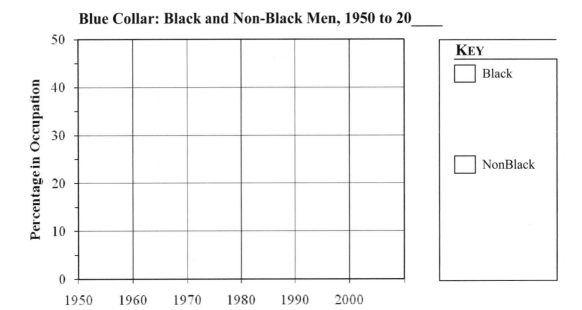

KEY

☐ Black

☐ NonBlack

Exercise 10 Are the racial gaps you explored in Exercise 9 different for women? Examine the occupational distribution of black and non-black women from 1950 to the present. Compare the distribution of these two groups to each other and to the trends for men. Why is it useful to look at men's and women's occupational trends separately?

▸ *Dataset*: EDUCOCCUP.TREND

▸ On your own, create four line graphs, one for each occupational category. Draw two lines in each chart, one for black women and one for non-black women, aged 35 to 44. Indicate the percentage of each group employed in the specified occupational category.

Exercise 11 Focusing on current data, look at the occupation distribution of 35-44 year-old black, non-Hispanic white, Asian, and Hispanic men and women. Between which racial/ethnic groups do you see the greatest differences?

▸ *Dataset*: OCCUP.DAT

▸ Create eight pie charts, one for men and one for women in each racial/ethnic group mentioned above, with divisions for each occupational category.

Occupational Distributions by Gender and Race/Ethnicity, 20____

White Men   White Women

KEY

☐ TopWC
☐ OtherWC
☐ TopBC
☐ OtherBC
☐ Service
☐ Farm

graphs continue on next page

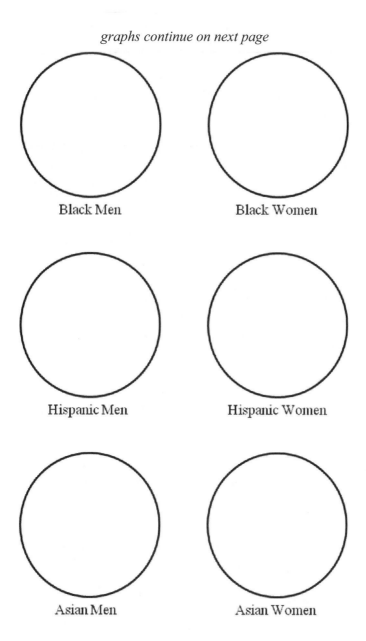

Black Men   Black Women

Hispanic Men   Hispanic Women

Asian Men   Asian Women

Exercise 12 Focusing on 35-44 year-old men, show the current occupational distribution for each Hispanic ethnic group. Describe the differences between occupational categories among the Hispanic groups. Overall, how does the occupational distribution of Hispanics compare with that of other racial/ethnic groups? What factors, if any, could account for the difference among groups? How about for the differences between occupational categories within each Hispanic group?

▶ *Dataset*: OCCUPHISPALL.DAT

▶ Create a stacked bar chart, stacked by each occupational category, showing occupational distribution within each specific Hispanic group.

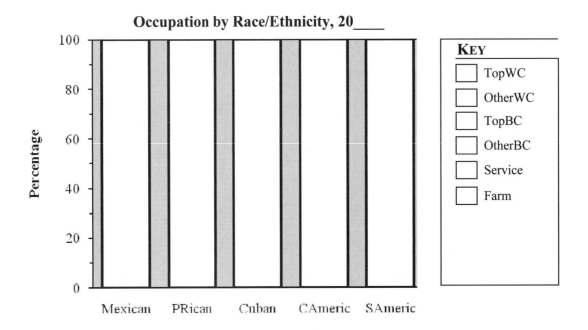

Occupation by Race/Ethnicity, 20____

KEY
- TopWC
- OtherWC
- TopBC
- OtherBC
- Service
- Farm

Exercise 13 On your own, repeat Exercise 12 for specific Asian groups.

▶ *Dataset*: OCCUPASIAN.DAT

Exercise 14 Using current data, show the occupational distribution of 35-44 year-old men and women based on their educational backgrounds. What does the relationship between education and occupational category appear to be?

▶ *Dataset*: OCCUPIMM-35.DAT

▶ Create a stacked bar chart with side-by-side bars for men and women. For each educational category, stack by occupational distribution.

Men's and Women's Occupations by Education, 20____

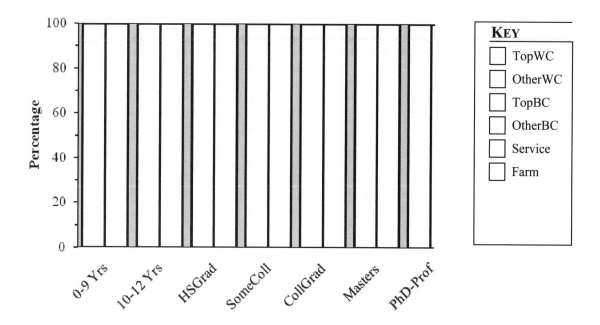

Exercise 15 Focusing on male college graduates aged 35-44 in the present year, examine the occupational distribution within each racial/ethnic group. Describe your findings.

  ‣ *Dataset*: OCCUPIMM-35.DAT

  ‣ Create a stacked bar chart showing the occupational distribution for each racial/ethnic group; stack by occupation.

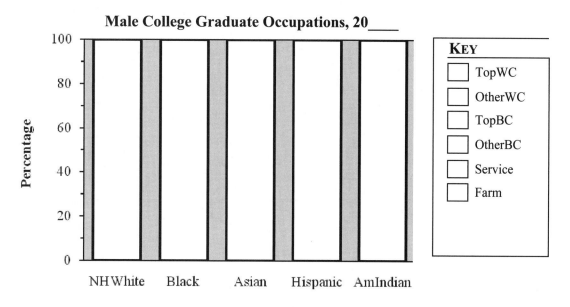

Exercise 16 Looking at female college graduates aged 35-44 in the present year, determine the occupational distribution within each racial/ethnic group. Describe your findings, and how they differ from the results of Exercise 15.

  ‣ *Dataset*: OCCUPIMM-35.DAT

  ‣ Create a stacked bar chart showing the occupational distribution within each racial/ethnic group; stack by occupation.

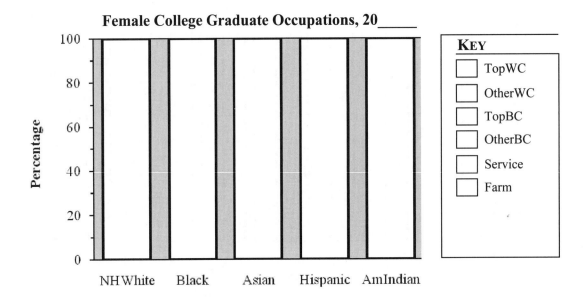

Female College Graduate Occupations, 20_____

KEY
- TopWC
- OtherWC
- TopBC
- OtherBC
- Service
- Farm

Exercise 17 Compare the racial/ethnic composition of medical doctors, ages 25-34, with those ages 55-64. How does the representation of each racial/ethnic group compare to the representation of that group in the population as a whole? Do you notice any differences between the two age groups?

▸ *Dataset*: DOCTORS.DAT

▸ Create two pie charts, one for each age group, with divisions for each racial/ethnic group.

Race/Ethnicity of Doctors, 20____

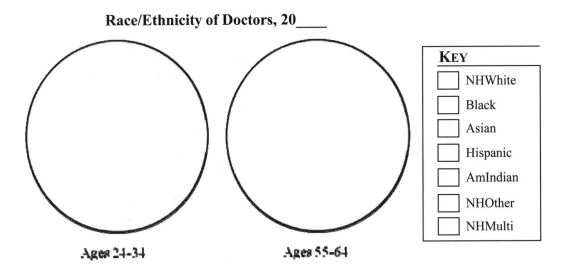

KEY
- NHWhite
- Black
- Asian
- Hispanic
- AmIndian
- NHOther
- NHMulti

Ages 24-34   Ages 55-64

Exercise 18 Focusing on those doctors, ages 25 to 34, in the present year, compare the racial/ethnic composition of male doctors with that of female doctors. How does controlling for gender affect the results from Exercise 17?

▸ *Dataset*: DOCTORS.DAT

▸ Create two pie charts, one for each gender, with divisions for each racial/ethnic group.

Race/Ethnicity Distribution of Doctors by Gender, 20_____

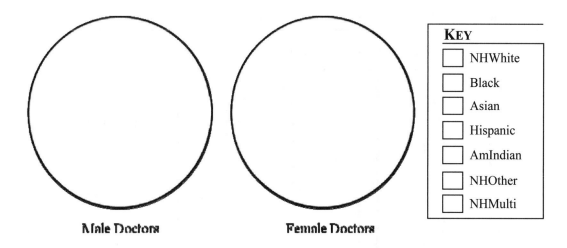

Male Doctors   **Female Doctors**

Exercise 19 On your own, repeat the previous two exercises for male and female lawyers, ages 2534, and 55-64, in the present. Describe the differences between age groups and between genders.

▶ *Dataset*: LAWYERS.DAT

Discussion Questions

1. Why do you think that occupational distributions vary between genders and among different races/ethnicities? What connection do you find between an individual's educational attainment and his or her occupation? Do you think that gender and race/ ethnicity affect the relationship between education and occupation?

2. How do you think historical events over the past hundred years have affected the overall occupational distribution? Think about changes in the percentage of workers with blue-collar jobs between 1950 and the present. What trends do you find in the composition of this category? Why do you think that there have been changes in the types of jobs people have?

C. Earnings Inequalities

Income rose for all racial/ethnic groups in the United States during the economic growth of the late 1990's, but despite this overall increase, a gap between the earnings of whites and minorities still persists. Many argue that this gap is due to the lower education levels and different occupational distribution of minorities; however, whites tend to earn more than their minority counterparts even when their education level and occupation are the same. In this section, you will examine earnings differences among persons of different racial/ethnic groups but with similar occupations and educational backgrounds.

Exercise 20 Using current data, examine the earnings distribution of men, ages 35-44, for each racial/ethnic group. Describe any significant differences that you find.

▶ *Dataset*: EARN.DAT

▸ Create a stacked bar chart with bars for each racial/ethnic group; stack by earnings.

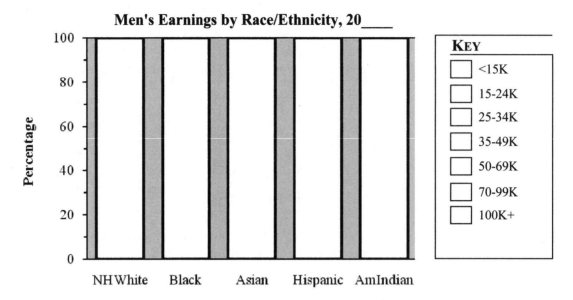

Men's Earnings by Race/Ethnicity, 20____

Exercise 21 How do women's earnings differ from those of their male counterparts? Are there similar differences among racial/ethnic groups? Using current data, illustrate the distribution of earnings among women, ages 35-44. Describe any significant differences among racial/ethnic groups.

▸ *Dataset*: EARN.DAT

▸ Create a stacked bar chart with bars for each racial/ethnic group; stack by earnings.

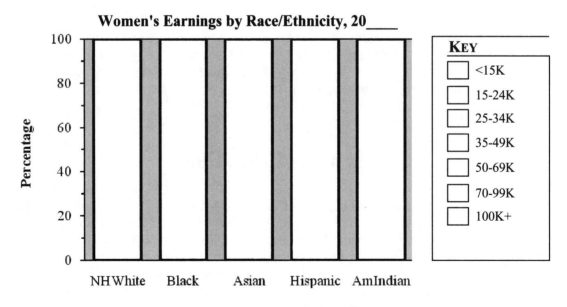

Women's Earnings by Race/Ethnicity, 20____

Exercise 22 Using current data, examine the earnings distribution in each occupational category. What relationship between earnings and occupation do you find? After determining the relationship between occupation and earnings, look specifically at the earnings of men, ages 35-44, in top white-collar occupations. Describe the differences you find among racial/ethnic groups.

- *Dataset*: WORK-35.DAT

  ▸ On your own, create a stacked bar chart with bars for each occupational category; stack by earnings.

  ▸ On your own, create a stacked bar chart only for men in top white-collar positions. Draw bars for each racial/ethnic group and stack by earnings.

Exercise 23 On your own, explore and describe earnings differences among specific Asian groups for men aged 35-44 years old in the present. How does the earnings distribution vary? Offer possible explanations for your findings.

  ▸ *Dataset*: EARNASIANALL.DAT

Exercise 24 On your own, repeat the previous exercise for specific Hispanic groups in the present.

  ▸ *Dataset*: EARNHISPALL.DAT

Exercise 25 On your own, focus on full-time, year-round male workers, ages 35-44. Determine if gaps in earnings along racial/ethnic lines are due mostly to a) racial/ethnic differences in educational attainment or b) differences in occupation among racial/ethnic groups.

  ▸ *Dataset*: WORK-35.DAT

Exercise 26 On your own, explore and describe earnings differences among 35-44 year-old women of specific Asian groups in the present. How does the earnings distribution vary? Offer possible explanations for your findings.

  ▸ *Dataset*: EARNASIANALL.DAT

Exercise 27 On your own, repeat the previous exercise for specific Hispanic groups in the present.

  ▸ *Dataset*: EARNHISPALL.DAT

Exercise 28 On your own, focus on full-time, year-round female workers, ages 35-44. Determine if gaps in earnings among racial/ethnic lines are due mostly to a) racial/ethnic differences in educational attainment or b) differences in occupation among racial/ethnic groups.

  ▸ *Dataset*: WORK-35.DAT

Exercise 29 Examine the earnings distribution of all doctors in the present.

  ▸ *Dataset*: DOCTORS.DAT

  ▸ Create a bar chart with bars indicating the percentage of doctors in each earnings category. (Hint: Use the Marginals command.)

Doctors' Earnings, 20____

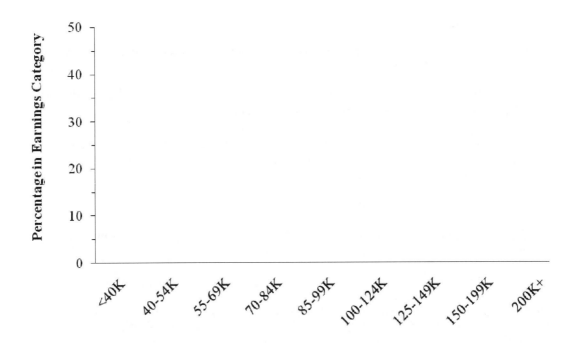

Exercise 30 Focusing on doctors, ages 25-34 and 55-64, examine earnings by race/ethnicity. What earnings differences do you see among racial/ethnic groups? Between the two age groups?

▸ *Dataset*: DOCTORS.DAT

▸ Create two stacked bar charts, one for each age group. Draw bars for each racial/ethnic group; stack by earnings.

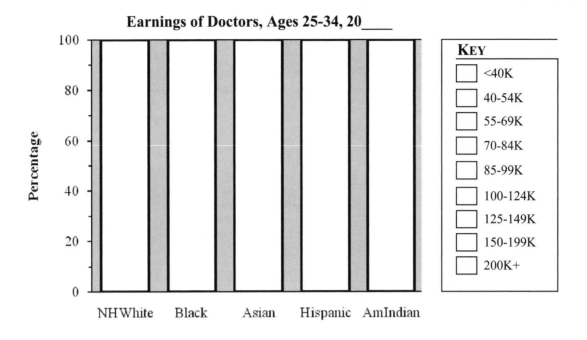

Earnings of Doctors, Ages 25-34, 20____

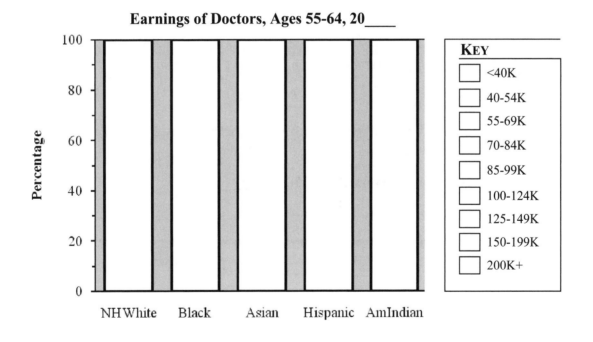

Earnings of Doctors, Ages 55-64, 20____

Exercise 31 Examine the earnings distribution for all lawyers in the present.

▶ *Dataset*: LAWYERS.DAT

▶ Create a bar chart with bars indicating the percentage of lawyers in each earnings category. (Hint: Use the Marginals command.)

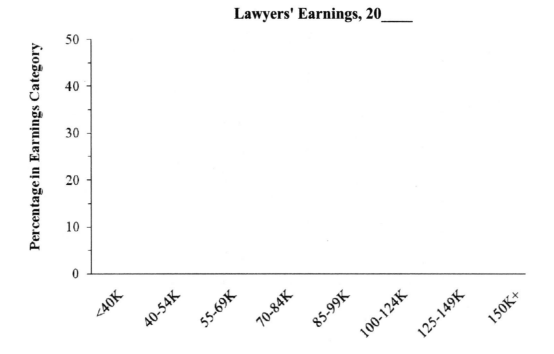

Lawyers' Earnings, 20____

Exercise 32 Focusing on lawyers, ages 25-34 and 55-64, show the earnings distribution by race/ethnicity. What differences in earnings do you find among racial/ethnic groups? Between age groups?

▸ *Dataset*: LAWYERS.DAT

▸ Create two stacked bar charts, one for each age group. Draw bars for each racial/ethnic group; stack by earnings.

Earnings of Lawyers, Ages 25-34, 20____

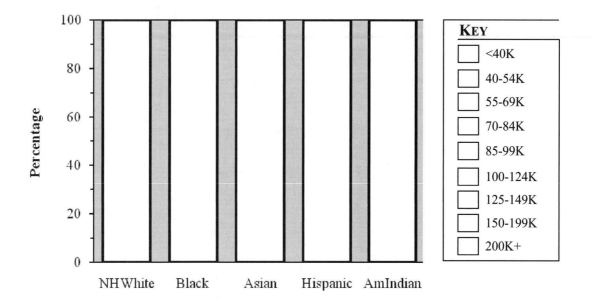

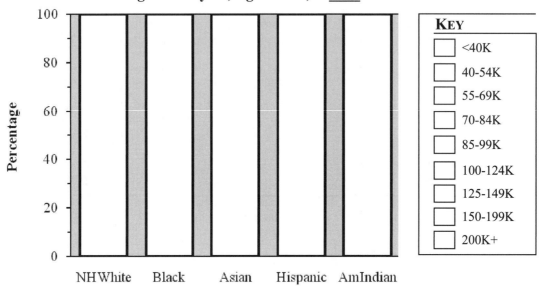

Earnings of Lawyers, Ages 55-64, 20____

KEY
- <40K
- 40-54K
- 55-69K
- 70-84K
- 85-99K
- 100-124K
- 125-149K
- 150-199K
- 200K+

Percentage (y-axis: 0, 20, 40, 60, 80, 100)

x-axis: NHWhite, Black, Asian, Hispanic, AmIndian

Discussion Questions

1. What differences in earnings exist among racial/ethnic groups? What role does educational attainment play in these differences? Do all racial/ethnic groups seem to experience similar "returns" on education?

2. How might you explain some of the differences discussed in the previous question? Why do you think these differences exist? Why have they persisted over time?

THINK
tank

1. Social critics argue that there has been a steady convergence among the races over the last few decades. Is the gap between blacks and whites narrowing in education, employment, and earnings? Do your results support the view that race is declining in significance, or indicate that further gains must be made before such optimism is justified? Would you say that Affirmative Action policies have outlived their usefulness?

2. Despite the increasing racial/ethnic diversity in the U.S., many housing markets are still highly segregated. Which racial/ethnic groups appear most likely to live in cities, suburbs, and non-metropolitan areas? Examine these racial/ethnic conditions by economic level. Do the more affluent segments of each racial/ethnic group live in the same place? What about the poor or middle income segments? What do you think influences housing segregation more: race/ethnicity or economic level?

chapter 3 IMMIGRANT ASSIMILATION

Immigration plays a vital role in shaping America's economic, political, and social landscape. Over the past fifty years, the most common source regions for immigrants have changed, as have their reasons for leaving and their choice of settlement areas within the U.S. Though the attention given to it by politicians and the public has waxed and waned over the years, immigration has remained a pertinent issue in the United States.

After the great influx of immigrants in the late nineteenth century, immigration had declined to historically low levels by the mid-twentieth century. However, with the 1965 Immigration Act and the easement of restrictive barriers to immigration, the number of immigrants entering the United States once again annually rose. Whereas in earlier periods most immigrants to the United States came from Eastern and Southern Europe and Canada, in recent decades the bulk of immigrants have come from Asia, Mexico, and other Latin American countries. This most recent trend is known as the "new immigration."

In any overview of immigration, the educational attainment, occupation, and earnings of the foreign-born population must be considered. Of particular interest to many social scientists is the relationship between the educational attainment of immigrants and their occupational choices and earnings. Furthermore, it can be extremely helpful to look at the types of jobs immigrants hold because of the impact that occupation has on income and social mobility. In turn, by looking at earnings, researchers can gauge the ease or difficulty immigrants have in reaching economic parity with native-born Americans.

In the following exercises, these and other factors will serve as your guide to studying immigration. You will look at who immigrates, where they settle in the United States, and what they do once they are here. You will consider current trends and how conditions for immigrants have changed over time. With these factors in mind, you will explore the degree to which immigrants have adopted the ideals and standards of the United States, and the degree to which they have maintained their own cultural heritage.

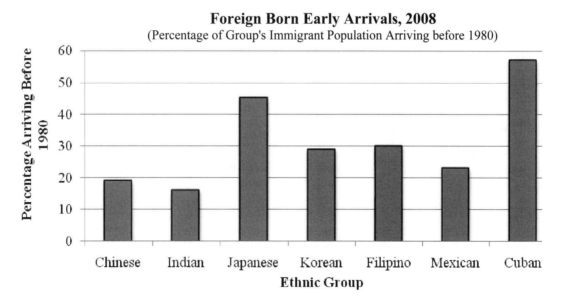

Foreign Born Early Arrivals, 2008
(Percentage of Group's Immigrant Population Arriving before 1980)

KEY

concepts

Immigration Status

U.S. residents can be classified as either native-born or foreign-born. The native-born population consists of persons born in the United States, including Puerto Rico and other outlying territories, as well as persons born abroad with at least one American parent. The foreign-born population includes all others born outside the United States. The foreign-born can be further classified by their year of entry into the U.S. The following categories are used here (dataset variable IMMIG) to classify the current U.S. population:

> Native-born
> Foreign-born entered before 1980
> Foreign-born entered 1980-1989
> Foreign-born entered 1990-1999
> Foreign-born entered 2000-present

NOTE: Dataset variables occasionally combine some of these categories

Origin Country

Foreign-born residents are classified by their country of birth. The following categories are used here (dataset variable ORIGIN6) to indicate the country or region of birth:

> Mexico
> OtrLatAm (Other Latin America)
> Asia
> Africa
> NAEurOcn (North America, Europe, and Oceania)

English Language Proficiency

The American Community Survey asks respondents if they speak only English at home and, if not, to indicate their own assessment of their English language ability. The following categories summarize possible responses for those who do not speak only English at home:

> Speaks English Very Well
> Speaks English Well
> Does Not Speak English Well
> Does Not Speak English at all

NOTE: The variable ENGSPK in the datasets abbreviates these responses as EngOnly (those who speak only English at home), Very well, Well, Not well, and Not at all.

A. The Immigrant Population

Over the last four decades, the racial/ethnic composition of the United States has steadily become more diverse. In fact, the United States is now one of the most multiethnic societies in the world. Immigration plays a significant role in this growing diversity.

The foreign-born population has increased absolutely and relatively since 1970. By 2008, the immigrant population accounted for twelve and a half percent of the total U.S. population, up from eleven percent in 2000 and eight percent in 1990. This "new immigration" is noteworthy not only because of its large size, but also because it represents a shift in source regions for immigration. Up through the mid-twentieth century, the majority of immigrants to the United States came from Canada and Europe. In the last fifty years, however, that population has declined steadily while the number of immigrants arriving in the United States from Latin America and Asia has continually increased.

Exercise 1 To set the stage for the issues you will explore in this chapter, look at the percentage of each racial/ethnic group made up of immigrants in the present. What general patterns do you find?

▸ *Dataset*: POP.TREND

▸ Create a pie chart for each racial/ethnic group. In each chart, make divisions based on immigration status.

Immigration Status Distribution by Race/Ethnicity, 20____

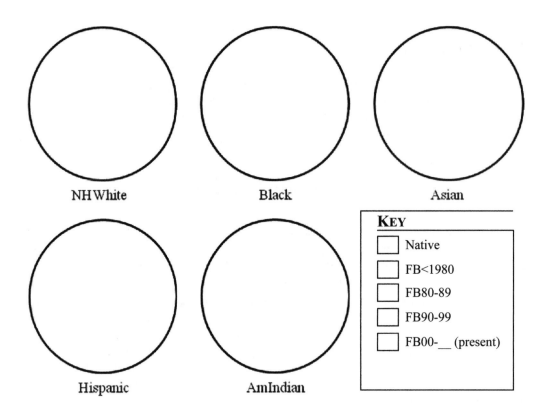

NH White   Black   Asian

Hispanic   AmIndian

KEY

☐ Native

☐ FB<1980

☐ FB80-89

☐ FB90-99

☐ FB00-__ (present)

Exercise 2 Now look at the immigration status of each specific Asian group. Which groups have the most native-born members? The most foreign-born? Which groups have the earliest immigrants? The most recent? Why do you think this is so?

▸ *Dataset*: ASIANPOP.DAT

▸ Create a stacked bar chart with bars for each specific Asian group. Stack by native-born, immigrated before 1980, immigrated between 1980 and 1989, immigrated between 1990 and 1999, and immigrated between 2000 and the present.

Immigration Status for Asian Groups, 20____

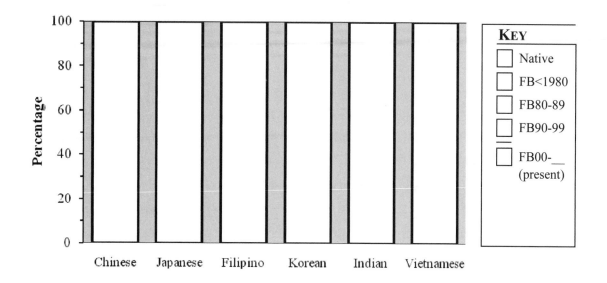

Exercise 3 Repeat the previous exercise for each specific Hispanic group.

▶ *Dataset*: HISPPOP.DAT

▶ Create a stacked bar chart with bars for each specific Hispanic group. Stack by native-born, immigrated before 1980, immigrated between 1980 and 1989, immigrated between 1990 and 1999, and immigrated between 2000 and the present.

Immigration Status for Hispanic Groups, 20____

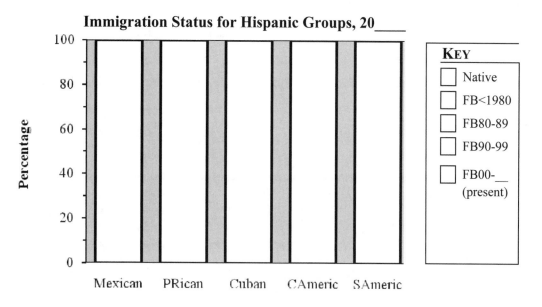

Exercise 4 Looking at people who immigrated to the United States since 2000, examine gender differences for each race/ethnicity. What differences do you find among the racial/ethnic groups?

▶ *Dataset*: IMMPOP.DAT

▶ Create a bar chart with side-by-side bars for men and women. For each racial/ethnic group, indicate the current number of immigrants.

Gender Differences in Recent Immigration by Race/Ethnicity, 20____

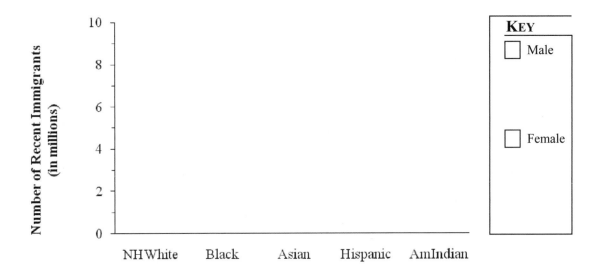

Exercise 5 Now look at the differences in numbers between men and women of specific Asian groups who have immigrated to the U.S. since 2000. What differences in numbers do you find between males and females? How does this vary for the different groups?

▸ *Dataset*: ASIANPOP.DAT

▸ On your own, create a bar chart with side-by-side bars for males and females and for each group, indicate the number of immigrants.

Exercise 6 Repeat the previous exercise for each specific Hispanic group.

▸ *Dataset*: HISPPOP.DAT

▸ On your own, create a bar chart with side-by-side bars for males and females and for each group, indicate the number of immigrants.

Discussion Questions

1. While reviewing your graphs showing the years in which different immigrant groups came to the U.S., consider the historical events that were occurring during the various time periods. What historical events do you think affected immigration the most?

2. What factors do you think influence the difference between the number of male and female immigrants? Conditions of native countries? Conditions in the U.S.? From what region does the largest group of female immigrants come from? Why do you think that this is the case?

B. **Immigrant Geographic Location**

Many immigrants settle near earlier immigrants from their country of origin who have already acclimated to life in the United States. The established support network present in such communities provides stability and crucial contacts for immigrants arriving in a completely new world. Additionally, since many people immigrate to the United States with the goal of improving their economic situation and that of their families, the availability of jobs also affects where immigrants choose to settle. Finally, immigrants tend to settle, at least initially, in or near ports of entry. Once all of these factors are taken it into account, it is not surprising that the areas with the largest immigrant populations are in or near large metropolitan cities. The cities with the largest immigrant populations are Los Angeles, New York, and Chicago.

Exercise 7 Compare the current immigration status distribution of Los Angeles to that of the United States as a whole. Are the distributions similar?

▸ *Datasets*: POP.TREND, POPLACNTY.DAT

▸ Create two pie charts, one for Los Angeles and one for the United States. In each chart, make divisions for native-born, immigrated before 1980, immigrated between 1980 and 1989, immigrated between 1990 and 1999, and immigrated between 2000 and the present.

Immigration Status Distribution in Los Angeles and the U.S., 20____

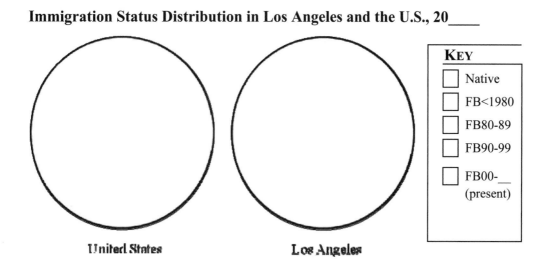

United States   Los Angeles

Exercise 8 Now look at the immigration status distribution of Los Angeles for each racial/ethnic group in the present. Which racial/ethnic groups have a greater number of recent immigrants? Which have a larger proportion of the earliest immigrants?

▸ *Dataset*: POPLACNTY.DAT

▸ Create a stacked bar chart for Los Angeles. In the chart, make bars for each racial/ethnic group; stack by immigration status.

Immigration Status Distribution of Los Angeles by Race/Ethnicity, 20____

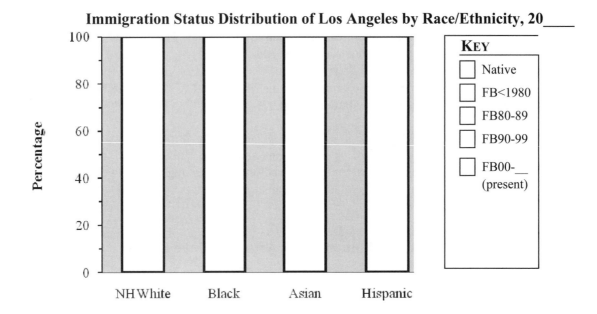

Exercise 9 Now look at the immigration status distribution for specific states in the present. Which states have the largest percentages of recent immigrants? Earliest immigrants?

▸ *Dataset*: IMMPOP.DAT

▸ Create a stacked bar chart with bars for each state; stack by immigration status.

Immigration Status by State, 20____

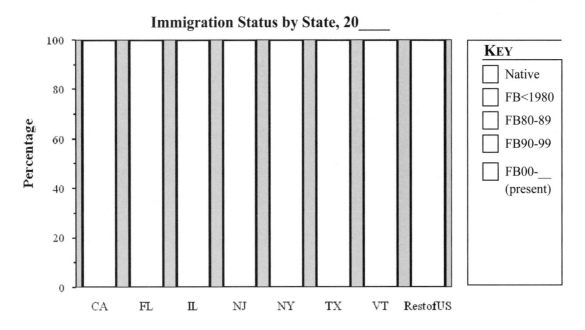

Exercise 10 On your own, explore how recent immigration has affected the racial/ethnic composition of certain states and the United States as a whole.

▸ *Dataset*: IMMPOP.DAT

C. Immigrant Age Structure

The age distribution of immigrants directly affects fertility, health care, education, and employment in society as a whole. For example, many Asian immigrants arrive during their child-bearing years and will have children after settling in the United States. As a result, the Asian population in the United States will grow at a faster rate than if the bulk of Asian immigrants arrived past their childbearing years.

An immigrant's age upon arrival also offers clues as to why he or she chose to come to the United States. Generally, younger immigrants cross the border into American with the hopes of financial and material success. Older immigrants, on the other hand, often seek reunification with relatives who have already immigrated to the United States.

Exercise 11 Look at the age distribution of the United States in the present and compare it to the age distribution of recent immigrants (those arriving in the U.S. since 2000). How are the distributions different?

‣ *Dataset*: POP.TREND

‣ Create two pie charts, one for the total U.S. population and one for the immigrant population arriving after 2000. Make divisions for ages 0-14, 15-34, 35-64, and 65+. (Hint: Add or combine age categories when necessary.)

Age Distribution of Recent Immigrants, 20____

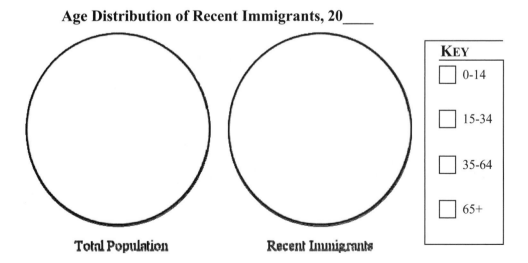

Total Population   Recent Immigrants

KEY
☐ 0-14
☐ 15-34
☐ 35-64
☐ 65+

Exercise 12 Focusing on foreign-born Asians in the present, compare the age distribution of immigrants in each specific Asian group. What trends do you find?

▸ *Dataset*: ASIANPOP.DAT

▸ Create a stacked bar chart with bars for immigrants of each Asian group. Stack by ages 0-14, 15-34, 35-64, and 65+. (Hint: Add or combine age categories when necessary.)

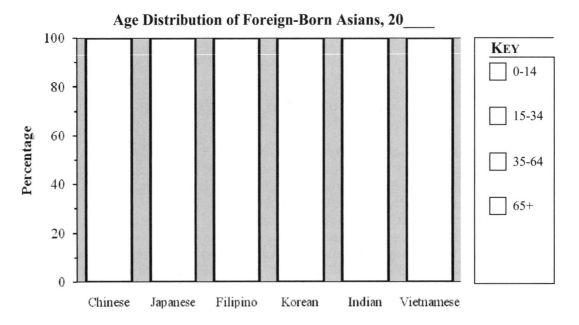

Age Distribution of Foreign-Born Asians, 20____

Exercise 13 Compare the current age distribution for foreign-born persons among specific Hispanic groups. What trends do you notice?

▸ *Dataset*: HISPPOP.DAT

▸ On your own, create a stacked bar chart with bars for immigrants of each Hispanic group. Stack by ages 0-14, 15-34, 35-64, and 65+.

Discussion Questions

1. Is the age distribution for those who immigrated to the U.S. between 1990 and the present similar to the age distribution of the U.S. as a whole? Why do you think this is so? How do you think the age distributions of earlier immigrants might have differed from those of later immigrants?

2. While looking at the Asian and Hispanic immigrant age distributions, consider why people arrive at the age they do. Do you think the reasons for coming to the United States vary among immigrants of different ages? Consider factors that might prompt people to immigrate such as seeking political asylum, work opportunities, and family reunification.

D. English Language Proficiency

An immigrant's command of English impacts his or her occupation, earnings, and adjustment to living in the United States. While most acknowledge that fluency in English is an important tool for immigrants, some Americans feel that immigrants should be required to speak English and some states have proposed paring down services offered in languages other than English. By looking at English proficiency among immigrant populations, you can investigate whom such policies would affect.

English fluency tends to vary according to an immigrant's region of origin. To a large extent, this variation reflects which immigrant groups are exposed to English before arriving in the United States. Generally speaking, English proficiency increases as duration of residence increases, thus, how long an immigrant resides in the United States plays a significant role in how proficient they are in the English language. However, an immigrant's age upon arrival, education level, and proximity to others who speak his or her native language all affect an immigrant's English proficiency level regardless of region of origin or duration of residence.

Exercise 14 Looking at all foreign-born Asians and Hispanics, show the distribution of degrees of English proficiency.

> ▸ *Datasets*: ENGHISP.DAT, ENGASIAN.DAT

> ▸ Create two pie charts, one for Asians and one for Hispanics. In each chart, make divisions for English proficiency categories.

English Proficiency Distribution of Foreign-Born Asians and Hispanics, 20____

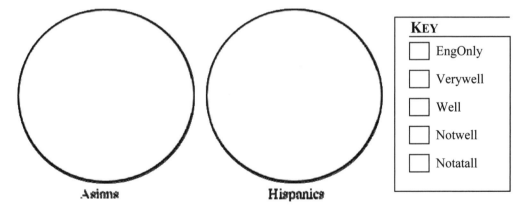

Exercise 15 Now look at English language proficiency among specific Asian groups. In which group does the largest percentage of members speak English? What group has the greatest percentage of individuals who do not speak English well or at all? What might account for these differences?

> ▸ *Dataset*: ENGASIAN.DAT

> ▸ Create a stacked bar chart with bars for each Asian group and stack by language proficiency.

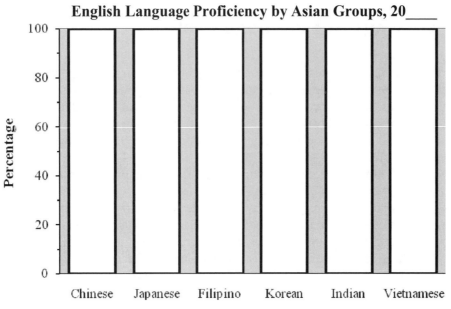

English Language Proficiency by Asian Groups, 20____

KEY

☐ EngOnly

☐ Verywell

☐ Well

☐ Notwell

☐ Notatall

Exercise 16 On your own, repeat the previous exercise for specific Hispanic groups.

▸ *Datasets*: ENGHISP.DAT

Exercise 17 Now consider the duration of residence for all foreign-born individuals in Asian and Hispanic groups. Examine the language proficiency of recent immigrants versus that of earlier immigrants. How does English proficiency change as immigrants are in the U.S. for longer periods of time?

▸ *Datasets*: ENGHISP.DAT, ENGASIAN.DAT

▸ On your own, create two stacked bar charts, one for Asians and one for Hispanics. In each chart, create bars for each immigrant status category and stack by language proficiency.

Discussion Questions

1. Recall Exercises 15 and 16, in which you looked at language proficiency for immigrants of different Asian and Hispanic groups. Which group has the highest percentage of members who are proficient English speakers? Why do you think this is the case? Cultural factors? Educational factors?

2. Now turn your attention to Exercise 17, in which you looked at the relative language proficiency of earlier and more recent immigrants. What factors do you think shape this distribution? Increased education? Attempts at assimilation? In general, does an immigrant's English proficiency always improve the longer he or she has been in the country? If not, provide some explanations for why proficiency in English might not always increase with the duration of residence in the U.S.

E. Education and Assimilation

Immigrants' education levels vary more than those of native-born Americans, with many immigrants at both extremes of educational attainment (PhDs and those without high school training). Among immigrant groups, there are some interesting patterns involving educational attainment. The proportion of immigrants who have attained a relatively high level of education is greater for men than it is for women. Immigrants' educational attainment also varies across regions of origin.

Exercise 18 Look at the educational attainment distribution for the entire U.S. population of individuals aged 25-34 in the present.

▸ *Dataset*: EDUCIMM.DAT

▸ Create a pie chart with divisions for education levels.

Educational Distribution of the U.S.: Ages 25-34, 20____

KEY
☐ 0-9 Yrs
☐ 10-12 Yrs
☐ HSGrad
☐ SomeColl
☐ CollGrad
☐ Masters
☐ PhD-Prof

Exercise 19 Now look at the differences in educational attainment among foreign-born individuals, ages 25-34, in specific Asian groups. In which group does the largest percentage of persons have a college degree? In which group is the rate of college graduation the lowest?

▸ *Dataset*: EDUCASIAN.DAT

▸ Create a stacked bar chart with bars for each group and stack by education level.

Educational Attainment of Foreign-Born Asian Groups, 20____

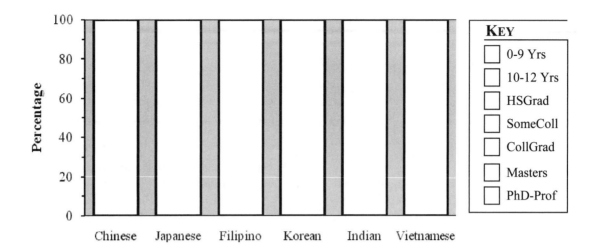

Exercise 20 Now take a look at the differences in educational attainment among foreign-born individuals, ages 25-34, in specific Hispanic groups. In which group does the largest percentage of persons have a college degree? In which group is the rate of college graduation the lowest?

▸ EDUCHISP.DAT

▸ Create a stacked bar chart with bars for each group and stack by education level.

Educational Attainment of Foreign-Born Hispanic Groups, 20____

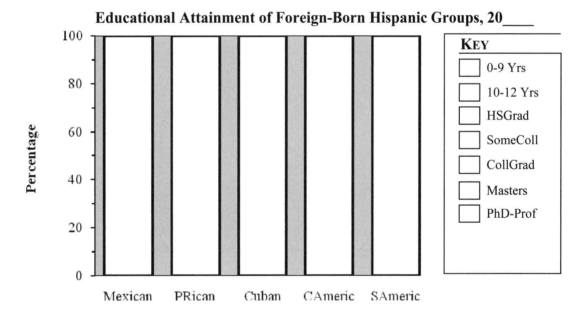

Exercise 21 Is the educational attainment of immigrants influenced by the duration of their residence in the United States? On your own, compare the educational attainment distribution of recent immigrants (2000 to the present) with that of those who came to the United States before 1980. Look at this relationship in a few racial/ethnic groups of your choice. Does the relationship between education and immigrant status vary among racial/ethnic groups?

▸ *Dataset*: EDUCIMM.DAT

Discussion Questions

1. Consider the educational attainment differences you found among specific Asian groups and specific Hispanic groups. What do you think could explain these differences? Cultural factors? Economic factors?

2. Consider the growing need in the U.S. for specific types of skilled and unskilled labor. Based on immigration patterns, are these needs being met by recent immigrants? Do you think that the needs of the labor force should influence the development of immigration policy?

F. Occupation and Assimilation

Variations in occupation among different groups of immigrants often reflect disparities in educational attainment and English language proficiency, two factors you have already considered. A large number of immigrants who have professional and managerial jobs are from Asia and Europe, while Hispanics comprise a significant proportion of the immigrants who have labor and service positions.

In addition to looking at how an immigrant's country of origin impacts occupational choices, it is important to look at gender differences and how they play out in the immigrant community. Today, male immigrants are heavily concentrated in service and agricultural jobs and have the lowest representation in managerial and sales positions. Female immigrants, on the other hand, tend to be concentrated in service and blue-collar employment.

Exercise 22 Focusing on men between the ages of 25 and 34, examine the occupational distribution of the entire U.S. population in the present. Compare it to the occupation distribution of men between the ages of 25 and 34 who immigrated to the U.S. since 2000. How are the distributions different?

▶ *Dataset*: OCCUPIMM-25.DAT *Dataset*: POP.TREND

▶ Create two pie charts, one for the U.S. and one for recent immigrants. Make divisions for the occupational categories.

Men's Occupations, 20____

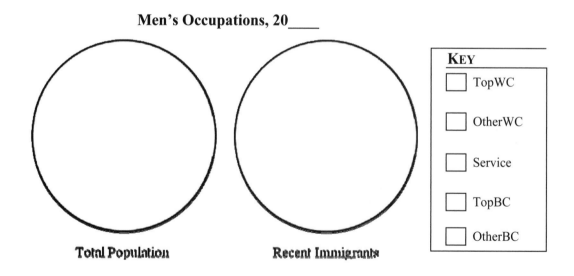

	KEY
☐	TopWC
☐	OtherWC
☐	Service
☐	TopBC
☐	OtherBC

Total Population   Recent Immigrants

Exercise 23 Still focusing on 25-34 year-old males, consider the ways in which occupational distribution changes as immigrants have been in the U.S. for longer periods of time. What sorts of immigrants are most likely to occupy top white-collar positions?

▶ *Dataset*: OCCUPIMM-25.DAT

▶ Create a stacked bar chart with bars for each immigration status; stack by occupation.

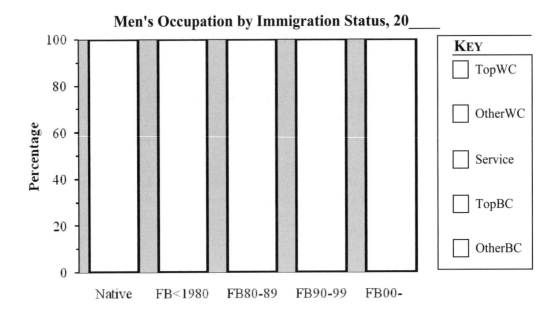

Men's Occupation by Immigration Status, 20____

Exercise 24 Look at the occupational distribution for 25-35 year-old Asian males and females. Compare the occupational distribution of recent immigrants to that of earlier immigrants. What are the gender differences?

▸ *Dataset*: EDUCIMM.DAT

▸ Create two stacked bar charts, one for men and one for women. In each chart, draw bars for each immigration status and stack by occupation.

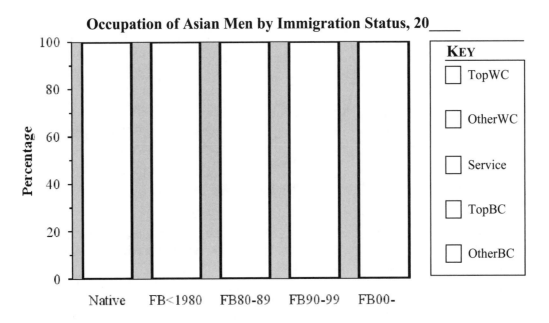

Occupation of Asian Men by Immigration Status, 20____

Occupation of Asian Women by Immigration Status, 20____

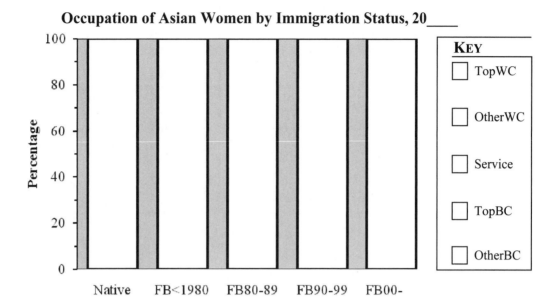

Exercise 25 On your own, repeat the previous exercise for Hispanics. How do Hispanics compare to Asians in terms of occupational distribution?

▸ *Dataset*: OCCUPIMM-25.DAT

Exercise 26 Now examine the occupational distribution of Asian and Hispanic immigrants at each educational level. You may focus on either males OR females, ages 25-34. As educational levels increase, what happens to the occupational distribution? Does the relationship between education and occupation vary between Asians and Hispanics?

▸ *Dataset*: OCCUPIMM-25.DAT

▸ Create two stacked bar charts, one for Asians and one for Hispanics. In each chart, draw bars for each educational level and stack by occupation. Specify whether you looked at males or females.

Occupation of Asians by Education, 20____

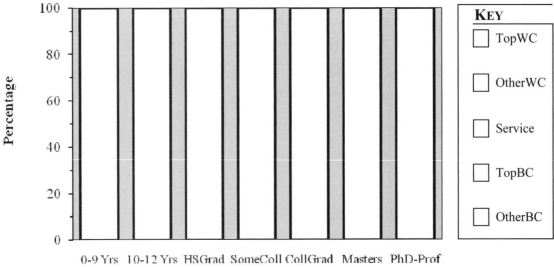

Occupation of Hispanics by Education, 20____

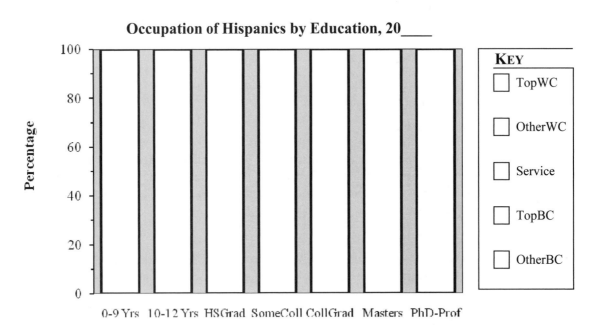

Discussion Questions

1. Consider the relationship between occupational distribution, English language proficiency, education, and duration of residence in the United States. Which factors do you think have the greatest influence on the occupational distribution of immigrants?

2. As education levels increased for immigrants, did their occupational distribution become more similar to the occupational distribution of the U.S. as a whole? If not, why do you think that this is the case?

G. Earnings and Assimilation

In addition to indicating economic status, earnings serve as an important measure of immigrants' adjustment to life in the United States and integration into the American economy. Overall, the earnings of male immigrants are significantly lower than that of their native-born counterparts, but immigrants' earnings do tend to increase as their duration of residence in the United States increases. This growth in earnings stems from a number of factors, including greater experience in the U.S. labor market, continued education following immigration, and better English language proficiency.

Like occupation, education, and English language proficiency, earnings vary by an immigrant's region of origin. Immigrants from Europe and Canada tend to have the highest earnings among foreign-born Americans, followed closely by Asian immigrants. On the other hand, earnings of Latin American immigrants tend to be lower than those of other immigrants. Part of this is due to the rise in earnings that comes with prolonged residence in the United States; European and Canadian immigrants, generally speaking, have resided in the United States for longer periods of time while their Latin American counterparts are more recent arrivals.

Exercise 27 Focusing on males aged 25-34, examine the earnings distribution of the entire U.S. population and compare it to the earnings distribution of those who immigrated to the U.S. since 2000. How do the distributions differ?

▸ *Dataset*: WORKIMM-25.DAT

▸ Create two pie charts, one for the U.S. as a whole and one for recent immigrants. In each chart, make divisions for earnings categories.

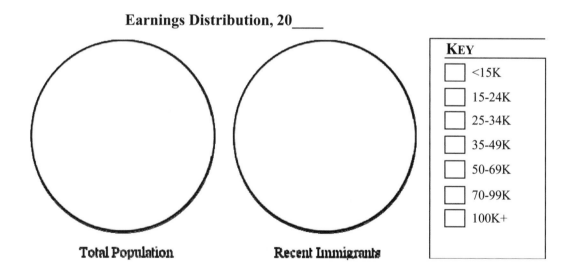

Exercise 28 Now look specifically at male college graduates, ages 25-34, in top white-collar positions. Compare the earnings of recent immigrants (since 2000) to the native-born population. Do the two groups show similar distributions? Why or why not?

▸ *Dataset*: WORKIMM-25.DAT

▸ Create two pie charts, one for recent immigrants and one for native-born Americans. In each chart, make divisions for earnings categories.

Earnings Distribution of College Graduates, Ages 25-34, 20____

Native Born   Recent Immigrants

KEY	
☐	<15K
☐	15-24K
☐	25-34K
☐	35-49K
☐	50-69K
☐	70-99K
☐	100K+

Exercise 29 Focusing on Hispanic men, ages 35-44 in the present, explore the earnings distribution as it relates to immigration status. Do earnings consistently increase as the duration of residence increases?

▸ *Dataset*: WORKHISP-35.DAT

▸ Create a stacked bar chart with bars for each immigration status category and stack by earnings

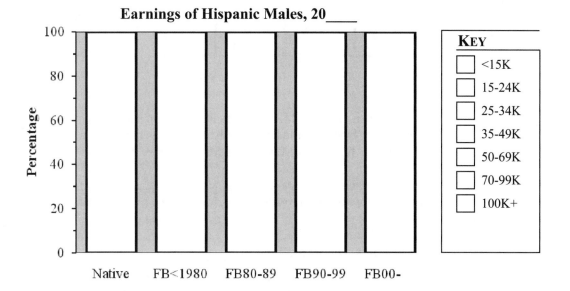

Exercise 30 Taking into account immigration status, determine the earnings distribution of Hispanic males, ages 35-44, in top white-collar positions in the present. What trends do you notice among those who earn more than $35,000 a year?

▸ *Dataset*: WORKHISP-35.DAT

▸ Create a stacked bar chart for Hispanic top white-collar male workers with bars for each immigration status category; stack by earnings.

Earnings of Top White Collar Hispanic Males, 20____

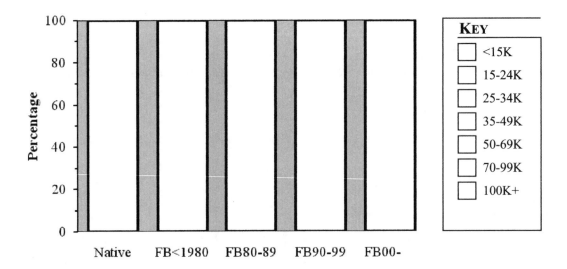

Exercise 31 Now look at Asian men, ages 35-44. How does immigration status affect the earnings distribution in this group? Does income consistently increase as the duration of residence increases? Compare your findings to your results from Exercise 29.

▸ *Dataset*: WORKASIAN-35.DAT

▸ Create a stacked bar chart with bars for each immigration status category; stack by earnings.

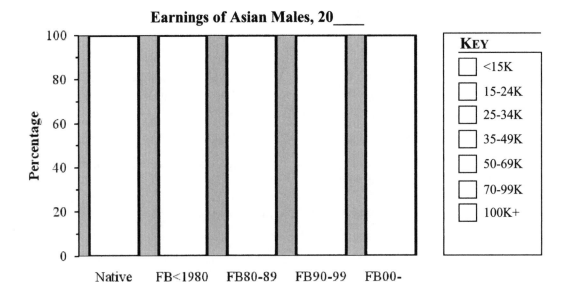

Earnings of Asian Males, 20____

Exercise 32 Taking immigration status into account, determine the earnings distribution for Asian males, ages 35-44, in top white-collar positions. What trends do you notice among those who make more than $35,000 a year?

▸ *Dataset*: WORKASIAN-35.DAT

▸ Create a stacked bar chart for Asian top white-collar male workers with bars for each immigration status category; stack by earnings.

Earnings of Top White Collar Asian Males, 20____

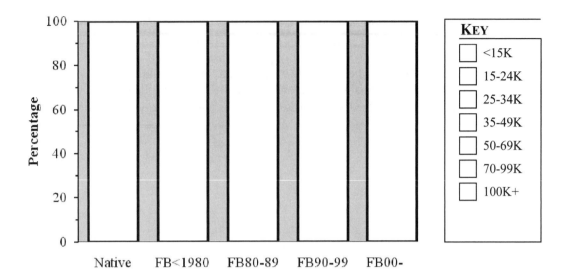

Discussion Questions

1. How do you think occupation, length of residence in the U.S., and education affect the earnings of immigrants? Do you think these factors, with the exception of length of residence, affect native-born residents in the same fashion? Why or why not?

2. Imagine you have a friend from one of the Asian or Hispanic groups studied in the text. They see the U.S. as the "land of opportunity" and plan to move here in order to make their "fortune." Using what you have learned from this section and the other chapters in this book, what advice would you give to this friend?

THINK
tank

1. Keeping in mind that most cultures have their own conceptions of gender and occupational roles, examine whether occupation, education, and earnings patterns are different for female and male immigrants. What similarities and differences do you see between native-born and foreign-born females? Does the labor market appear to be biased against immigrants in general or perhaps specifically against female immigrants? Use the data from this chapter to explain and defend your answer.

2. Some people think that immigrants to the United States get more government "hand-outs" than they deserve. Other people argue that immigrants "pay for themselves" and make a positive contribution to our economy. Do you think immigration is good for the U.S.? Should current policies be changed to allow more or fewer immigrants? Why or why not? What are the potential social, economic, and political implications of current trends in immigration? Use the data to make inferences and support your position.

chapter
4 LABOR FORCE

How many times has someone asked you, "What do you do?" or "What are you going to do after you graduate?" By "do", the questioner usually means, "work". Since so many Americans consider their work an integral part of who they are, it is not surprising that this is a question that surfaces repeatedly in the lives of many young people.

Bearing in mind the role that work plays in our lives as an indicator of both economic and personal success, we begin this chapter with a look at labor force participation trends. A person is considered to be in the labor force if he or she is currently working or looking for work. Persons not in the labor force typically include students, homemakers, retirees and disabled people.

Of those in the labor force, the percentage of persons who are unemployed can vary greatly among gender, age, and racial/ethnic groups. Yet the unemployment trends of all of these groups are strongly affected by periods of economic growth and recession. For example, in the early 1950s, unemployment rates were quite low but rose during a recession in the latter part of the decade. The "guns and butter" period of the late 60s saw low unemployment levels that increased sharply during the recession of 1973-1975. Similar fluctuations occurred throughout the 1980s and early 90s as workers scrambled to acquire new skills to meet the needs generated by economic restructuring. The economic boom of the mid-to-late-1990s saw record lows in unemployment but these numbers had risen by the decade's end,  spurred in part by the inevitable economic downturn. Though the economy moderately improved at the start of the 21st century, unemployment reached extremely high levels following the 2008 recession.

Although all groups are affected by economic changes, some groups have historically been affected more than others. Usually, blacks suffer a sharper, quicker increase in unemployment than non-blacks during periods of economic decline, but when the economy picks up again, unemployment rates drop faster among blacks than non-blacks. Economic changes also impact different age groups in varying ways. Due to seniority status, older people can often avoid layoffs during recession. On the other hand, since employers are less likely to hire someone who they think is going to retire soon, economic upswings have little impact upon older people's unemployment rates. A shift in the needs of the labor market can cause different rates of unemployment between men and women. An economy based in heavy industry, for example, may employ fewer female workers than an economy based in service and information.

While unemployment trends closely follow the peaks and valleys of the economy, labor force participation itself is not as strongly affected by economic changes. Still, there have been gradual changes in the racial and gender gaps in labor force participation. This chapter will introduce you to labor force concepts and trends, beginning with the general population, and then consider the unique characteristics of the male and female labor forces. Though much of this chapter focuses on the gender gap in the labor force, during the course of these exercises you will study how labor force participation and employment varies across a number of different groups in society.

KEY
concepts

Labor Force Status

The civilian labor force includes persons ages 16 and over who either have a job (employed) or are able to work and looking for employment (unemployed). The labor force can be grouped into the following categories:

> **In Labor Force-Employed**—Persons with a full-time or part-time job

> **In Labor Force-Unemployed**—Persons who are able to work and who are looking for work or laid off from a job.

> **Not in the Labor Force**—Persons without a job and not available for work (e.g. retirees, homemakers, full-time students, etc.)

Percent in Labor Force (Labor Force Participation Rate)

Calculated from the above categories as:

$$\frac{\text{Employed} + \text{Unemployed}}{\text{Employed} + \text{Unemployed} + \text{Not in Labor Force}} \times 100$$

Percent Unemployed (Unemployment Rate)

Calculated from above categories as:

$$\frac{\text{Unemployed}}{\text{Employed} + \text{Unemployed}} \times 100$$

Full-time/Part-time Workers

Employed workers are considered to be full-time workers if they usually work more than 35 hours per week. Part-time workers work less than 35 hours per week but can be classified more specifically based on the number of hours that they usually work. The WORKHRS variable in the datasets groups workers according to the following categories based on the average number of hours worked each week:

Full35 (Full-time workers)	10-19
20-34	Under 10

NOTE: The EMP4 variable distinguishes between full-time and part-time workers using the categories EmpFull and EmpPart

Year-round Full-time Workers

Employed workers who work more than 35 hours per week for 50 or more weeks per year.

OTHER concepts

Race/Ethnicity (Chapter Two)   **Marital Status** (Chapter Five)
Education (Chapter Two)

A. Overall Trends

Labor force participation rates have changed in important ways since 1950, especially for young women and older men. However, despite the progress achieved during the Civil Rights Movement and other societal changes, racial gaps in labor force participation are increasing among men. Black women, on the other hand, have held a unique position in the labor force for several decades.

In the following exercises, you will look at labor force participation and unemployment in terms of gender, race/ethnicity, and age. Since women exit and reenter the labor force more often than men, and these fluctuations would skew overall trends, we will look at men's and women's labor force participation separately.

Exercise 1 How has the percentage of men and the percentage of women in the labor force changed over time? Using data from 1950 to the present, look at the percentage of men and women, ages 16 and older, in the labor force. Describe any significant trends that you find.

▸ *Dataset*: EMPLOY.TREND

▸ Create a line graph with two lines, one for men and one for women, ages 16 and older. For each year, indicate the percentage of each gender in the labor force. (Hint: Add or combine "employed" with "unemployed" to create the Total Labor Force category.)

Exercise 2 How has the percentage of men and women who are in the labor force but unemployed changed over time? Using data from 1950 to the present, look at the percentage of men and women, ages 16 and older, that are unemployed. What trends do you notice?

▸ *Dataset*: EMPLOY.TREND

▸ Create a line graph with two lines, one for men and one for women, ages 16 and older. For each year, indicate the percentage of each group that was unemployed. (Hint: Remember to omit NILF from your calculations; see the "Percent Unemployed" equation in this chapter's Key Concepts.)

Unemployment of Men and Women in the Labor Force, 1950 to 20____

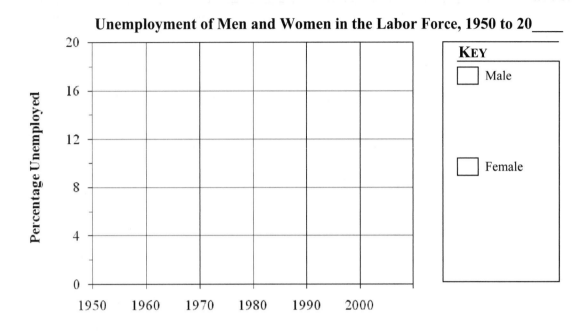

Exercise 3 Now look at the relationship between race and the percentage of men and women in the labor force. Using data from 1950 to the present, look at the percentage of black and non-black men and women, ages 16 and older, who were in the labor force in each year. How do these trends differ from those you observed in previous exercises?

▶ *Dataset*: EMPLOY.TREND

▶ Create a line graph with four lines: one for black men, one for non-black men, one for black women, and one for non-black women. For each year, indicate the percentage of each of those groups in the labor force.

Blacks and Non-Blacks in the Labor Force, 1950 to 20____

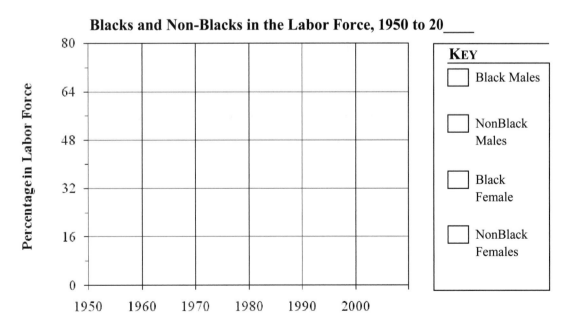

Exercise 4 What is the relationship between race, unemployment, and gender? Using data from 1950 to the present look at the percentage of black and non-black men and women, ages 16 and older, that were unemployed. How do these trends differ from those you observed in previous exercises?

▶ *Dataset*: EMPLOY.TREND

▶ Create a line graph with four lines: one for black men, one for non-black men, one for black women, and one for non-black women. For each year, indicate the percentage of each of those groups unemployed at the time of the census.

Unemployment of Blacks and Non-Blacks, 1950 to 20____

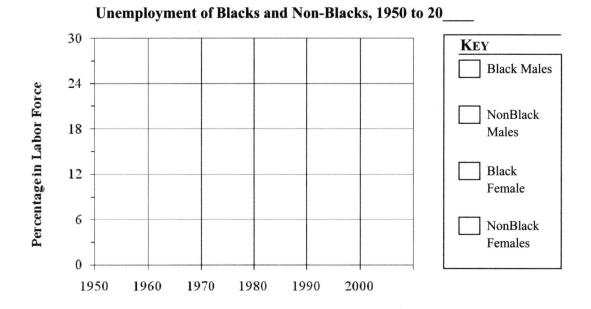

Exercise 5 Focusing on the present, examine the relationship between gender, race/ethnicity, and labor force participation. When looking at men and women, ages 16 and older, what differences do you see in labor force participation between genders and among racial/ethnic groups?

▶ *Dataset*: EMPEDUC.DAT

▶ Create a bar chart with side-by-side bars for men and women. For each racial/ethnic group, indicate the percentage of men and women in that group in the labor force.

Men and Women in the Labor Force by Race/Ethnicity, 20____

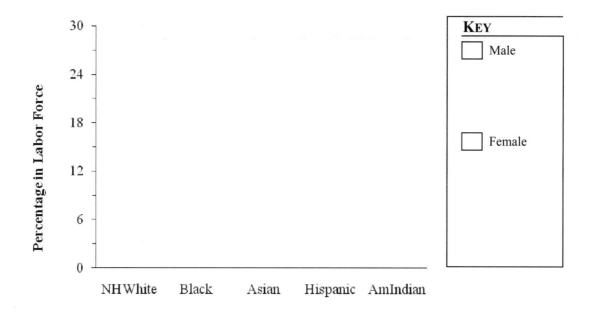

Exercise 6 Focusing on the present, examine the relationship between gender, race/ethnicity, and unemployment. When looking at men and women, ages 16 and older, what differences in unemployment rates do you notice between genders and among racial/ethnic groups?

▸ *Dataset*: EMPEDUC.DAT

▸ Create a bar chart with side-by-side bars for men and women. For each racial/ethnic group, indicate the percentage of men and women unemployed.

Unemployment for Men and Women by Race/Ethnicity, 20____

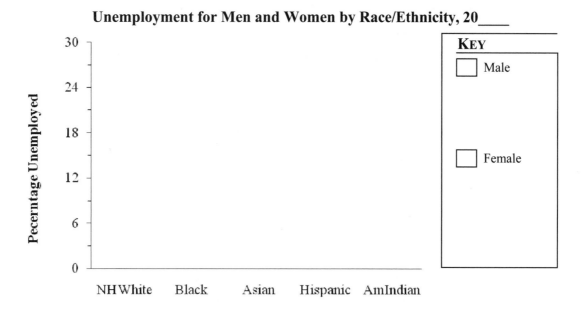

Exercise 7 Looking just at 1950 and current data, determine the percentage of women in each age group who are in the labor force. What are the differences between these years?

▸ *Dataset*: EMPLOY.TREND

▸ Create two bar charts, one for 1950 and one for the present. In each chart, indicate the percentage of women in each age group who are in the labor force.

Women in the Labor Force, 1950 20____

Women in the Labor Force,

Exercise 8 Does gender influence an individual's work hours? Focus on men's and women, ages 18 and older, in the labor force in the present. What differences do you find in men and women's full-time/part-time work status? What might account for the difference between the number of hours worked by men and the number of hours worked by women?

▸ *Dataset*: WORKEDUC.DAT

▸ Create two pie charts, one for men and one for women. In each chart, make divisions for work hour status.

Full and Part Time Workers, 20____

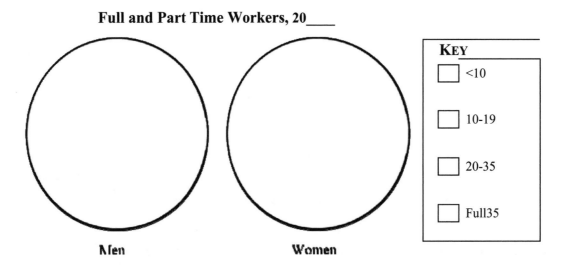

Men   Women

KEY
☐ <10
☐ 10-19
☐ 20-35
☐ Full35

B. Men's Labor Force Participation

While women have experienced a noticeable increase in labor force participation in the past sixty years, men's participation in the labor force has actually decreased. Though this change has not been especially dramatic in the population as a whole, some groups have been affected more than others. Changes in Social Security, pension, and early retirement have led to a reduction in older men's labor force participation while at the same time, young black men have experienced both a decrease in labor force participation and an increase in unemployment.

As you work through the following exercises, consider why some groups of men have experienced more dramatic decreases in labor force participation than other groups. When looking at unemployment trends, think about how and why certain economic changes may have affected some groups more than others.

Exercise 9 Look at the percentage of black males, ages 16-24, in the labor force from 1950 to present. How has the percentage of young black males in the labor force changed over time? What might account for these changes?

▸ *Dataset*: EMPLOY.TREND

▸ Create a line graph indicating the percentage of black men, ages 16-24, for each year in the labor force.

Black Males in the Labor Force, Ages 16-24, 1950 to 20____

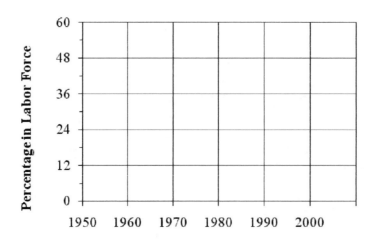

Exercise 10 Look at the percentage of black males, ages 16-24, unemployed from 1950 to the present. How has the percentage of young black males who are unemployed changed over time? What might explain these changes?

▸ *Dataset*: EMPLOY.TREND

▸ Create a line graph indicating the percentage of black males, ages 16-24, unemployed in each year.

Unemployed Black Males, Ages 16-24, 1950 to 20____

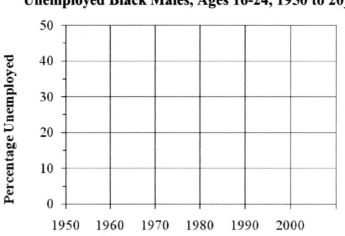

Exercise 11 Focusing on the present, look at men ages 16-24, 35-44, and 55-64 in each racial/ethnic group. What percentage of each group was in the labor force? Among which racial/ethnic age groups do you see the greatest differences?

▸ *Dataset*: EMPEDUC.DAT

▸ Create a bar chart with side-by-side bars for each of the three age groups listed above. For each racial/ethnic group, indicate the percentage of each group in the labor force.

Age of Men in Labor Force by Race/Ethnicity, 20____

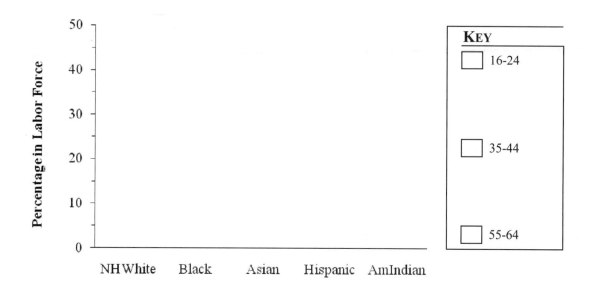

Exercise 12 Now focus on 35-44 year-old male Asians and Hispanics who were in the labor force in the present. Looking at each specific Asian and Hispanic group, note any significant differences you find among the groups.

▸ *Datasets*: EMPASIANALL.DAT, EMPHISPALL.DAT

▸ On your own, create a bar chart with bars for each specific Asian and Hispanic group. For each group, indicate the percentage of men, ages 35-44, who were in the labor force in the present.

Exercise 13 Is there a relationship between educational attainment and unemployment? Examine the education level of men, ages 35-44, who were unemployed in the present. Which levels of educational attainment had the highest rates of unemployment?

▸ *Dataset*: EMPEDUC.DAT

▸ On your own, create a bar chart with bars for each specific Asian and Hispanic group. For each group, indicate the percentage of men, ages 35-44, who were in the labor force in the present.

Exercise 14 Does the relationship between education and unemployment vary among racial/ethnic groups? Focusing on men, ages 35-44, in the present, look at unemployment rates for those with less than a high school education, a high school diploma and a college degree.

▸ *Dataset*: EMPEDUC.DAT

▸ Create a bar chart with side-by-side bars for three education categories: less than high school, high school graduates, and college graduates. For each racial/ethnic group, indicate the percentage of 35-44 year-old men at each education level who were unemployed in 2000.

Education of Unemployed Men, Ages 35-44, by Race/Ethnicity, 20____

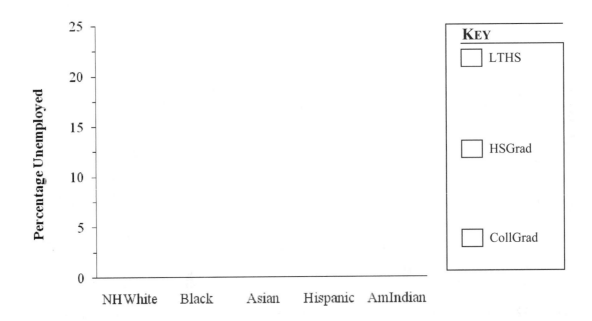

Exercise 15 Using current data, look at the full-time/part-time work status of males in each age group. How does the work hour status distribution vary with age?

▸ *Dataset*: WORKEDUC.DAT

▸ Create a stacked bar chart with bars for each age group; stack by employment status.

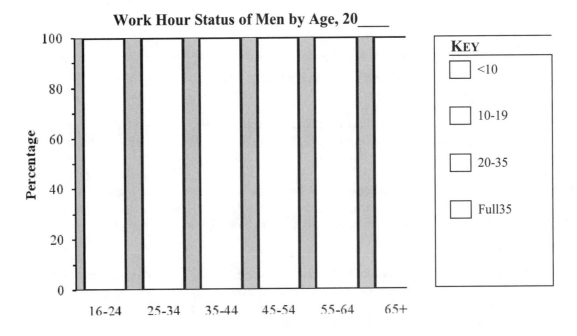

Exercise 16 Is there a relationship between race/ethnicity and an individual's full-time/part-time work status? Using current data, look at the work hour status distribution of males 35-44 in each racial/ethnic group. How does the hourly status distribution vary?

▸ *Dataset*: WORKEDUC.DAT

▸ Create a stacked bar chart with bars for each racial/ethnic group; stack by work hour status.

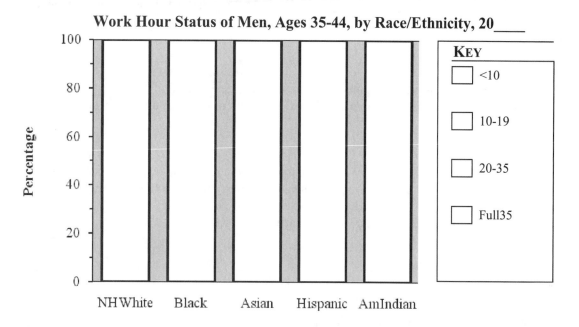

Work Hour Status of Men, Ages 35-44, by Race/Ethnicity, 20____

Discussion Questions

1. Think about unemployment among young black males. What are some possible reasons for this group's past and present position in the labor market? Explain why some economic trends may have had a greater impact on this particular group's job opportunities than they had on the opportunities of other racial/ethnic age groups.

2. Explore the differences in labor force participation between Asian and Hispanic groups. Discuss the position of these groups in the labor market, both overall and relative to other racial/ethnic groups. Offer possible explanations for the differences you found.

C. Women's Labor Force Participation

Over the last few decades, the participation of women in the labor force has increased dramatically. The growth of the female labor force constitutes mostly middle and upper class women who have sought and found employment outside the home. Part of the increase in the number of women working outside the home can be attributed to rising economic demands on families, coupled with women's desire for independent income. In the 1970s, the Women's Rights Movement provided women with the support they needed to enter the labor force. Today, women represent the majority of college enrollees, and most enter the workforce after graduation.

Although women are joining the labor force in greater numbers, they also exit and reenter the labor force more often than men; a pattern that can be partially explained by women's childbearing and family responsibilities. Lower earnings and fewer opportunities for advancement may also play a role in a woman's likelihood to exit the labor force. Still, it is clear that the relationship between childbearing and labor force participation has changed, considering that a majority of women now work outside the home during their childbearing years.

In the following exercises, you will examine overall gender differences in employment status and labor participation, as well as the gender stratification among various racial/ethnic groups.

Exercise 17 How does the percentage of women in the labor force vary with race/ethnicity? Focusing on the present, look at the percentage of women, ages 16-24 and 25-34, in the labor force in each racial/ethnic group. Do you find any significant differences among racial/ethnic groups?

▸ *Dataset*: EMPLOY.DAT

▸ Create a bar chart with side-by-side bars for the two age groups you examined. For each racial/ethnic group, indicate the percentage of women participating in the labor force.

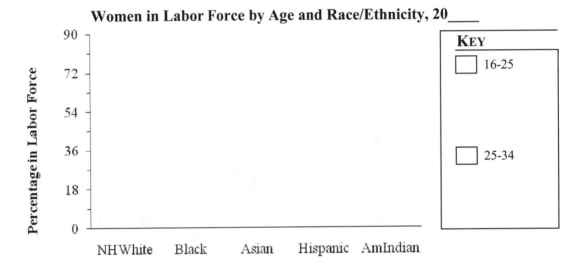

Women in Labor Force by Age and Race/Ethnicity, 20____

Exercise 18 On your own, explore the relationship between unemployment, race/ethnicity, and age among women in the present. Repeat the previous exercise, but indicate the percentage unemployed rather than the percentage in the labor force.

▸ *Dataset*: EMPLOY.DAT

Exercise 19 Focusing on women, ages 25-34, in the present, consider labor force participation among specific Hispanic groups. What percentage of women in each of these groups is currently in the labor force? Describe any significant differences you find among the groups.

▸ *Dataset*: EMPHISPALL.DAT

▸ Create a bar chart with bars for each specific Hispanic group, indicating the percentage of 25-34 year-old women in the labor force.

Hispanic Women in the Labor Force, Ages 25-34, 20____

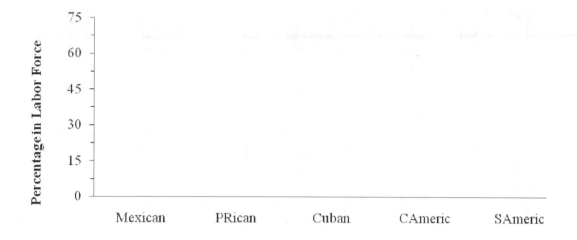

Exercise 20 Focusing on women, ages 25-34 in the present, look at labor force participation for each specific Asian group. What percentage of women in each of these groups was in the labor force in the present? Describe any significant differences you find among the groups.

▶ *Dataset*: EMPASIANALL.DAT

▶ Create a bar chart with bars for each specific Asian group, indicating the percentage of 25-34 year-old women in the labor force.

Exercise 21 Using current data, look at the hourly work status of women by age group. How does full-time/part-time work status vary by age for women? What might account for these variations?

▶ *Dataset*: WORKEDUC.DAT

▶ Create a stacked bar chart with bars for each age group; stack by work hour status.

Work Hour Status of Females by Age, 20____

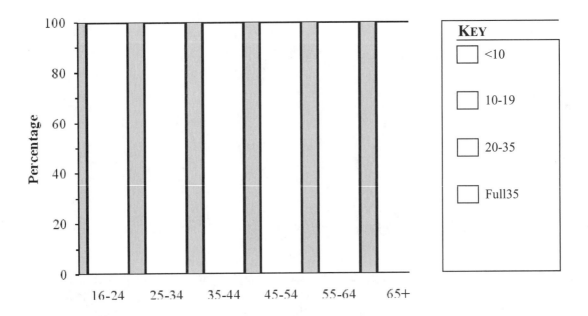

Exercise 22 Is there a relationship between race/ethnicity and full-time/part-time work status for women? Using current data, look at the work hour status distribution of females, ages 35-44, in each racial/ethnic group. Describe any differences you find among the groups, and offer a possible explanation as to why these differences might occur.

▸ *Dataset*: WORKEDUC.DAT

▸ Create a stacked bar chart with bars for each racial/ethnic group; stack by hourly work status.

Women's Work Hour Status by Race/Ethnicity, Ages 35-44, 20____

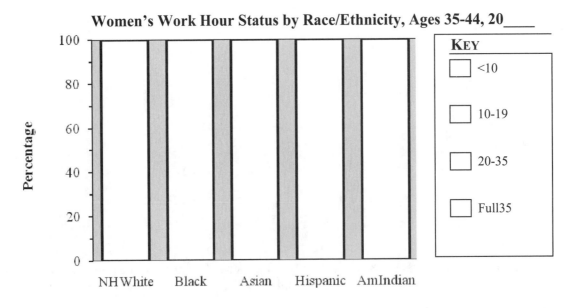

Exercise 23 Is there a relationship between a woman's educational attainment and the number of hours she works? Focusing on the present, examine the work hour status distribution of 25-34 year-old women for each educational level. What factors related to education might affect how many hours a woman works?

▸ *Dataset*: WORKEDUC.dat

▸ Create a stacked bar chart with bars for each racial/ethnic group; stack by hourly work status.

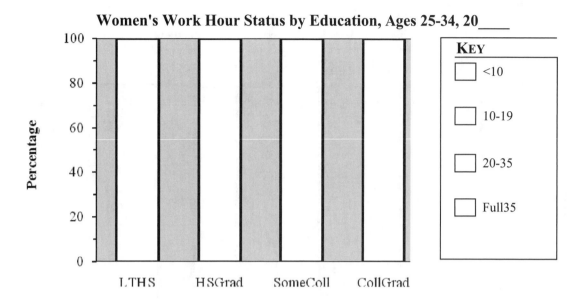

Women's Work Hour Status by Education, Ages 25-34, 20____

KEY
- <10
- 10-19
- 20-35
- Full35

Exercise 24 Is there a relationship between a woman's educational attainment and her participation in the labor force? Focusing on the present, examine the percentage of 25-34 year-old women in the labor force for each education level.

▸ *Dataset*: EMPEDUC.DAT

▸ Create a bar chart with bars for each education level indicating the percentage of women, ages 25-34, in the labor force.

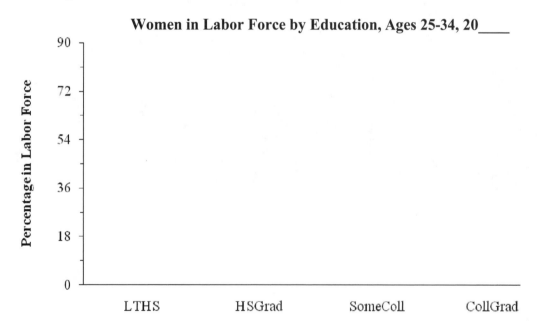

Women in Labor Force by Education, Ages 25-34, 20____

Exercise 25 Now look at the relationship between educational attainment and marital status. Focusing on women, ages 25-34, in the present, look at the marital status distribution at each education level. Compare your findings from this exercise to your results from previous exercises.

▸ *Dataset*: MAREDUC.DAT

▸ Create a stacked bar chart with bars for each education level; stack by marital status.

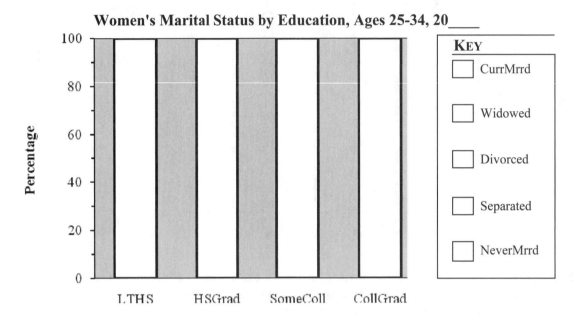

Women's Marital Status by Education, Ages 25-34, 20____

KEY
- CurrMrrd
- Widowed
- Divorced
- Separated
- NeverMrrd

Discussion Questions

1. Between 1950 and the current year, what was the overall trend in the percentage of women working outside the home? How does this compare with the employment patterns of men since 1950? How has the gap between the percentage of women and the percentage of men in the labor force changed over the past several decades? What factors do you think may have influenced these changes?

2. Provide possible explanations for the labor force participation patterns of Black, Asian, Hispanic and American Indian women.

3. Considering your findings for the current year, predict the gender and racial/ethnic distribution of the labor force in 2020.

THINK
tank

1. Many Americans believe that a good education leads to a stable job, and more education inevitably leads to a higher paying job. While this seems to be the general trend, does education always "pay off" in the labor market? Do some individuals with fewer years of schooling earn more than certain individuals with college or graduate degrees? Explain why this might happen. Do you think schools, colleges, and universities do an adequate job of preparing people for the labor force? If not, what should be changed? Do you think the public education system prepares some types of students for college or a well-paying job better than it prepares others? If so, who benefits the most? Why?

2. Some people believe that those who are poor simply do not want to work. However, a large number of people below the poverty level do have steady employment or are actively looking for a job. Describe the working poor. Who are they? What are some other reasons why people who work or want to work may be poor or in poverty? Should all individuals who work the same number of hours enjoy the same standard of living? Why or why not?

chapter 5

MARRIAGE, DIVORCE, AND COHABITATION

In the 1950s, television shows like "Ozzie and Harriet" and "Leave It to Beaver" portrayed the nuclear family as consisting of two parents, married and living together, with at least two children. Though they seem anachronistic to contemporary viewers, these TV shows were accurate representations of married life in this period. Marriage rates were high and rising, divorce rates were low, and the birth rate was skyrocketing.

While June and Ward Cleaver epitomized the behaviors and values of postwar America, many people mistakenly think the demographics of this period were merely a continuation of earlier marriage and birth patterns, but this is not quite the case. The end of World War II

precipitated the dramatic increase in births known as the Baby Boom that continued into the early 1960s. During this period, five out of six women in peak childbearing years gave birth to two or more children. Americans were also marrying early and staying married.

As the Baby Boomers matured, however, they did not follow their parents' marriage and childbearing patterns. More and more people delayed marriage until their late twenties or early thirties. Those couples that did marry often delayed having children and ultimately had fewer children than their parents' generation. During this period, divorce rates increased as well.

As the number of marriages decreased and divorce became more common, the number of people "cohabiting"—living together without being married—steadily climbed. Cohabitation became an option not only for young people, but also an alternative for divorced adults not ready to remarry. Americans' choices in marriage partners have also changed. In the years during and following the Civil Rights movement, the number of Americans marrying people of different racial/ethnic backgrounds increased substantially. Today, as more people delay marriage or remarry later in their lives, Americans have also become more likely to choose marriage partners with education levels similar to their own.

There no longer seems to be a "typical" family lifestyle that can be portrayed by a single TV show. In this chapter, you will look at marital status trends: marriage choices, divorce, and cohabitation. Your findings will give you a clearer picture of how marriage in America is changing, and what it might become in the future.

KEY
concepts

Marital Status

Refers to whether a person was "now married", "widowed", "divorced", "separated", or "never married" at the time of the census.

> **Never Married**—Includes all persons who have never been married, including persons whose only marriage(s) was annulled.

> **Separated**—Includes persons legally separated or otherwise absent from their spouse because of marital discord.

> **Widowed**—Widows and widowers who have not remarried.

> **Divorced**—Legally divorced persons who have not remarried.

> **Currently Married**—All persons married at the time of the census.

Cohabitator (Unmarried Partner)

A not currently married adult who shares living quarters and has a close personal relationship with another adult.

OTHER concepts

Cohort (Chapter One)	**Race/Ethnicity** (Chapter Two)
Education (Chapter Two)	**Labor Force Status** (Chapter Four)

A. Marital Trends

Though marriage and fertility rates in the United States have been in overall decline since the 1950s, these trends have not affected all groups equally. Today, it remains important to examine how trends in marriage and fertility impact individuals of different races, cohorts, and education levels. Within these groups, are people more likely to never get married, or are they simply putting off marriage? Is a person's educational attainment related to his or her marital status and/or the age at which he or she marries?

In the following exercises you will look at changes in marital status distribution over time, racial/ethnic differences in marital trends, the shift in the average age of marriage, and the relationship between educational attainment and marriage.

<u>Exercise 1</u> Examine the marital status distribution of Americans from 1950 to the present. What types of patterns do you see?

> ▸ *Dataset*: MARITAL.TREND

> ▸ Create a stacked bar chart; for each year, stack by marital status.

Marital Status, 1950 to 20____

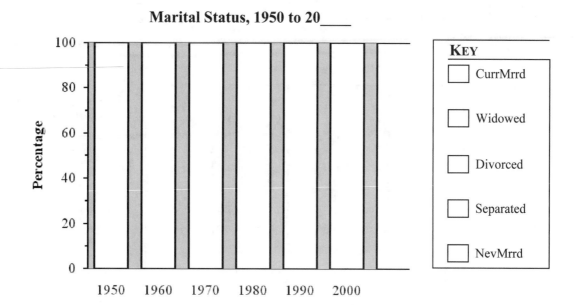

Exercise 2 Using data from 1950 to the present, look specifically at the marital status distribution of people, ages 15-24. What trends do you notice?

▶ *Dataset*: MARITAL.TREND

▶ Create a line graph with three lines: one for currently married, one for divorced, and one for never married individuals. For each year, indicate the percentage of 15-24 year-olds in each marital category.

Marital Status, Ages 15-24, 1950 to 20____

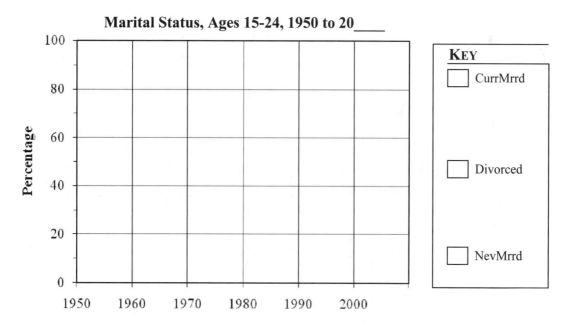

Exercise 3 In the past, it was expected that people would marry between the ages of 18 and 21. Has that changed? Using current data show the marital status distribution for each age group. What is the dominant marital status in each age group? Do your findings surprise you?

▶ *Dataset*: MARITAL.TREND

▸ Create a stacked bar chart with bars for each age group. Within each age group, stack by marital status.

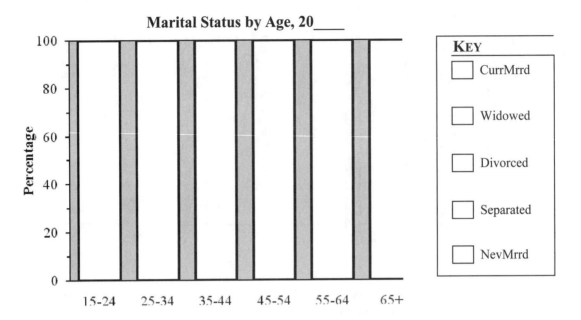

Marital Status by Age, 20____

Exercise 4 Examine the marital status differences between blacks and non-blacks.

▸ *Dataset*: MARITAL.TREND

▸ Create a stacked bar chart with side-by-side bars for blacks and non-blacks. For each year, stack by marital status.

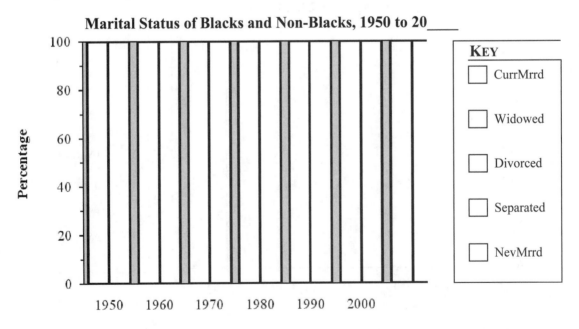

Marital Status of Blacks and Non-Blacks, 1950 to 20____

Exercise 5 Focusing on the present, compare the marital status of non-Hispanic Whites, Blacks, Asians, Hispanics, and American Indians. Describe any significant findings.

▸ *Dataset*: MARITAL.DAT

‣ Create a stacked bar chart with a bar for each racial/ethnic group, stacking by marital status.

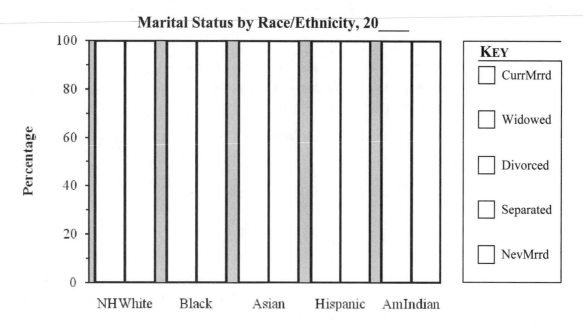

Marital Status by Race/Ethnicity, 20____

KEY
☐ CurrMrrd
☐ Widowed
☐ Divorced
☐ Separated
☐ NevMrrd

Exercise 6 Using current data, examine the education levels of 23-28 year-old women who have never been married. Describe any significant findings.

‣ *Dataset*: MAR-W.DAT

‣ Create a bar chart with side-by-side bars for high school and college graduates. For each age, show the percentage of those at each education level who have never been married.

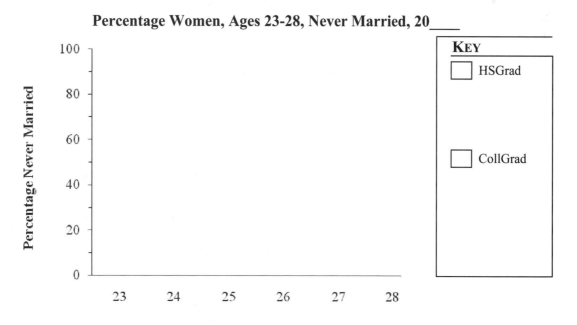

Percentage Women, Ages 23-28, Never Married, 20____

KEY
☐ HSGrad
☐ CollGrad

Exercise 7 On your own, repeat the previous exercise for women of a specific racial/ethnic group.

▶ *Dataset*: MAR-W.DAT

B. Marriage Choices

As Americans' attitudes about age, race/ethnicity, and education have changed, so have their marriage preferences. While the terms "intermarriage" and "mixed marriage" are usually only applied to the marriage of two people of different racial/ethnic backgrounds, race/ethnicity are not the only factors that might vary between two spouses. Age and educational attainment can play equally important roles in marriage choices.

In the following exercises, you will look at marriage choices in terms of age, race/ethnicity, and education. While completing these exercises, you should consider the ways in which the typical marriage partners have become more different from each other in recent years, and how they may have become more similar.

Exercise 8 Compare the age distribution of married women to that of married men. Are there any significant differences?

▶ *Dataset*: MARITAL.DAT

▶ Create two pie charts, one for married men and one for married women. In each chart make divisions for each age category.

Age Distribution by Gender, 20____

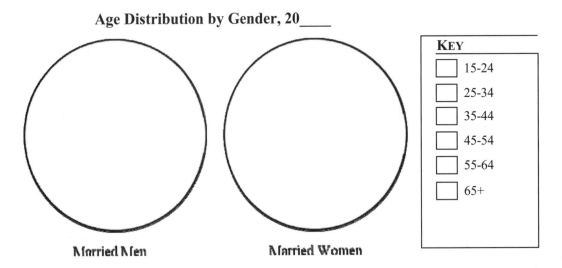

| KEY |
| 15-24 |
| 25-34 |
| 35-44 |
| 45-54 |
| 55-64 |
| 65+ |

Married Men   Married Women

Exercise 9 Look at the ages of the spouses of 25 year-old men and women. Do men tend to marry women who are younger or older than they are? How about women?

▸ *Datasets*: SPOAGE-M.DAT, SPOAGE-W.DAT

▸ Create a stacked bar chart with bars for 25 year-old men and 25 year-old women showing the age distribution of their spouses.

Spouse Ages of 25 Year-Old Men and Women, 20____

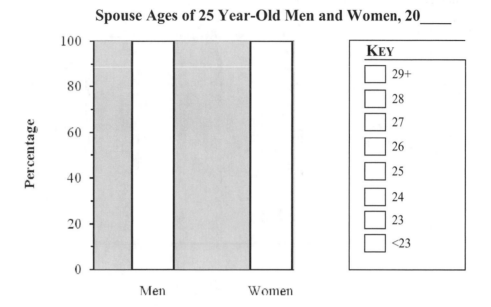

Exercise 10 What proportion of non-Hispanic white men are choosing to marry a woman of a different racial/ethnic group? How does the percentage of non-Hispanic white men with a wife of a different racial/ethnic group vary by age group?

▸ *Dataset*: SPORACE-M.DAT

▸ Create a bar chart. For each age group, indicate the percentage of non-Hispanic white men who are married to a woman of a different race/ethnicity.

Percentage Intermarried for Men by Age, 20____

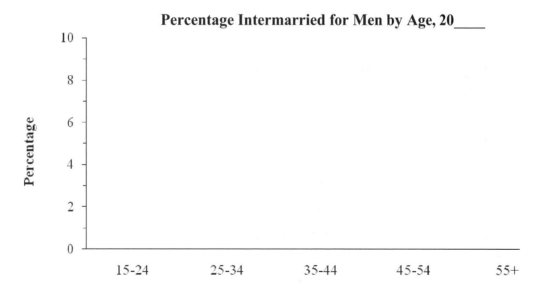

Exercise 11 Look at the race/ethnicity distribution of husbands of non-Hispanic white, black, Asian, and Hispanic women, ages 25-34 in the present. What differences among racial/ethnic groups do you notice?

▸ *Dataset*: SPOEDUC-W.DAT

▸ Create a stacked bar chart for each racial/ethnic group of wives, ages 25-34, and stack by the race/ethnicity of the husbands.

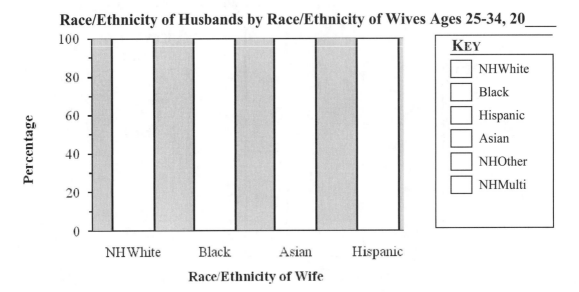

Race/Ethnicity of Husbands by Race/Ethnicity of Wives Ages 25-34, 20____

Exercise 12 In addition to age and race, education plays a role in marriage choices. Focusing on women who were between the ages of 25 and 34 in the present, look at the educational attainment distribution of their husbands. Do women tend to marry men who have similar educational backgrounds?

▸ *Dataset*: SPOEDUC-W.DAT

▸ Create a stacked bar chart and for each education level of married women, ages 25-34, stack by the education level of their husbands.

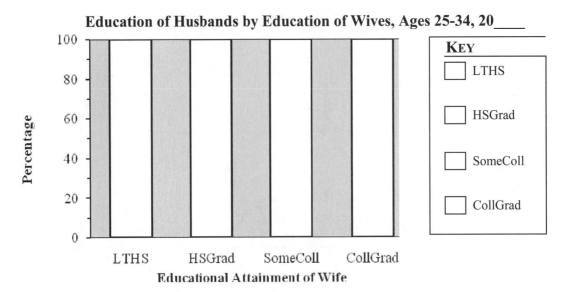

Education of Husbands by Education of Wives, Ages 25-34, 20____

Exercise 13 According to current data, what are the demographics of the husband of a 25 to 30 year-old black woman with a college degree most likely to be? What are the most likely demographics of the husband of a 25 to 34 year-old Hispanic with a college degree? On your own, compare the marriage choices of Hispanic and black women with college degrees aged 25-34. (Hint: you must look at race/ethnicity and education separately.)

▶ *Datasets*: SPORACE-W.DAT, SPOEDUC-W.DAT

Discussion Questions

1. Why do you think there are differences in the age distributions of married men and women?

2. Which historical events may have influenced the recent increase in interracial couples and marriages? Looking at marriage patterns, determine which age group seems to have been most affected by these events.

3. Imagine yourself five years from now. Given your age, race, gender, and expected educational attainment, if you were to marry, what would be the most likely demographics of your spouse? How do the answers suggested by the data you looked at in this section differ from your expectations?

4. How might you explain recent trends in marriage choices? How do the preferences of certain groups differ from those of their elders? What factors may have influenced changes in people's preferences regarding the age, race/ethnicity, and educational attainment of their partners?

C. Divorce

In order to obtain a divorce prior 1969, an individual living in the United States had to prove that his or her spouse was guilty of adultery, desertion, physical or mental abuse, habitual drunkenness, or a felony conviction. In 1969, however, the divorce laws were changed, allowing for a "no-fault" divorce. Rather than placing blame on one particular spouse, a no-fault divorce acknowledges mutual responsibility for the dissolution of the marriage.

While sociologists and historians continue to debate whether no-fault divorce laws have been responsible for increased divorce rates, one thing is certain: divorce rates doubled between 1966 and 1976. But who makes up the growing population of divorced Americans? Do divorce rates vary among racial/ethnic groups? Age groups? Is someone with a high school diploma more likely to get divorced than someone with a PhD? Is there a relationship between divorce and labor force participation among women?

In the following exercises you will look at trends in divorce in terms of age, race/ethnicity, education, and labor force participation.

Exercise 14 Examine the current percentage of divorced people in each age group. Do the older age groups' patterns necessarily indicate the percentage of people in your own age group who will be divorced as your cohort ages? Why or why not?

▶ *Dataset*: MARITAL.DAT

▸ Create a bar chart and for each age group, indicate the percentage of the population that has been divorced.

Percentage Divorced by Age, 20____

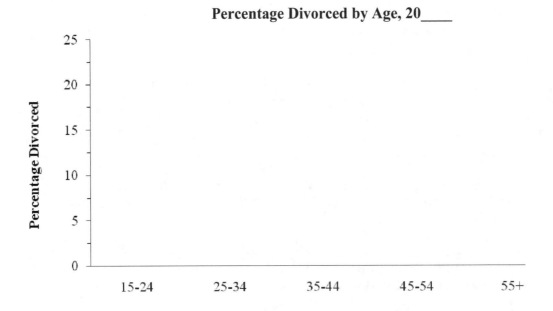

Exercise 15 Using data from 1950 to the present, analyze the differences in the proportion of divorced people among blacks and non-blacks. Discuss significant differences between these two groups, and note any changes over time.

▸ *Dataset*: MARITAL.TREND

▸ Create a line graph with separate lines for blacks and non-blacks. For each year, indicate the percentage of the population that has been divorced.

Percentage Divorced, Blacks and Non-blacks, 1950 to 20____

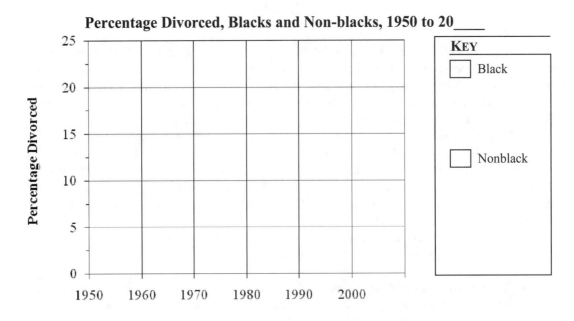

Exercise 16 Looking at persons ages 35-44, compare the current percentages of people divorced and separated in each racial/ethnic group. Why do you think these differences exist?

- *Dataset*: MARITAL.DAT
- Create a bar chart with side-by-side bars for divorce and separation. For each racial/ethnic group, indicate the percentage of people divorced and separated.

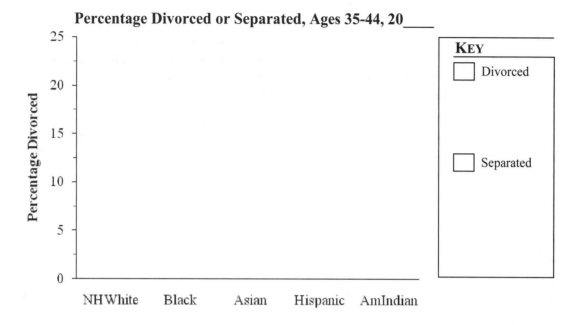

Percentage Divorced or Separated, Ages 35-44, 20____

Exercise 17 To what extent does there seem to be a connection between educational attainment and divorce? Do people with higher levels of education seem more likely to get divorced?

- *Dataset*: MAREDUC.DAT
- Create a bar chart with side-by-side bars for three education levels (LTHS, HSGrad, and CollGrad). For each age group, indicate the percentage divorced in each education level.

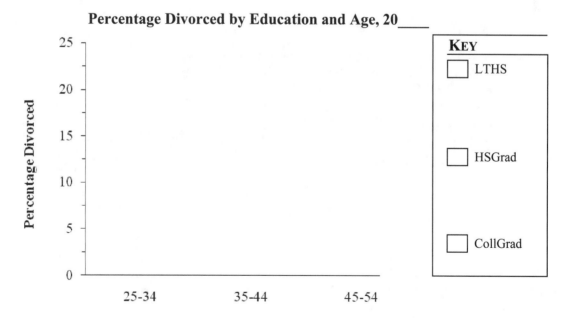

Percentage Divorced by Education and Age, 20____

Exercise 18 Focusing on women, ages 25-34 in the present, describe the relationship between marital status and labor force participation. Do a greater percentage of divorced women than married women participate in the labor force? Keeping in mind the patterns you saw in the labor force chapter, describe and offer possible explanations for your findings.

▸ *Dataset*: MARPOV-W.DAT

▸ Create a bar chart; for each marital status, indicate the percentage of women in the labor force. (Hint: You will need to add the percentage of women employed full-time, the percentage employed part-time, and the percentage unemployed to find the total percentage of women in each group in the labor force.)

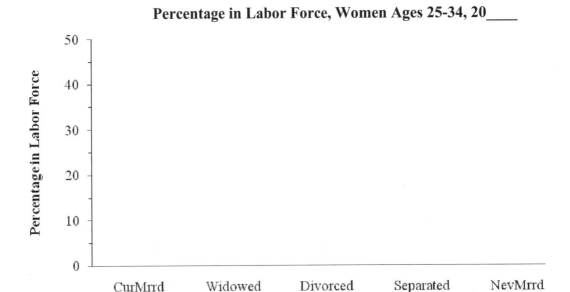

Percentage in Labor Force, Women Ages 25-34, 20____

Discussion Questions

1. How might the women's rights movement of the 1970s and more recent trends in gender equality have influenced women's labor force participation, marital status, and the relationship between the two?

2. Explain how gender relations, race relations, economic trends, labor force participation rates, and changing social attitudes might affect divorce rates.

D. Cohabitation

The rise in cohabitation rates seems in many ways to be connected with the maturation of the Baby Boomers. But just who is cohabiting? Young college students? Divorced people who don't want to remarry just yet? Is cohabiting a way to "try out" a relationship before marriage, or is it a long-term alternative to marriage?

In the following exercises you will examine the characteristics of cohabitants. By looking at the age, race/ethnicity, education, and marital status of cohabitants, you will gain a clearer picture of the role of cohabitation in contemporary trends in family structure.

Exercise 19 Examine the age distribution of people who are currently cohabiting. Do your findings support your expectations? Are there any notable differences in the age distributions of men and women who are cohabiting?

▶ *Datasets*: COHAB-M.DAT, COHAB-W.DAT

▶ Create two pie charts, one for each gender, make divisions for age groups.

Age Distribution of Cohabitants, 20____

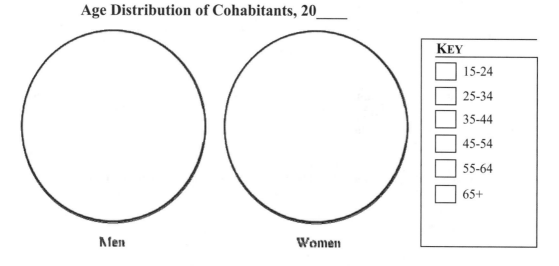

Men   Women

KEY
☐ 15-24
☐ 25-34
☐ 35-44
☐ 45-54
☐ 55-64
☐ 65+

Exercise 20 Does the current age distribution of cohabitants differ by race? Look at the age distribution of female cohabitants in each racial/ethnic group. Are there any significant differences? Give possible explanations for why some groups may be more or less likely to cohabitate.

▶ *Dataset*: COHAB-W.DAT

▶ Create a stacked bar chart and for each racial/ethnic group, stack by the age of cohabitants.

Ages of Women Cohabitants by Race/Ethnicity, 20____

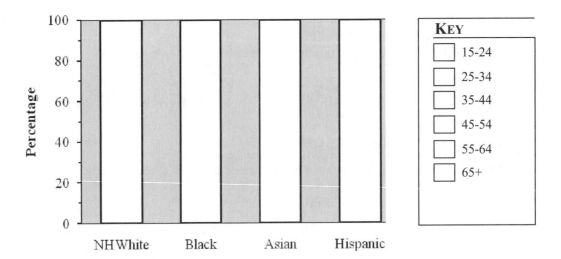

Exercise 21 When many people think about cohabitors, they picture college students or recent graduates living together for a short period of time before marriage. Examine and describe the relationship between educational attainment and cohabitation for women.

▸ *Dataset*: COHAB-W.DAT

▸ Create a pie chart for women cohabitants in the present with divisions for education levels.

Educational Distribution for Women Cohabitants, 20____

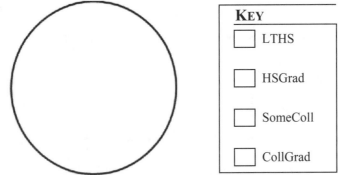

Discussion Questions

1. Describe the overall characteristics of cohabiting Americans. Who is most likely to be cohabiting? Offer possible explanations for your findings.

2. Do you think that you are likely to cohabit? Under what circumstances? Did or do either or your parents or grandparents cohabitate? Why do you think cohabitation has become more common and acceptable?

THINK

tank

1. Compare the race/ethnicity, age, poverty, and employment characteristics of three groups of unmarried women: those never married, those who are divorced, and those who are widowed. Would you say that these groups are similar? What are the most significant differences between the groups, and how do you account for these differences?

2. Some social critics suggest that the "form" of marriage is less important than the "function". In other words, it is more important that marriages are loving, trusting, respectful, supportive relationships, and less important that they reflect the traditional context of one man and one woman in a relationship legally recognized by the state. Do you agree with this premise? Are there significant differences between male-female marriages, gay and lesbian unions, or cohabiting couples? What are the social, economic, and political implications of broadening the 'form' of marriage in the U.S.?

chapter 6 GENDER INEQUALITY

The image of the "typical" American woman has changed dramatically since the 1950s. As the gap between the number of women and the number of men graduating from college and joining the labor force continues to shrink, there has been a significant decrease in the number of women who choose to devote all of their energy to raising a family. Yet, personal choices are not always as clear-cut as the overall trends may indicate. Even today, many women still grapple with how to balance their personal and professional lives.

The changes in women's roles in society that have occurred over the past fifty years are strongly related to historical events and economic trends. While working class women have always worked outside the home, many women from the middle and even upper classes entered the workforce during World War II to replace male workers then serving overseas. Though many

of these women enjoyed their newfound independence and responsibilities, most were forced to leave their positions at the end of the war in order to create jobs for returning GIs. While there were limited opportunities for women to work outside the home in postwar America, the strong economy of the 1960s and increased federal support for higher education enabled many women in the Baby Boom cohort to attend college. With increased educational attainment, women became more likely to delay marriage and childbearing in order to pursue a career; a trend that has become increasingly pronounced in recent decades. Since 1970, women's occupational choices have been determined in large part by the industrial shift from manufacturing to services and by economic ups and downs. During recent decades, many families have found that they cannot survive on the earnings of one breadwinner. The need for a second salary has not only had a significant impact on women, but has also changed the way that society as a whole views women in the labor force.

Despite many gains, women are still not equally represented in all fields and income brackets. In order to understand gender inequality in the workplace, you will examine the earnings and occupational choices of men and women with the same level of education. Furthermore, you will consider whether the gender gap in earnings results from discriminatory practices such as the "glass ceiling" and the "old boy's network," or from factors such as real qualification differences between men and women.

By charting trends in women's educational attainment, occupational choices and earnings, you will consider how, why, and to what extent women's lives have changed since 1950.

KEY

concepts

Gender
Male or Female

OTHER concepts

Cohort (Chapter One)
Earnings (Chapter Two)
Education (Chapter Two)

Race/Ethnicity (Chapter Two)
Occupation (Chapter Two)

A. Educational Attainment

Until the 1950s, the cost of a college education limited enrollment to mostly students from wealthy families. Often, if a family could afford the tuition for only one child, they would choose to send their son. However, an abundance of jobs and higher salaries in the 1950s and 1960s enabled families to send more children to college. Additionally, beginning in the 1960s, increased federal support for higher education created more opportunities for men and women. In the last few decades, women, as well as previously underrepresented racial/ethnic groups, have begun to attend college in much larger numbers.

In addition to being affected by economic trends, many people believe the educational attainment of women in turn impacts childbearing trends. During the past few decades, as their education levels have increased, women have been having fewer children and giving birth later in life.

In the following exercises, you will examine trends in educational attainment since 1950, including differences by gender and difference between men and women across racial/ethnic groups. You will also look at the relationship between childbearing and educational attainment.

<u>Exercise 1</u> Using data from 1950 to the present, examine changes in the percentage of men and women ages 25-34 that have a high school education or more. Describe the role gender seems to play in educational attainment, and how the gender gap may have changed over time. Do you think it is useful to focus on this particular age group? Why or why not?

▸ *Dataset*: EDUC.TREND

▸ Create a line graph with a line for women and a line for men. For each year, indicate the percentage of 25-34 year-old men and women with a high school education or more. (Hint: You will need to add the percentage of high school graduates, those with some college, and college graduates in order to find the total percentage of each group that has graduated from high school.)

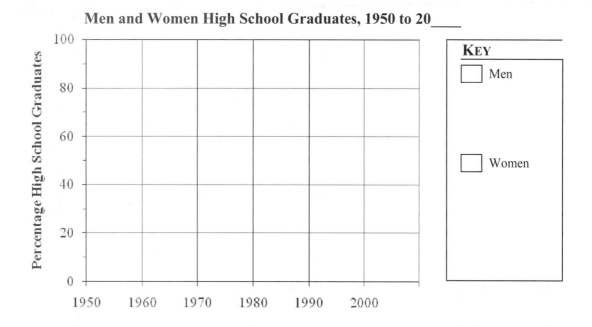

Men and Women High School Graduates, 1950 to 20____

Percentage High School Graduates

100

80

60

40

20

0

1950   1960   1970   1980   1990   2000

KEY

☐ Men

☐ Women

Exercise 2 Using data from 1950 and the present, look at the difference between the percentage of high school graduates among black and non-black men and women, ages 25-34. Describe any significant differences.

▸ *Dataset*: EDUC.TREND

▸ Create two bar charts, one for blacks and one for non-blacks, with side-by-side bars for men and women. In each chart show, for 1950 and the present, the percentage of 25-34 year-old men and women with a high school education or more. (Hint: You will need to add the percentage of high school graduates, those with some college and college graduates in order to find the total percent of each group that has graduated from high school.)

High School Graduates: Black Men and Women, 20____

High School Graduates: Non-Black Men and Women, 20____

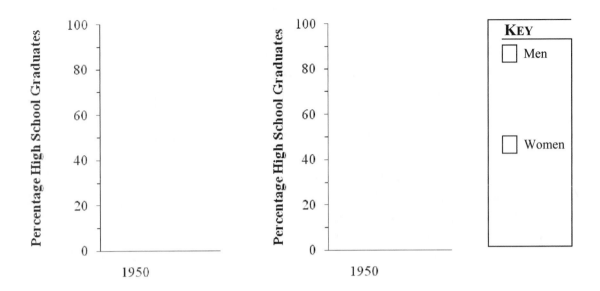

Exercise 3 Using data from 1950 to the present, examine changes in the percentages of men and women, ages 25-34, who have graduated from college. Is the gap between men and women at this level of educational attainment significantly different from the gender gap at the high school diploma level?

▸ *Dataset*: EDUC.TREND

▸ Create a line graph with a line for women and a line for men, ages 25-34. For each year, indicate the percentage of each group that has graduated from college.

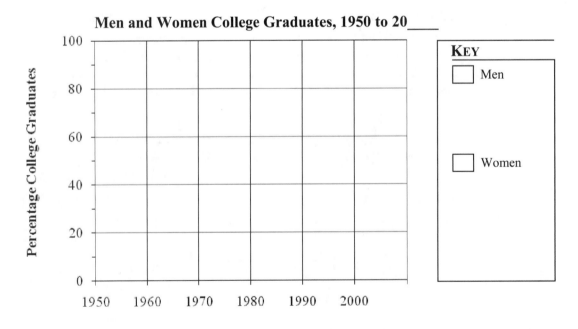

Men and Women College Graduates, 1950 to 20____

Exercise 4 What are the differences in college degree attainment between black and non-black women and men, ages 25-34, from 1950 to the present? Are the gender and race gaps between these four groups significantly different from the gaps at the high school diploma level?

▸ *Dataset*: EDUC.TREND

On your own, create two bar charts, one for blacks and one for non-blacks, with side-by-side bars for men and women. In each chart, for each census year from 1950 to the present, show the percentage of 25-34 year-old men and women with a college degree or more.

Exercise 5 On your own, examine the educational attainment of women ages 25 and above in the present. Describe the differences between the younger and older cohorts. Which cohorts of women appear to have made the greatest gains in educational attainment?

▸ *Dataset*: EDUCIMM.DAT

Exercise 6 Focusing on the present, show the educational attainment distribution of men and women, ages 25-34, for all racial/ethnic groups. How does the gender gap differ across these groups?

▸ *Dataset*: EDUCIMM.DAT

▸ Create a stacked bar chart with side-by-side bars for men and women, ages 25-34. For each racial/ethnic group, stack by educational attainment.

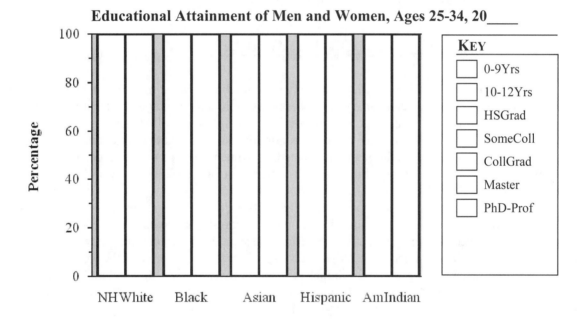

Educational Attainment of Men and Women, Ages 25-34, 20____

Exercise 7 On your own, focus on people with Masters and PhD's and describe the gender gap among those with higher levels of educational attainment in the present.

▸ *Dataset*: EDUCIMM.DAT

B. Occupation and Gender

Historically, there has been a very clear division of labor between men and women. Until recently, most women in the labor force entered the fields of nursing, social work, teaching, service, and domestic work. Today, women are moving into all fields, and the number of male and female professionals entering the workforce is more or less equal. At the same time as, men are slowly moving into fields traditionally dominated by women. Even as the representation of women and men becomes more equal in many jobs, internal gender differences are still evident within occupations.

Many believe that a "double standard" still affects the role of women in the workplace, especially in upper management positions. For example, a man striving to climb the corporate ladder may be viewed as "ambitious," while his equally driven female counterpart may be considered "pushy." Women, more often than men, are still sexually harassed in the workplace.

Despite fathers' increased contributions to their family responsibilities and the growing popularity of flextime and day care, many women have not been able to devote all of their energy to their careers due to their role as the family's primary caretaker. In the following exercises, you will examine trends in occupational choices among men and women. You will also look at how these gender divisions play out in different racial/ethnic groups.

__Exercise 8__ Using data from 1950 to the present, look at the changing percentages of women and men, ages 35-44, in each occupational category. Do men and women appear to be concentrated in different occupational categories? How has that distribution changed over time?

▸ *Dataset*: EDUCOCCUP.TREND

▸ Create two bar charts, one for 1950 and one for the present. Using side-by-side bars for men and women, ages 35-44, indicate the percentage in each occupational category.

Occupations in 1950:
Men and Women, Ages 35-44

Occupations in 20____:
Men and Women, Ages 35-44

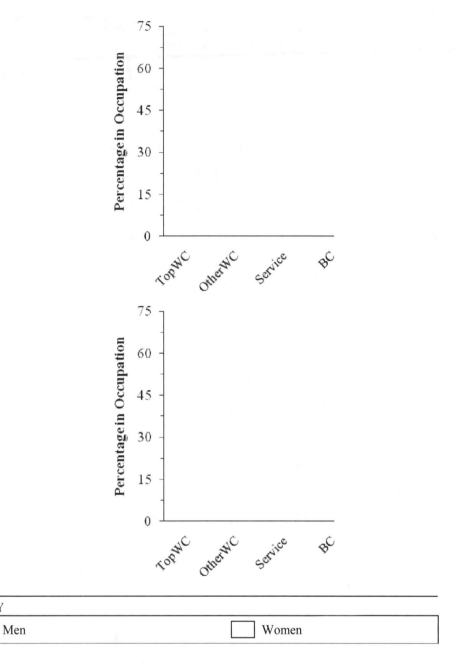

Exercise 9 How does the occupation distribution vary for black and non-black men and women, ages 35-44, over time? In which occupations are black men and women more likely to work? On your own, examine gender differences within each race and then compare your findings to the gender gaps in the entire population (Exercise 8).

  ▶ *Dataset*: EDUCOCCUP.TREND

Exercise 10 Investigate gender differences in occupations for specific Asian groups, ages 35-44, in the present. Describe your findings and compare them to the gender gaps in other racial/ethnic groups.

  ▶ *Dataset*: OCCUPASIANALL.DAT

▸ On your own, create a stacked bar chart with side-by-side bars for women and men, ages 35-44, in each specific Asian group; stack by occupation category.

Exercise 11 Compare the gender distribution of doctors, ages 25-34, to doctors, ages 55-64. Is there any difference between the two groups?

▸ *Dataset*: DOCTORS.DAT

▸ Create two pie charts, one for each age group, with divisions for gender.

Gender Distribution of Doctors by Age, 20____

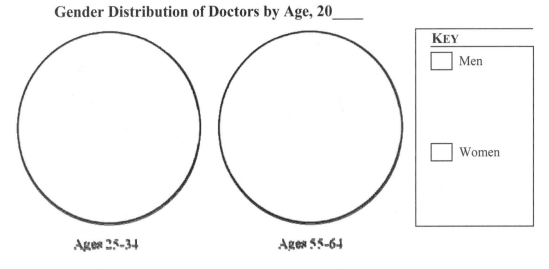

Exercise 12 Compare the gender distribution of lawyers, ages 25-34, with that of lawyers, ages 55-64. Is there any difference between the two groups?

▸ *Dataset*: LAWYERS.DAT

▸ Create two pie charts, one for each age group, with divisions for gender.

Gender Distribution of Lawyers by Age, 20____

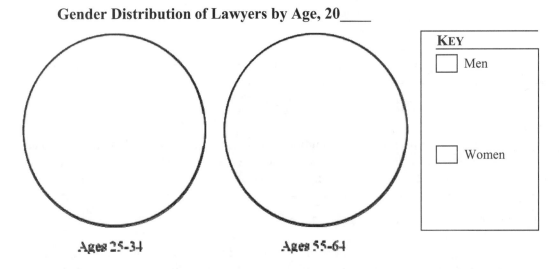

Exercise 13 Look at the gender distribution of doctors and lawyers, ages 25-34 and 55-64, for each racial/ethnic group. Compare these findings to the gender distribution for the overall population of doctors and lawyers that you examined in Exercises 11 and 12.

▸ *Datasets*: DOCTORS.DAT, LAWYERS.DAT

- On your own, create a stacked bar chart showing the gender distribution of doctors in each racial/ethnic group. Use side-by-side bars for each age group and stack by gender.

- On your own, create a stacked bar chart showing the gender distribution of lawyers in each racial/ethnic group. Use side-by-side bars for each age group and stack by gender.

Discussion Questions

1. What factors do you think affect a woman's occupational choice? A man's?

2. How does society perceive occupations traditionally held by women as different from those traditionally held by men? Do you think that society today continues to value certain occupations more than others?

3. Why do you think that a great number of women have moved into fields previously dominated by men, whereas a relatively small number of men have moved into fields previously dominated by women?

4. Why do you think that men are disproportionately represented among the higher ranks of employees in fields dominated by women, such as nursing?

C. Education and Occupation

An individual's educational attainment strongly affects his or her choice of occupation. Until recently, men and women tended to enter different fields. Similarly, men and women in college tend to pursue different areas of study, and do not pursue graduate degrees at equal rates. Although the gender differences in educational attainment and occupational choice are becoming narrower, they still affect many areas of study and work. In the following exercises, you will explore how educational attainment affects occupational choice, and how both of these factors are influenced by gender.

Exercise 14 Using data from 1970 and the present; examine how educational attainment affects the occupational status distribution of working men and women, ages 35-44. Compare the percentage of female college graduates who have top white-collar employment to the percentage of male college graduates who have top white-collar employment. Has there been any change over time? Why is it helpful to focus on 1970 and the present?

- *Dataset*: EDUCOCCUP.TREND

- Create a stacked bar chart with side-by-side bars for male and female college graduates, ages 35-44; for each year, stack by occupational status.

Occupations of Male and Female College Graduates, 1970 and 20____

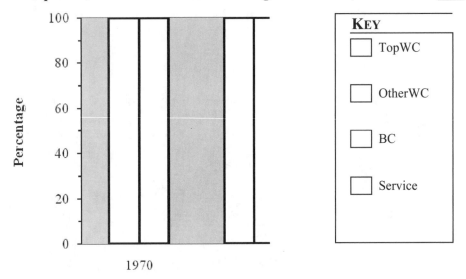

Exercise 15 On your own, look at the data in Exercise 14 in terms of race/ethnicity. Are there gender differences within and among different racial/ethnic groups? Describe your findings.

▸ *Dataset*: EDUCOCCUP.TREND

Discussion Questions

1. How do you think your gender has affected your study and career plans?

2. How do your own career plans compare with your parents' and grandparents' occupational choices? What factors might affect the occupational choices of different generations?

3. Do you think the impact educational attainment has on women's career choices is different than the impact it has on men's choices? If so, how?

4. In the future, do you think the occupational choices of men and women with comparable educational backgrounds will become more similar? What social and economic factors might affect trends in occupational choice?

D. The Gender Gap in Earnings

Over the last few decades, women have earned more money as their level of educational attainment and occupational status has increased. However, a gap between male and female earnings still exists. As individuals, a woman often earns less than a man in an identical position in the same company. These differences can be attributed to gender discrimination, such as the "glass ceiling" or the "old boy network." However, as shown in the chapter on Labor Force, women with similar credentials sometimes have fewer years of full-time work experience than men because they left the labor force because of family or other commitments. Thus, comparisons between groups are sometimes difficult. In the following exercises, you will compare the earnings of men and women who work full-time, year-round. You will take a closer look how education and occupation impact the earnings gap.

Exercise 16 Using current data, compare the earnings of women and men, ages 25-34, to those of women and men, ages 35-44. Describe any differences and offer possible explanations for them.

▶ *Dataset*: EARN.DAT

▶ Create a stacked bar chart with side-by-side bars for men and women. Draw a bar for 25-34 year-olds and a bar for 35-44 year-olds; stack by current earnings.

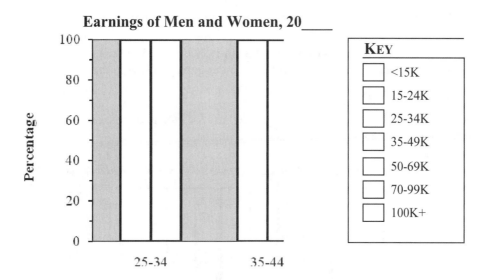

Earnings of Men and Women, 20____

Exercise 17 Look at the current earnings of men and women, ages 35-44, for each racial/ethnic group. What are the gender differences within and among racial/ethnic groups?

▶ *Dataset*: EARN.DAT

▶ Create a stacked bar chart with side-by-side bars for men and women. For each racial/ethnic group, stack by earnings.

Earnings of Men and Women, Ages 35-44, by Race/Ethnicity, 20____

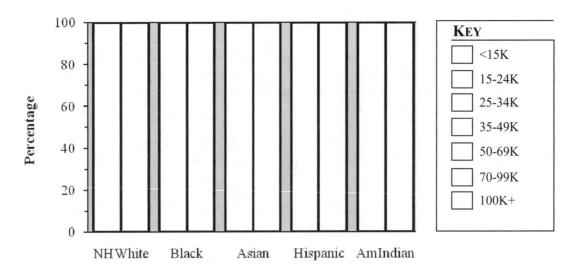

Exercise 18 Looking at the earnings of men and women, ages 35-44 in the present, focus on education. Does educational attainment affect the gender gaps you saw in the previous exercises?

▶ *Dataset*: WORK-35.DAT

▶ Create a stacked bar chart with side-by-side bars for men and women. For each educational level, stack by earnings.

Earnings of Men and Women, Ages 35-44, by Education, 20____

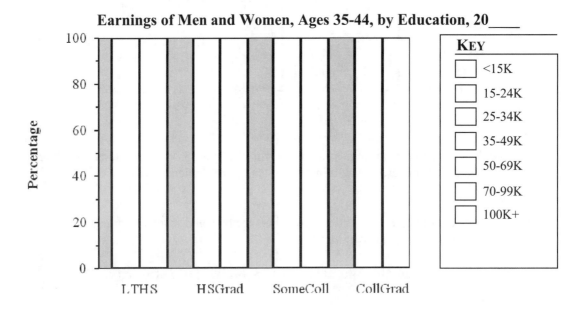

Exercise 19 On your own, determine whether or not a college education decreases the gender gap in earnings for 35-44 year-olds in all racial/ethnic groups. If not, why do you think some differences persist?

▶ *Datasets*: WORK-35.DAT, WORKHISP-35.DAT, WORKASIAN-35.DAT

Exercise 20 Is it possible to erase the gender gap by focusing only on those who not only have college degrees, but also hold top professional positions? On your own, examine the gender gap in the earnings of 35-44 year-olds with a college education in top professional positions. Do you continue to see differences between women and men? Do both genders seem to be experiencing an equal "return" on their education in this situation?

▸ *Dataset*: WORK-35.DAT

Exercise 21 Using current data, examine the gender gap in doctors' earnings. Look at doctors, ages 25-34 and 45-64, and compare the differences in men's and women's earnings in this profession. Do the patterns seem to be any different from those you found when looking at all occupations? How does the gender gap vary by age?

▸ *Dataset*: DOCTORS.DAT

▸ On your own, create four pie charts for doctors: one for men aged 25-34, one for men aged 45-64, one for women aged 25-35, and one for women aged 45-64. In each chart, show the earnings distribution.

Exercise 22 On your own, repeat the previous exercise for lawyers.

▸ *Dataset*: LAWYERS.DAT

Discussion Questions

1. Why do earning differences between genders exist? Do you think the differences are increasing or diminishing? What leads you to that conclusion?

2. Why do you think that white men are disproportionately represented in the highest earnings categories? How might this fact affect women and other minorities?

3. How would you explain the fact that fields traditionally dominated by women tend to pay less than other fields? Do you think these fields pay less because they are less valued by society, or do they pay less because of historical discrimination against the women who work in them? How do you think pay would change if men dominated these fields?

4. Building upon Question 3, some women believe that if they convince men to enter fields that have traditionally been "women's work," more respect and money will follow. Do you think that this would happen? Can you think of any fields in which this has happened or been attempted?

5. Looking back at trends in gender differences in earnings, what do you think the earnings distribution between the genders will look like twenty years from now? Up until now, how have your own earnings compared to those of people of the opposite sex? How do you think your gender and race affect your earnings potential?

THINK
tank

1. The respective roles of men and women can vary a great deal among cultures and racial/ethnic groups. Although the U.S. Census is not designed to directly investigate gender attitudes or expectations, it does offer a great deal of information about the daily lives of men and women. Based on your examination of the data, does it appear that gender differences vary by race/ethnicity? What evidence can you produce to support or disprove the notion that different cultures perceive gender in different ways?

2. The relatively low number of women in high level corporate positions has sometimes been attributed to the "glass ceiling"—characterized by restricted access to upper-level positions because of gender. However, some critics suggest that differences in women and men's rate of promotion are not due to biased workplace policies, but rather are due to the disruptive effects of childbearing and other family responsibilities. Is this a valid argument? What evidence can you produce to support or disprove this theory? What policies could businesses implement to help women and men balance career and family? Would such policies be good for business? Why or why not?

chapter 7 HOUSEHOLDS AND FAMILIES

This chapter is somewhat different from topics covered in previous chapters because you will not be examining Americans as individuals, but rather looking at groups of individuals who live in households. American households have taken on a variety of forms since the 1950s, and though married-couple families with children are still prominent, most researchers and social observers would agree that households and families have undergone a great deal of change since the days of "Ozzie and Harriet."

While you will be exploring household composition trends from 1950 to the present, it is important to understand that the nuclear family households of the 1950s were actually somewhat of an anomaly in terms of household history. Between 1900 and 1930, the United States experienced a steady decline in fertility and, consequently, shrinking household sizes (the Great Depression of the 1930s caused marriage rates to plummet and births fell to a record low as economic uncertainty prompted many couples to delay marriage and childbearing). Furthermore, many singles and families were forced to share housing units and, as a result, the number of new households formed dropped considerably.

Throughout the late 1930s and early 1940s, the economy and job market began to improve. The improved economic situation enabled more people to purchase single-family homes, encouraging an increase in marriage and birth rates. Over the twenty years between 1940 and 1960, the population under the age of five doubled, ushering in an era commonly known as the "Baby Boom". As households grew, a large crop of new homes built in the 1950s—more than double the number built during the previous decade—paved the way for mass migration to suburban America. Small single-family homes became the housing standard, and the nuclear family came to represent the "typical" American household. Although the 1950s may not have been the "golden age" that some nostalgic observers suggest, it certainly was an era of economic and demographic growth.

By the mid-sixties, however, as the baby boomers matured, marriage and birth rates plummeted while divorce rates rose drastically. These shifts, in turn, had a significant impact on household composition and formation. The corresponding increase in single parent households and non-family households sparked considerable public debate that has continued up to the present.

Household

A household refers to all of the persons (one or more) who occupy a single housing unit. The two main types of households - family and non-family - are defined below. For census purposes, one person in each household is designated as a "householder". The householder typically is the person, or one of the persons, who owns or rents the home.

NOTE: Datasets include variables that pertain to family households only (FAMTYPE) or all household types, including both family and non-family households (HHTYPE).

Family Households

A family consists of a householder and one or more other persons living in the same household who are related to the householder by birth, marriage, or adoption. All persons who are related to the householder are regarded as members of his or her family. Family households can be classified as follows:

> **Married-Couple Families**—These include the householder and his or her spouse, as well as any children related to the householder by birth, marriage, or adoption. Such households may also include other relatives or non-relatives.

> **Single-Mother Families**—Households headed by an unmarried female and including one or more children related to the householder by birth, marriage, or adoption. Such households may also include other relatives or non-relatives.

> **Single-Father Families**—Households headed by an unmarried male and including one or more children related to the householder by birth, marriage, or adoption. Such households may also include other relatives or non-relatives.

Non-Family Households

Any person or group of persons not living with relatives and occupying separate living quarters would qualify as a non-family household. Male-headed non-family households include single-male households as well as male householders living with one or more non-relatives. Likewise, female-headed non-family households include single-female households as well as female householders living with one or more non-relatives. Non-family household members might include housemates, roommates, borders, cohabiting couples of the same or opposite sex, and unmarried partners.

Presence of Children Under 18

Households can be classified by the number of children under the age of 18 related to the householder and residing in the household. The following groupings are used here:

> No related children present
> At least one child under age 6 (may include other children over the age of 6)
> At least one child 6-17 years old, with none under age 6

NOTE: Dataset variable KID abbreviates these categories as: None, Kids<6, and KidsOther

Household Size
Number of persons per household, with categories 1, 2, 3, 4, and 5+.

Dual Earner Family Status
Married-couple families are classified by the husband and wife's labor force status as follows:

Dual Earner   Single Earner Female
Single Earner Male   No Earner Family

Housing Type
An occupied housing unit is a house, apartment, a mobile home, a group of rooms, or a single room that is occupied as separate living quarters. Housing type will be classified here as:

House   Mobile home or trailer
Apartment in building with 2-9 units   Other including houseboats, campers, vans, etc.
Apartment in building with 10+ units

NOTE: Dataset variable HOUSING abbreviates these categories as House, APT2-9, APT10+, MobHome, and Other.

Ownership-Rentership
Classifies households according to the ownership of the housing unit.

Owner—Denotes the householder or another household member owns or co-owns the unit, even if it is mortgaged or still being paid for.

Renter—All other households

OTHER concepts

Race/Ethnicity (Chapter Two)
Poverty Status of Family (Chapter Eight)

Today, alternative household arrangements and changing conceptions of family and marriage challenge previously held norms regarding adoption, health insurance coverage for unmarried partners, and tax deductions. Controversy over these issues has led many to question what defines a "normal" family.

As you work through this chapter, think of historical events, changes in social attitudes, and economic trends that affect households and families. By looking at overall household trends, the characteristics of non-family households, married couples, female-headed and male-headed households, and housing types, you will gain an understanding of the evolution of the American household since the iconic days of the 1950s.

A. Household Trends

For the past fifty years, the two-parent "standard" of the 1950s has been slowly giving way to a greater proportion of smaller, non-family and single-parent family households. Moreover, since 1950, there has been a significant increase in the number of households made up of only one or two people. The following exercises reveal a trend towards an increasingly complex mosaic of family and non-family arrangements.

Exercise 1 During which time period since 1950 has the number of households increased the most? During which decade did the total U.S. population increase the most? Using data from 1950 to the present, look at the changes in number of households and the number of people in the United States. Why do trends differ between the two measures?

▸ *Datasets*: POP.TREND, HOUSEHOLDS.TREND

▸ Create a line graph with two lines, one for the number of households (in millions) and one for the U.S. population (in millions). For each year, indicate the number of households and the number of people living in the United States.

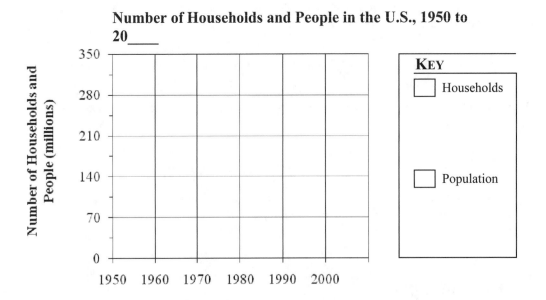

Number of Households and People in the U.S., 1950 to 20____

Exercise 2 Look at the changes in household size since 1950. Overall, has household size increased or decreased? How do you account for your findings?

▸ *Dataset*: HOUSEHOLDS.TREND

▸ Create a stacked bar chart with bars for each year; stack by the percentage of households with a given number of persons.

Number of Persons Per Household, 1950 to 20____

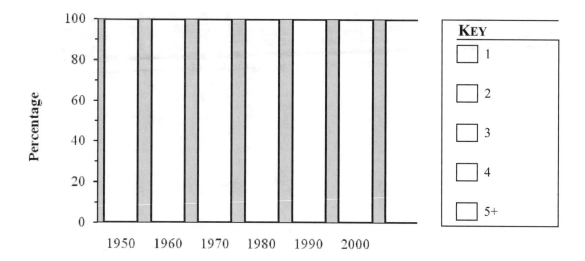

Exercise 3 How has the composition of U.S. households changed over time? Determine the percentage of households of each type since 1950, and discuss any significant increases or decreases among types.

▸ *Dataset*: HOUSEHOLDS.TREND

▸ Create a stacked bar chart with bars for each year, stacking by household type.

Household Type, 1950 to 20____

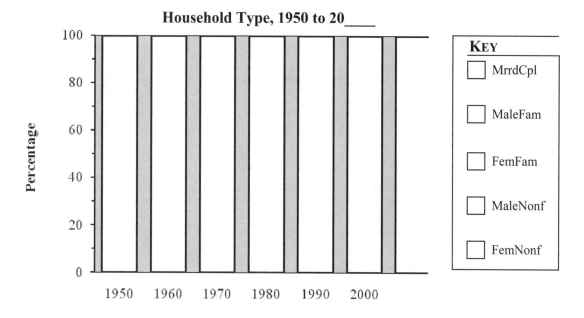

Exercise 4 Using your findings from the previous exercise, describe the changes that occurred for each household type since 1950. Discuss changes in the prevalence of different types of family and non-family households.

▸ *Dataset*: HOUSEHOLDS.TREND

B. Non-Family Households

One of the most significant trends in the last few decades has been a rapid increase in the number of non-family households. Most of this increase stems from the growing number of single-person householders, many of whom are older and financially better off than singles in previous eras. This increase, coupled with declining fertility, has been a major contributor to the overall decline in household size. The following exercises look at the composition of non-family households in terms of gender, age, race/ethnicity, and economic well-being.

Exercise 5 What percentage of households in the present were non-family households? What has happened to the percentage of non-family households since 1950?

▸ *Dataset*: HOUSEHOLDS.TREND

▸ Create a line graph indicating the percentage of non-family households from 1950 to the present.

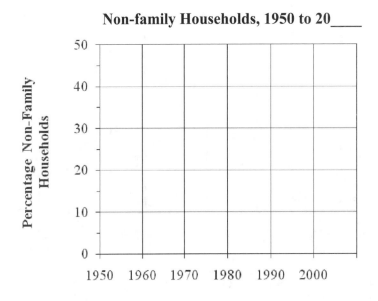

Exercise 6 Using data from 1950 to the present, determine whether there have ever been as many female-headed non-family households as male-headed non-family households. What are the trends over time, and what might account for the differences?

▸ *Dataset*: HOUSEHOLDS.TREND

▸ Create a bar chart with side-by-side bars for male-headed non-family and female-headed non-family households. For each year, indicate the percentage of all households that are in each of these two categories.

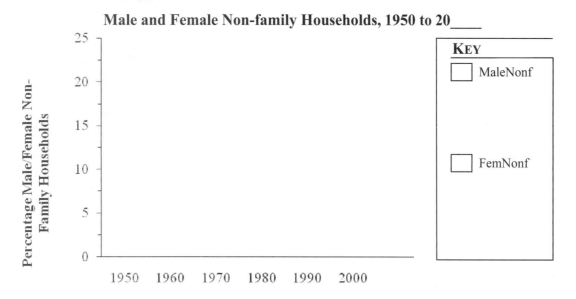

Male and Female Non-family Households, 1950 to 20____

Exercise 7 Why might a householder's age affect whether he or she lives in a non-family household? How does this tendency differ by gender?

▸ *Dataset*: HOUSEHOLDS.DAT

▸ Create a bar chart with side-by-side bars for men and women. For each householder age group, indicate the percentage living in non-family households.

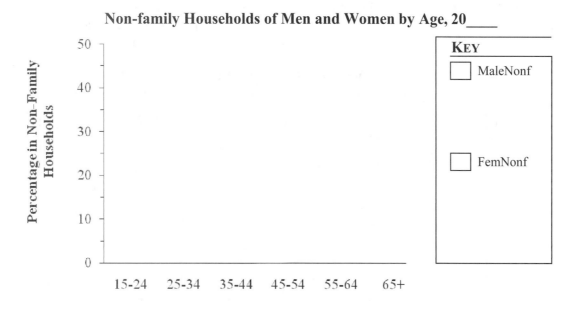

Non-family Households of Men and Women by Age, 20____

Exercise 8 Using data from 1950 to the present, examine trends over time in the percentage of male and female non-family households for blacks and non-blacks. Describe any trends that you find significant and suggest factors that might account for these trends.

▸ *Dataset*: HOUSEHOLDS.TREND

▸ Create a line graph indicating the percentage of male-headed non-family households and female-headed non-family households for blacks and non-blacks, 1950 to the present.

Male and Female Non-family Households by Race, 1950 to 20____

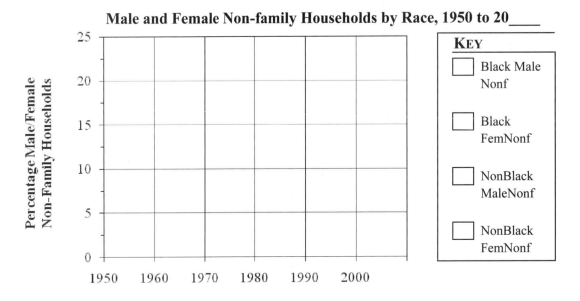

Exercise 9 Focusing on the present, determine the percentage of family, male-headed non-family, and female-headed non-family households for each racial/ethnic group. Describe any significant differences among the groups.

▸ *Dataset*: HOUSEHOLDS.DAT

▸ Create a stacked bar chart with bars for each racial/ethnic group and stack by the percentage of family, male-headed and female-headed non-family households. (Hint: You will need to add the percentage of married-couple households to the percentages of male- and female-headed households to find the total percentage of family households.)

Family and Non-family Households by Race/Ethnicity, 20____

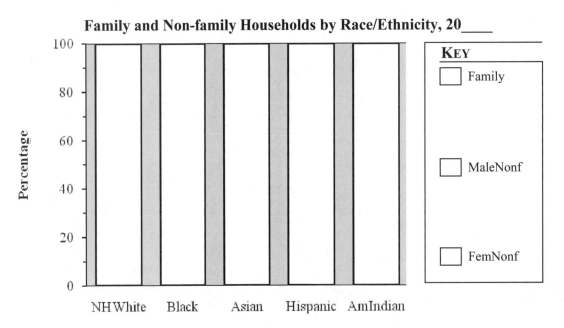

C. Married-Couple Families

Despite changing trends in marriage, childbearing, divorce, and cohabitation, the majority of households in the United States are still family households. Most of these family households include married-couples, a majority of whom are in their first marriage, but many include individuals that have been divorced and remarried. While the current trend among young adults is to delay marriage until the mid or late twenties, demographers estimate that the vast majority of Americans will eventually marry.

Exercise 10 Bearing in mind changes in the number of married-couple households over time (see Exercise 3), describe the distribution of family types among family households in the present. What percentage of family households are married couples, male-headed, and female-headed?

▸ *Dataset*: FAMILY.DAT

▸ Create a pie chart with divisions for each type of family household.

Family Household Distribution, 20____

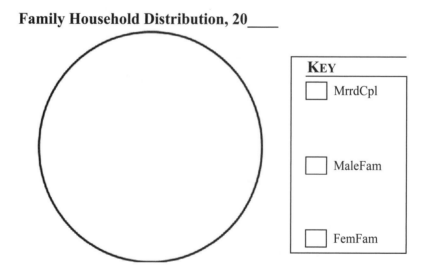

KEY

☐ MrrdCpl

☐ MaleFam

☐ FemFam

Exercise 11 Using current data, look at the percentage of households headed by a married couple.

▸ *Dataset*: FAMILY.DAT

▶ Create a stacked bar chart with bars for each racial/ethnic group, stacking by the percentage of married couples and "other" family types in the present. (Hint: Non-married-couple families include male-headed families and female-headed families.)

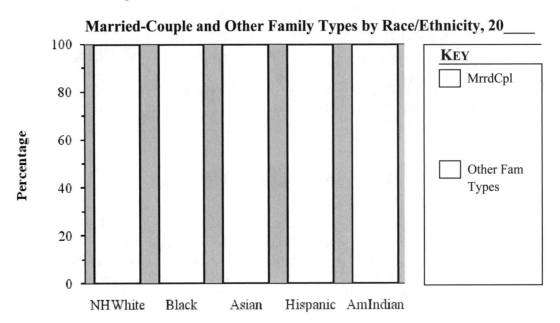

Married-Couple and Other Family Types by Race/Ethnicity, 20____

Exercise 12 Were children under 18 a part of most married-couple families in the present?

▸ *Dataset*: FAMILY.DAT

▸ Create a pie chart for married-couple families showing the proportion of such families with no children, children under age 6, and other children. See the "Key Concepts" section for an explanation of these categories.

Presence of Children in Married-Couple Families, 20_____

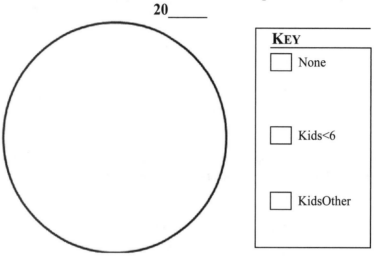

Exercise 13 On your own, using current data, explore differences among racial/ethnic groups in the percentage of married couples who have children.

▸ *Dataset*: FAMILY.DAT

Exercise 14 In 1950, the typical married-couple family was supported by a male single-earner. Is this true in the present? In the present what percentage of married-couple families were supported by a male single-earner? What percentage was supported by dual earners?

▸ *Dataset*: FAMILY.DAT

▸ Create a pie chart for married couples with divisions for single-earner females, single-earner males, dual earners, and no-earners.

Earner Distribution of Married-Couple Families, 20____

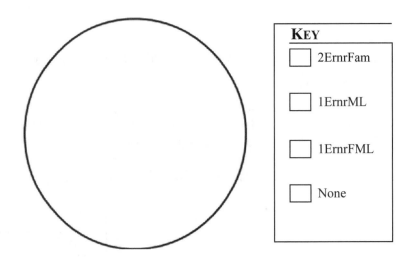

KEY

☐ 2ErnrFam

☐ 1ErnrML

☐ 1ErnrFML

☐ None

Exercise 15 How did the distribution of types of earners in married-couple families vary by age group in the present? What might account for these differences?

▸ *Dataset*: FAMEARN.DAT

▸ Create a stacked bar chart with bars for each age group. For each age group, stack by the percentage of single-earner females, single-earner males, dual earners, and no-earner families in the present.

Earners in Married-Couple Families by Age, 20____

KEY

☐ 2ErnrFam

☐ 1ErnrML

☐ 1ErnrFML

☐ None

Exercise 16 How did earnings arrangements in married-couple families vary among racial/ethnic groups? Which racial/ethnic group had the highest percentage of dual earner married couples? The lowest? What are some possible differences between dual earner and single-earner families?

▸ *Dataset*: FAMEARN.DAT

▸ Create a stacked bar chart with bars for each racial/ethnic group, stacking by the percentage of dual earner, single-earner male, single-earner female, and no-earner married-couple families in the present.

Earners in Married-Couple Families by Race/Ethnicity, 20____

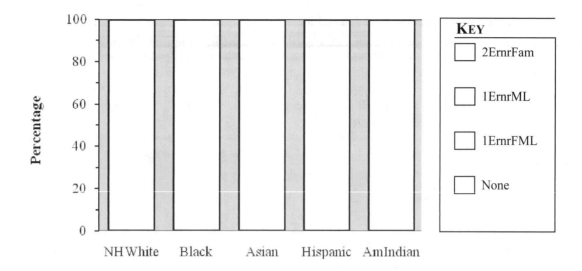

Exercise 17 Are married-couple families less likely to be living in poverty than other family types? Using current data, examine the percentage of households living in poverty among married-couple families, female-headed families, and male-headed families.

▸ *Dataset*: FAMILY.DAT

▸ On your own, create three pie charts: one for married couples, one for female-headed families, and one for male-headed families. In each chart, make divisions for poverty and non-poverty households.

Discussion Questions

1. In the 1950s, most families reflected the "Ozzie and Harriet" image of a married-couple family headed by a single male earner. How do current trends in earnings arrangements compare to those of the 50s? What might account for these changes?

2. What is the relationship between household composition and poverty status? Are married couples necessarily better off economically?

D. Male- and Female-Headed Families

Most male- or female-headed family households are single-parent families. While the number of male-headed family households has grown, they remain a small percentage of total family households. Most male-headed family households are comprised of single, divorced fathers living with their children.

Part of the growth in male-headed family households can be attributed to more sympathetic views of paternal custody, but most children with divorced parents live with their mothers. An emphasis on maternal custody resulted in a surge of female-headed family households, comprised of single mothers living with their children. Although some female-headed households, as well as male-headed households, are the result of the death of a spouse, the majority of single mothers are divorced and work to support their children.

Single parenthood continues to generate controversy and debate among political pundits and social scientists alike. Some argue that children living with single parents do not receive all of the support they need. Others argue that living in a household filled with marital conflict is more detrimental than living in a single-parent household. Whatever the case may be, male- and female-headed households are becoming more prevalent in American society. In the following exercises, you will look at the overall trends, racial/ethnic composition, and economic well being of male- and female-headed households.

Exercise 18 Considering the overall trends in household type since 1950 (See Exercise 3), discuss the trends in male-headed families since 1950.

▸ *Dataset*: HOUSEHOLDS.TREND

Exercise 19 Focusing on the present, determine which racial/ethnic groups have the highest and lowest percentage of male-headed families. Discuss the differences among groups and what might account for this variation.

▸ *Dataset*: FAMILY.DAT

▸ Create a bar chart with bars for each racial/ethnic group indicating what percentage of family households is comprised of male-headed families.

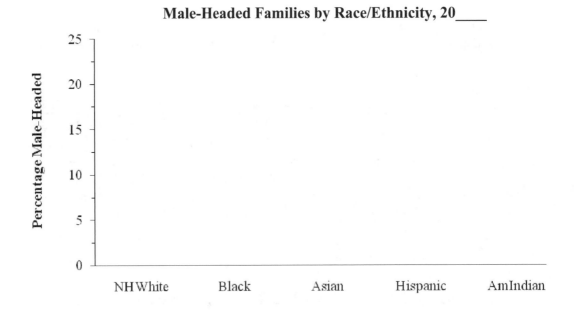

Male-Headed Families by Race/Ethnicity, 20_____

Exercise 20 Do male-headed families tend to be above the poverty level regardless of race/ethnicity?

▸ *Dataset*: FAMILY.DAT

▸ Create a stacked bar chart with bars for each racial/ethnic group, stacking by male-headed families living above and below the poverty threshold in the present. (Hint: To find the percentage of families living above poverty, add the percentage of those who are "near poor" to the percentage of those who are in the "middle" or "comfortable" categories.)

Male-Headed Families and Poverty Status, 20____

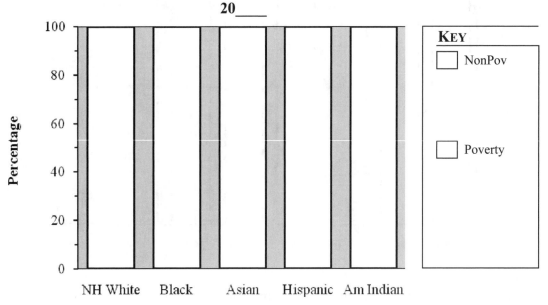

Exercise 21 How has the number of female-headed families changed since 1950? What was the number of female-headed family households in 1950? In the present? What might account for changes over time?

▸ *Dataset*: HOUSEHOLDS.TREND

▸ Create a line graph indicating the number of female-headed families in each year.

Female-Headed Families, 1950 to 20____

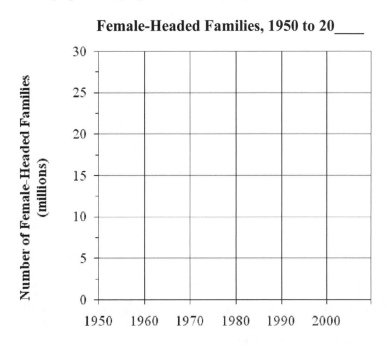

▸ Create a stacked bar chart with bars for each year, stacking by female-headed and other family households.

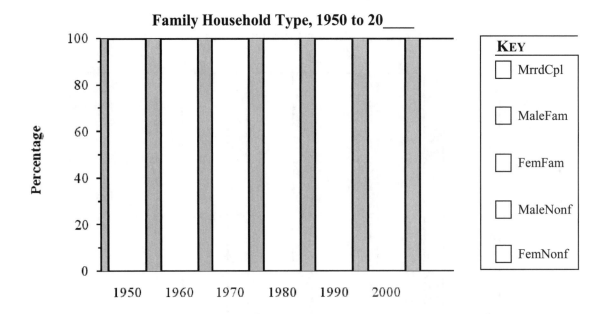

Family Household Type, 1950 to 20____

Exercise 22 What percentage of female-headed families has young children (less than 6 years)? Does this percentage vary by race/ethnicity?

▸ *Dataset*: FAMILY.DAT

▸ Create a bar chart with bars for each racial/ethnic group. For each group, indicate the percentage of female-headed families with children under the age of 6 in the present.

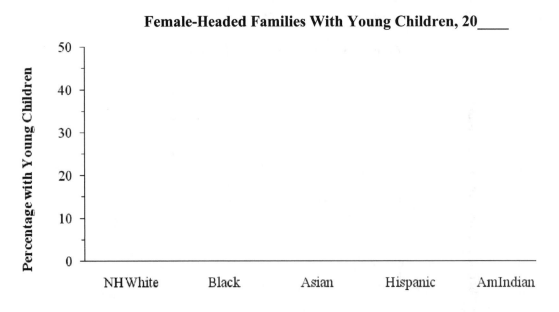

Female-Headed Families With Young Children, 20____

Exercise 23 How did the age distribution of householders in female-headed families vary among racial/ethnic groups in the present? Describe any significant findings and what might account for the differences in age across racial/ethnic groups.

▸ *Dataset*: FAMILY.DAT

▸ Create a stacked bar chart with bars for each racial/ethnic group, stacking by age categories.

Current Age Distribution of Female-Headed Families by Race/Ethnicity, 20____

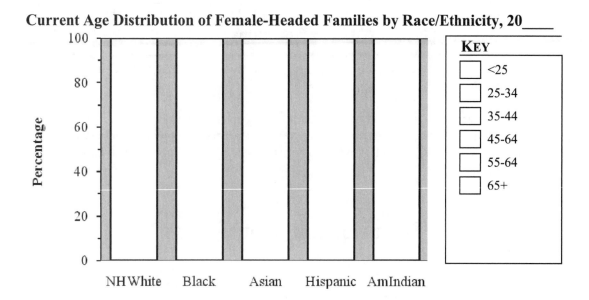

Exercise 24 What percentage of female-headed families was in poverty in the present? Is race/ethnicity a factor in the poverty status of female-headed families?

▸ *Dataset*: FAMILY.DAT

▸ Create a stacked bar chart with bars for each racial/ethnic group, stacking by the percentage of female-headed families living above and below the poverty threshold in the present.

Female-Headed Families and Poverty Status, 20____

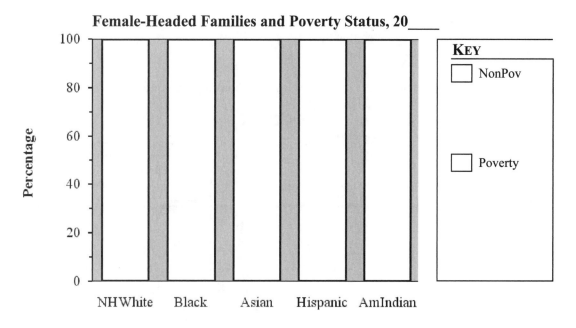

Exercise 25 Write a brief comparison of male-headed and female-headed families since 1990.

E. Housing and Households

Household and housing trends are interrelated. If household rates grow, housing construction increases; if rates decline, so does the housing market. Young, single adults require different housing than large families; thus population demographics impact housing construction. For example, the small, "starter" homes built in the late 1950s were specifically designed to accommodate demographic changes. The number of houses built during the 1950s was double that of the 1940s due to skyrocketing marriage and birth rates accompanied by a soaring economy. The following exercises explore this relationship between household characteristics and housing type. We will limit our inquiry to four basic types of housing units: houses, apartments in buildings with 2-9 units, apartments in buildings with 10 units or more, and mobile homes.

Exercise 26 Which types of housing are most common for U.S. households in the present? Does the most prevalent type vary by race/ethnicity?

▸ *Dataset*: HOUSING.DAT

▸ Create a pie chart showing the percentage of each housing type in the present.

Housing Type Distribution, 20____

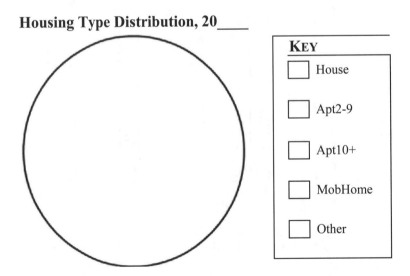

KEY

☐ House

☐ Apt2-9

☐ Apt10+

☐ MobHome

☐ Other

▸ On your own, create a stacked bar chart with bars for each racial/ethnic group, stacking by the percentage of housing types in the present.

Investigating Change in American Society | 158

Exercise 27 Currently, how does housing type vary depending on the age of the householder? What might account for these differences?

▸ *Dataset*: HOUSING.DAT

▸ Create a stacked bar chart with bars for each age group, stacking by housing type.

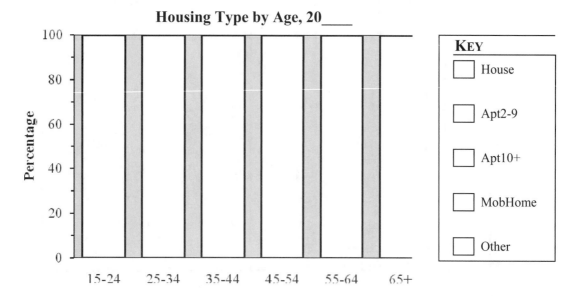

Exercise 28 Focusing on the present, determine whether or not families and non-families tend to live in the same kind of housing. Offer explanations for any differences you find.

▸ *Dataset*: HOUSING.DAT

▸ Create two pie charts, one for families and one for non-families. In each chart, show the housing type distribution.

Housing Type Distribution for Families and Non-families, 20_____

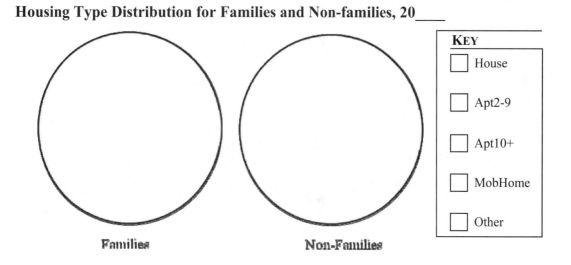

Exercise 29 Using current data, determine whether housing type varies by race/ethnicity. Describe your findings.

▸ *Dataset*: HOUSING.DAT

▸ Create a stacked bar chart with bars for each racial/ethnic group; stack by housing type distribution.

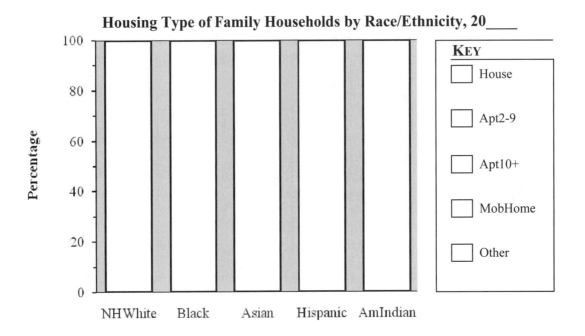

Housing Type of Family Households by Race/Ethnicity, 20____

Exercise 30 What is the relationship between home ownership and family composition? Are female-headed families as likely to own a home as married couples?

▸ *Dataset*: HOUSING.DAT

▸ On your own, create three pie charts: one for female-headed families, one for male-headed families, and one for married couples. In each chart, show the percentage of homeowners and non-homeowners.

Discussion Questions

1. Home ownership is considered by many to be an integral part of the "American dream." Do you think this view is justified? Should affordable housing be made available to all Americans?

2. How does age influence housing choices and living arrangements? Consider a "typical" person at each of the following ages: 10, 20, 30, 40, 50, 60, and 70+. How might his or her housing arrangements change over time? What factors might cause people or households to change their type of residence?

THINK
tank

1. Single-parent families are generally less economically well off than married-couple families. However, the age and education level of the household head also affects the economic well being of a family, regardless of the marital status of the householder. Provide evidence to support or refute the claim that children in single-parent families may be better off economically than children in married-couple families, depending on a parent's age and education level. Are there other aspects of 'well being' (beside economic) that would be important to explore in order to determine differences between single parent and married-couple families? If you could design a study to examine the effects of family structure on children, what other aspects of well being would you want to know about, and how would you measure them?

2. While reading your local newspaper, you notice a cantankerous letter to the editor suggesting that certain neighborhoods should be zoned for families only. According to the author of the letter, all non-family households are composed of young college students, and their late hours disrupt the peace of neighborhoods. Do you think this type of zoning is fair? Why or why not? Write an informative response to the letter that illustrates who would be affected by such zoning.

POVERTY

Many Americans are unaware of the current state of poverty in the United States. While overall poverty levels have decreased significantly since the late 1940s, in recent years they have consistently risen. Though popular conceptions about who is in poverty might suggest that this trend ought to concern only certain groups, in truth poverty is an important and relevant issue for all Americans.

Before assessing the overall situation, however, it is necessary to look at the ways in which poverty is defined. The federal government bases its definition of poverty upon a Department of Agriculture nutritional study conducted in 1961 that established that the average non-farm family spends one-third of its income on food. In light of this information, the researchers developed an "Economy Food Plan" that established the minimum cost for fulfilling a family's basic nutritional needs. The poverty level is determined by multiplying the cost of the "Economy Food Plan" by three. Families with earnings below three times the amount of the "Economy Food Plan" are considered to be living in poverty. Naturally, the calculations take inflation and family size into account.

While the results of this study are still used to measure poverty today, many politicians and researchers contend that this system for determining poverty status is flawed. Critics of the measurement argue that it is outdated, does not consider changes in the nation's consumption patterns, and does not account for regional differences in the cost of living. For example, food is much more expensive in urban areas than rural areas. But regardless of how poverty is measured, the fact remains that a large number of Americans lack the economic resources to meet their basic living costs. In the face of this problem, we look at who is in poverty, why they are in poverty, and what is being done to assist them.

The Poverty Rate for Children and the Older Population, 1966-2008

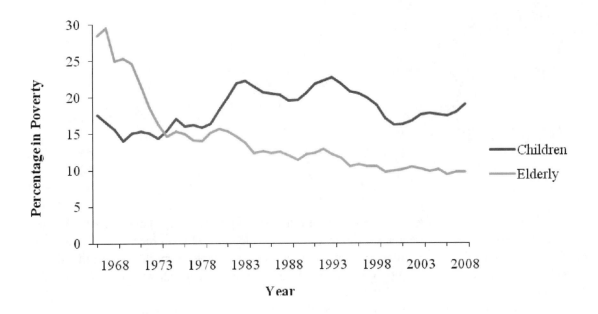

KEY
concepts

Poverty Status of a Family

At its core, the federal government's poverty classification is a family-based measure. A family's poverty status (either "in poverty" or "not in poverty") is determined on the basis of the family's total income and whether or not that amount falls below the "poverty cut-off" (the income threshold below which is considered poverty income). The "poverty cut-off" is based on the assumed costs of a family's living expenses and differs according to a family's size and composition. Because poverty status is based on the combined income of the family, considerations such as the number of earners in a family are important factors in determining its poverty status.

Poverty Status of an Individual

Although poverty status is a family-based concept, persons can also be classified as "in poverty" or "not in poverty" whether they live in family or non-family households. Persons living in family households are simply assigned the poverty status of their family, while persons residing in non-family households are treated as individuals. Their poverty status is determined on the basis of individual level "poverty cut-offs". When using poverty status information for individuals, bear in mind that the statistics reflect income for the entire family rather than individual income (for those who live in a family).

Income Relative to Poverty Cut-off

While the "poverty cut-off" distinguishes between poverty and non-poverty incomes, it can also be used to interpret different levels of non-poverty income. This involves determining the ratio of actual income to the "poverty cut-off." For example, in 2008, if the poverty cut-off for a family of four is $21,834, a family with an income of up to 1.5x the poverty cut-off ($32,751) might be considered "near poor," while a family with an income more than five times the poverty threshold ($109,170) would be considered "comfortable." For a smaller family with a lower poverty cut-off, a "comfortable" income would be somewhat lower; for a larger family it would be somewhat higher. Adopting a formula developed by Judith Treas and Ramon Torrecilia, we use the following "Income to Poverty Cut-off" conversion:

> **Poor**—Family income below the poverty cut-off.
>
> **Near-Poor**—Family income between 1x and 1.5x the poverty cut-off.
>
> **Middle**—Family income between 1.5x and 5x the poverty cut-off
>
> **Comfortable**—Family income more than 5x the poverty cut-off

OTHER concepts

City-Suburb-Nonmetropolitan (Chapter One) **Region** (Chapter Three)
Education (Chapter Two) **Family Household** (Chapter Seven)
Race/Ethnicity (Chapter Two)

Many people have a vague concept of "welfare" as the government's solution to poverty. In the United States, "welfare" is actually comprised of several different federal programs, each with distinct qualifying guidelines. Many of these programs were developed during the New Deal era, including Social Security Retirement, Social Security Disability Insurance, Unemployment Insurance and Aid to Families with Dependent Children (AFDC). In the 1960s, President Johnson's "War on Poverty" gave birth to a second wave of reforms: Supplemental Security Income, the School Lunch Program, Medicaid, Medicare and the Food Stamp Program.

Despite government assistance programs, societal and economic changes in recent decades have led to an increase in the number of people in poverty. During the late 70s and early 80s, real wages were depressed due to a recession and an influx of Baby Boomers looking for work. Furthermore, in the face of tougher competition, those with lower education levels had difficulty securing employment. Besides changing economic trends, the evolving composition of the American family household has also influenced poverty levels. Over the past three decades, an increase in divorce rates has led to an increase in single-parent families, the vast majority of which are female-headed. The increase in single mothers, coupled with the lower overall earnings of females, has created a unique trend known as the feminization of poverty.

The year 1996 marked an important change in the U.S. welfare system and the way the government addressed poverty. President Bill Clinton, who promised to "end welfare as we know it" in 1992, signed into law the Personal Responsibility and Work Opportunity Reconciliation Act (PRWORA), which replaced the AFDC with Temporary Assistance for Needy Families (TANF). The new system eliminated welfare as an entitlement, established work requirements, and imposed a lifetime time-limit restriction on assistance. The new system also shifted a large amount of the responsibility for welfare away from the federal government and onto the state governments.

The welfare reforms of 1996 led to a large decline in "welfare rolls" (i.e. the number of persons receiving welfare benefits). Using this as a marker, welfare reform has been deemed successful by some policy-makers. However, changing economic conditions and long-term impacts have brought its success into question. A large number of social scientists are currently studying the effects of welfare reform more closely. Better evidence for the success or failure of these reforms is expected in the coming years.

In this chapter, you will explore overall poverty trends and focus on patterns in terms of race/ethnicity, family type, gender, age, educational attainment, and geographic location of people in poverty. As you work through these exercises, consider the economic trends and historical events that may have influenced the current state of poverty in America.

A. The Race/Ethnicity of Poverty

Despite changing attitudes about race and an overall improvement in the economic status of most minorities, there is still a strong relationship between a household's race/ethnicity and the likelihood it is classified below the poverty level. In the following exercises, you will look at overall poverty trends in terms of race/ethnicity and focus on the state of poverty among different racial/ethnic groups in the present. As you complete these exercises, recall other factors connected to race/ethnicity—for example, educational attainment and earnings—that may partially account for your findings.

Exercise 1 Look at the percentage of black and non-black family households in poverty from 1970 to the present. Describe your findings.

▸ *Dataset*: FAMPOV.TREND

▸ Create a line graph with a line for blacks and a line for non-blacks; for each year, indicate the percentage of family households in poverty.

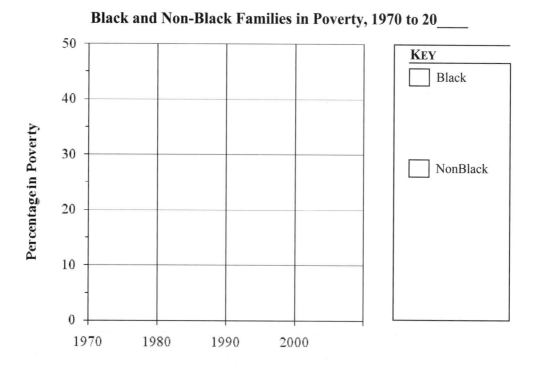

Exercise 2 Focusing on the present, consider the racial/ethnic distribution of poverty and non-poverty families. Which racial/ethnic group comprises the largest portion of families in poverty? Describe any significant differences in the race/ethnicity of poverty and non-poverty families.

▸ *Dataset*: FAMILY.DAT

▸ Create two pie charts, one for poverty and one for non-poverty families, with divisions for each racial/ethnic group. (Hint: Add the percentage of "near poor," "middle," and "comfortable" income families to find the total percent of families not in poverty.)

Race/Ethnicity Distributions of Families, 20____

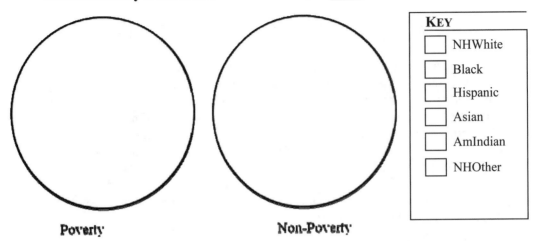

KEY

☐ NHWhite
☐ Black
☐ Hispanic
☐ Asian
☐ AmIndian
☐ NHOther

Poverty   Non-Poverty

Exercise 3 Consider the previous exercise from a different angle. Using current data look at the percentage of families in each racial/ethnic group that are in poverty. Describe any differences among the racial/ethnic groups you examine.

▶ *Dataset*: FAMILY.DAT

▶ Create a bar chart with bars for each racial/ethnic group. For each group, indicate the percentage of families in poverty in the present.

Poverty by Race/Ethnicity, 20____

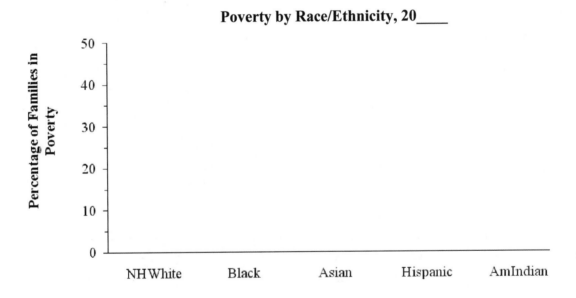

Exercise 4 Using current data, look at the percentage of families in poverty within each specific Hispanic group. Which groups have the highest percentage of families in poverty? The lowest? What are some possible explanations for these differences?

▶ *Dataset*: FAMPOVHISP.DAT

▶ Create a bar chart with bars for each specific Hispanic group; for each group, indicate the percentage of families in poverty in the present.

Families in Poverty for Hispanic Group, 20____

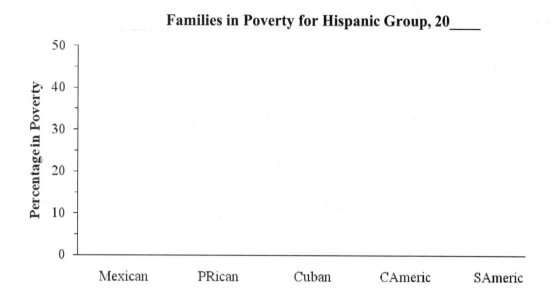

Exercise 5 Using current data, look at the percentage of families in poverty within each specific Asian group. Which groups have the highest poverty level for families? The lowest? What are some possible explanations for these differences?

▸ *Dataset*: FAMPOVASIAN.DAT

▸ Create a bar chart with bars for each specific Asian group; for each group, indicate the percentage of families in poverty in the present.

Families in Poverty for Asian Groups, 20____

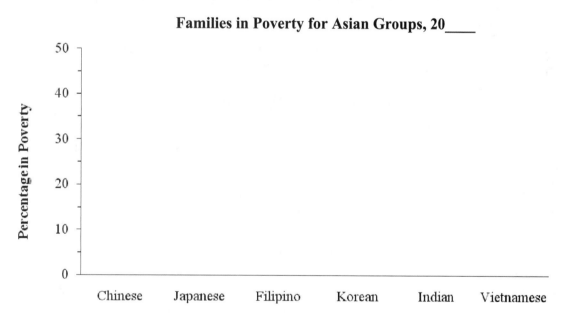

Discussion Questions

1. Can you think of any historical events that might have had an impact on the number of Americans living in poverty?

2. Did the results from Exercise 2 surprise you? How do the results differ from popular conceptions of people in poverty? Can you think of explanations for the patterns you found in Exercise 2?

B. Households and Poverty

Over the last fifty years, economic changes have combined with trends in marriage, divorce, and childbearing rates to alter the structure and composition of American households. While most exercises in the following section focus on poverty in female-headed family households, these exercises will provide an overview of the relationship between poverty and all household types.

While you work through these exercises, consider if certain households are more likely to be living in poverty. Does this vary by race/ethnicity? As you explore the connection between poverty and household type, recall other factors related to household type that might also influence socio-economic status.

Exercise 6 Using data from 1970 to the present, look at the prevalence of poverty in different types of families. Which family types experience the highest rates of poverty? The lowest?

▸ *Dataset*: FAMPOV.TREND

▸ Create a bar chart with side-by-side bars for each family type. For each year, indicate the percentage of each family type living in poverty.

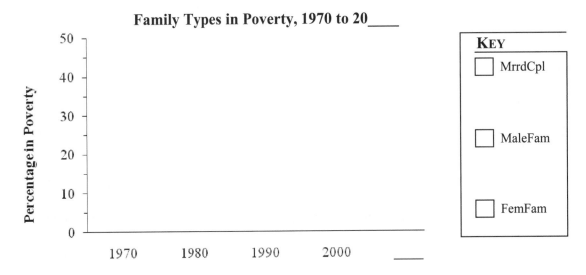

Family Types in Poverty, 1970 to 20____

Exercise 7 Using data from 1970 to the present, look at poverty in black and non-black families. Describe the trends. Does poverty seem more influenced by race/ethnicity or by family type?

▶ *Dataset*: FAMPOV.TREND

▶ Create two line graphs, one for blacks and one for non-blacks. In the graphs, draw a line for each family type. Indicate the percentage of each family type in poverty for each year.

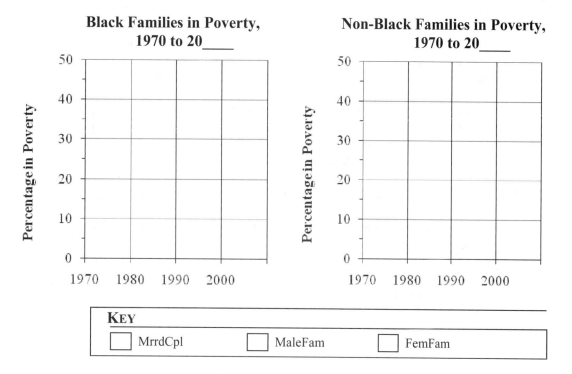

Black Families in Poverty, 1970 to 20____

Non-Black Families in Poverty, 1970 to 20____

KEY		
☐ MrrdCpl	☐ MaleFam	☐ FemFam

Exercise 8 Do you think that racial/ethnic differences in poverty rates are related to racial/ethnic differences in family structure? Focusing on the present, consider the percentage of families living in poverty in each racial/ethnic group and how it might be related to the percentage of female-headed households in each racial/ethnic group. Describe any significant findings.

▶ *Dataset*: FAMILY.DAT.

▶ On your own, create two bar charts. The first chart should indicate the percentage of female-headed families in each racial/ethnic group. The second chart should indicate the percentage of families living in poverty in each racial/ethnic group.

Discussion Questions

1. Why do you think that different family types experience varying levels of poverty?

2. To what extent do you think that family type factors into the increased poverty rate among blacks?

3. What factors other than family type might influence poverty levels among minority groups?

C. Gender and the Feminization of Poverty

Over the last fifty years, researchers have been observing the relationship between gender and poverty, coining the phrase *feminization of poverty* to describe the increasingly strong relationship between the two. In order to understand how and why this trend has emerged, we must first consider the relationship between household composition and socio-economic status. Half of the female-headed households living in poverty have undergone a household composition change, usually divorce. Thus, as long as divorce rates continue to rise, so will the number of female-headed households. The prevalence of divorce also means that many of these female household heads are completely responsible for supporting children. Finally, in the past thirty years there has been a marked increase in out-of-wedlock births that, like divorce, frequently leave the mother as the only means of financial support.

Exercise 9 What might account for the fact that female-headed families constitute the majority of all families in poverty? Using data from 1970 to the present, look at what percentage of all family households are female-headed. Then, look at the percentage of all family households in poverty that are female-headed. Describe your findings.

▶ *Dataset*: FAMPOV.TREND

▶ Create two bar charts, one for all families and one for families in poverty. In the first chart, indicate what percentage of all families is female-headed. In the second chart, indicate what percentage of all families in poverty is female-headed.

Female-Headed Families as Percent of All Families, 20____

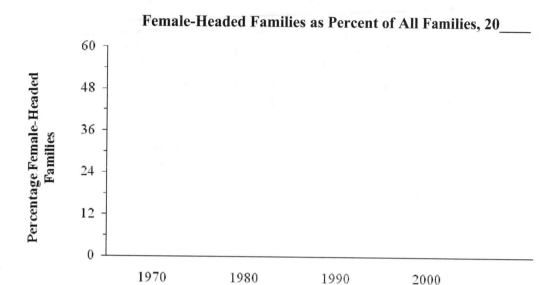

Female-Headed Families as a Percentage of Families in Poverty, 20____

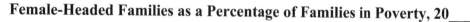

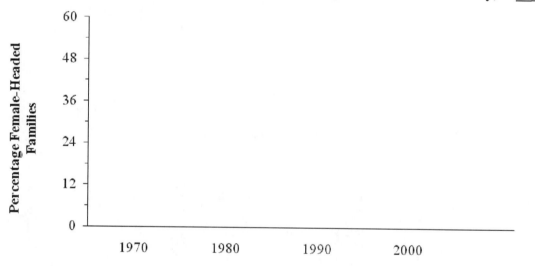

Exercise 10 On your own, repeat the previous exercise for black families only. Compare your findings to your results for Exercise 9.

▶ *Dataset*: FAMPOV.TREND

Exercise 11 How does the poverty of female-headed families vary by race/ethnicity? Compare the overall percentage of female-headed families to the percentage of female-headed families in poverty for each racial/ethnic group in the present. Describe any differences you find among the groups.

▶ *Dataset*: FAMILY.DAT

▶ On your own, create two bar charts, one for all families and one for families in poverty. In the first chart, indicate for each racial/ethnic group the percentage of families that are female-headed. In the second chart, indicate for each racial/ethnic group the percentage of families in poverty that are female-headed.

Exercise 12 In this exercise, we will focus on persons rather than families (See the "Key Concepts" section in this chapter for the distinction between the poverty status of families and that of persons). Looking only at persons 18 years old and older in the present, consider how poverty rates differ between genders and among racial/ethnic groups. Which groups have the highest rates of poverty? The lowest? Offer explanations for your findings.

▸ *Dataset*: POVGEO.DAT

▸ Create a bar chart with side-by-side bars for men and women. For each racial/ethnic group, indicate the percentage of men and women living in poverty.

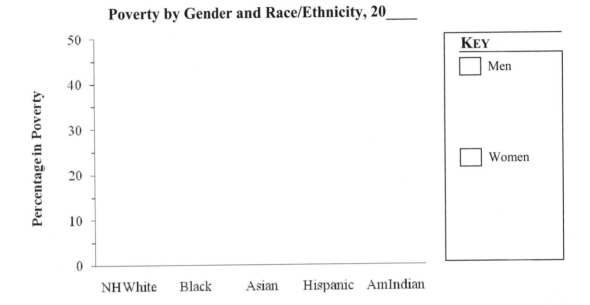

Poverty by Gender and Race/Ethnicity, 20____

Discussion Questions

1. Do you agree that the "feminization of poverty" is an accurate label for recent trends in poverty? Why or why not?

2. Does the feminization of poverty affect racial/ethnic groups differently? If so, how?

D. Age and Poverty

Over the last fifty years, social assistance programs like Social Security have helped many elderly people stay above the poverty level. As the situation for the eldest American citizens has improved, the story for children has been one of reduced benefits and small overall reduction in poverty levels. The increasing number of female-headed family households, a trend that you explored in the previous section, only partially explains this phenomenon.

This section will look at poverty in all age groups, but will focus on the elderly and children. As you examine the relationship between age and poverty, recall other factors related to age such as education, marital status, and earnings. Consider how they might affect an individual's poverty status.

Exercise 13 Focusing on the present, compare the percentage of people in poverty in each age group. Which ages have the highest percentage of people in poverty? The lowest? What might account for your findings?

▶ *Dataset*: POVGEO.DAT

▶ Create a bar chart indicating the percentage of people in poverty in each age group in the present.

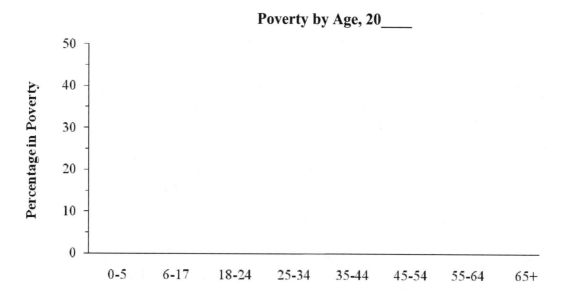

Poverty by Age, 20____

Exercise 14 Using current data, look at the percentage of children (ages 0-17) and elderly (ages 65 and above) in poverty within each racial/ethnic group. Describe your findings.

▶ *Dataset*: POVGEO.DAT

▶ Create a bar chart with side-by-side bars for children (Hint: add the numbers or combine categories of ages 0-5 and ages 6-17) and the elderly. For each racial/ethnic group, indicate the percentage of children (by age group) and the elderly in poverty in the present.

Poverty of Children and the Elderly by Race/Ethnicity, 20____

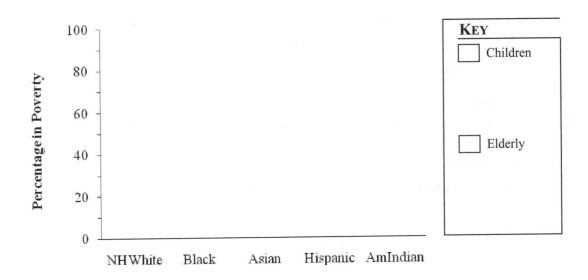

Exercise 15 Focusing on the present, compare the percentage of elderly men living in poverty to the percentage of elderly women living in poverty. Is this gender gap significantly different from the overall gender gap in poverty?

▶ *Dataset*: POVEDUC.DAT

▶ Create two pie charts: one for elderly men and one for elderly women. In each chart, show the percentage living in poverty and the percentage not in poverty.

Poverty Status of Elderly Men and Elderly Women, 20____

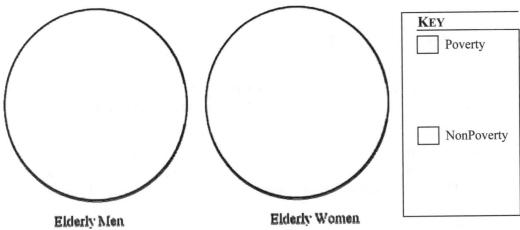

Discussion Questions

1. Why do children and the elderly have different levels of poverty? How do the poverty levels in these two age groups differ from the poverty level for the overall population?

2. Do you think that future cohorts will follow the same age-related pattern of poverty?

E. Education and Poverty

In recent years the American labor market has undergone significant restructuring at an ever increasing rate. Blue collar positions, which were once the mainstay of the U.S. economy, now make up a smaller portion of existing jobs as an increase in education levels has allowed for more white collared jobs. Technological changes, coupled with the downsizing of industry, have led to a demand for workers with higher education levels. Overall, in the face of tougher competition, those with lower education levels have had difficulty securing well-paying employment.

In this section, you will examine the relationship between poverty and educational attainment. As you examine this relationship, keep in mind other factors related to education, such as gender and race/ethnicity.

Exercise 16 Focusing on the present, explore the relationship between educational attainment and poverty for people aged 25-34. What does the relationship seem to be?

▶ *Dataset*: POVEDUC.DAT

▶ Create a bar chart for 25-34 year-olds indicating the current percentage in poverty for each educational attainment level.

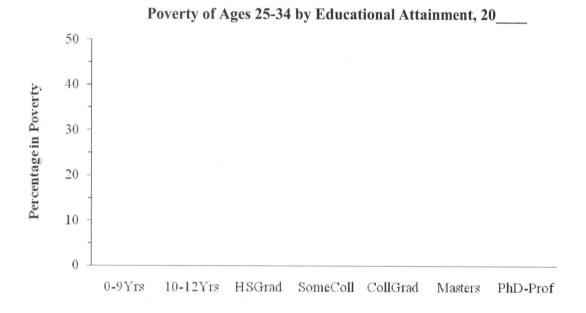

Poverty of Ages 25-34 by Educational Attainment, 20____

Exercise 17 Using current data, examine the relationship between education and poverty in terms of race/ethnicity. Looking only at 25-34 year-old college graduates and those with less than a high school education determine the percentage in poverty in each racial/ethnic group. What differences do you find among the different groups?

▶ *Dataset*: POVEDUC.DAT

▶ Create a bar chart with side-by-side bars, one for 25-34 year-old college graduates and one for people of the same age with less than a high school education. Indicate the percentage of people in poverty at each education level for each racial/ethnic group.

Poverty Among Ages 25-34 by Educational Attainment and Race/Ethnicity, 20____

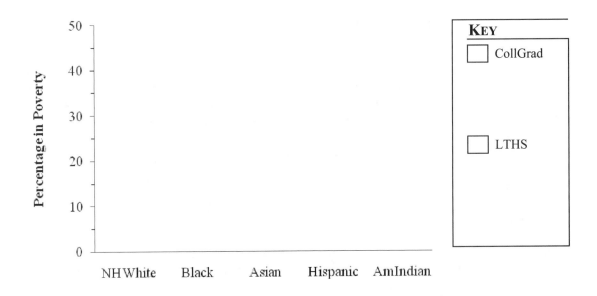

Discussion Questions

1. Is the relationship between education and poverty what you expected it to be? What other factors, besides race/ethnicity, might affect the relationship between education and poverty?

2. Why does the relationship between education and poverty vary among racial/ethnic groups?

F. Geography and Poverty

Over the past sixty years, certain regions have experienced significant growth in population and job market size, while others have experienced equally remarkable losses. These shifts, especially those associated with industrial downsizing, create inequality differences across regions.

After considering regional differences, you will compare the percentage of people living in poverty in metropolitan, non-metropolitan, and rural areas. As you complete these exercises, think about how and why employment opportunities and the incomes associated with them may vary between regions and areas.

<u>Exercise 18</u> Focusing on the present, show how the percentage of families in poverty differs in city, suburban, and non-metropolitan areas. Which type of area has the highest percentage of families in poverty? The lowest? Did you expect to find a different sort of pattern?

▸ *Dataset*: FAMPOVGEO.DAT

▸ Create a bar chart indicating the percentage of family households in poverty for each type of geography.

Percent in Poverty by Geography, 20____

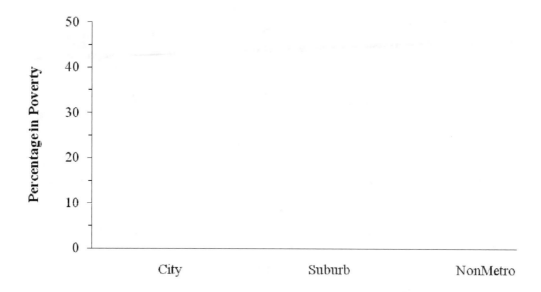

Exercise 19 Is the percentage of households in poverty in cities, suburbs, and non-metropolitan areas similar for blacks and non-blacks? Focusing on the present, compare the percentage of black and non-black families in poverty in city, suburban, and non-metropolitan areas.

▶ *Dataset*: FAMPOVGEO.DAT

▶ Create two bar charts. In the first chart, indicate the percentage of black families in poverty in each area. In the second chart, indicate the percentage of non-black families in poverty in each area.

Black Families in Poverty by Geography, 20____

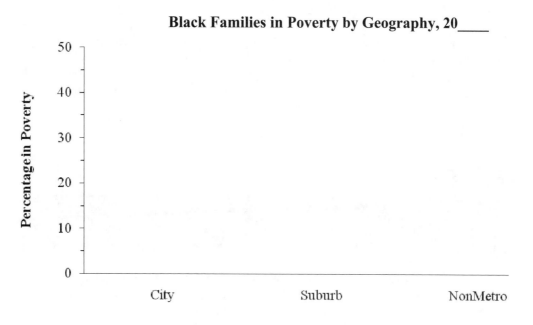

Non-Black Families in Poverty by Geography, 20____

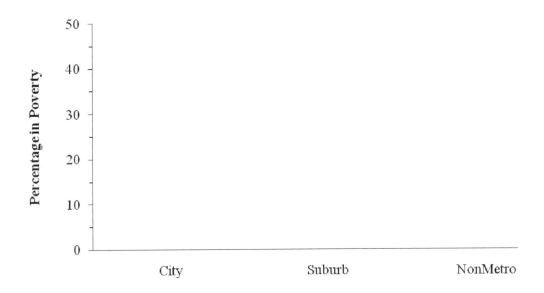

Exercise 20 On your own, select another racial/ethnic group you would like to focus on and repeat the previous exercise for that particular group.

▶ *Dataset*: FAMPOVGEO.DAT

Discussion Questions

1. Are the conditions associated with poverty in cities similar to the conditions associated with poverty in non-metropolitan areas?

2. How do you think the percentage of family households in poverty varies across regions in the United States? Which region, Northeast, South, Midwest, or West, do you think has the highest percentage of family households in poverty?

THINK
tank

1. Consider what you have learned about the relationship between poverty and age, gender, race/ethnicity, household structure, education, and metropolitan geography. Given what you have learned, what strategies do you think would help reduce poverty levels? Make two or three recommendations for policy changes at the local, state, and federal levels. What are some of the benefits and shortcomings to each of these strategies?

2. What has happened to the respective poverty levels of the old and the young over the last few decades? Why have these changes occurred? Given that governments allocate limited resources to combat poverty, is it better to allocate funds to impoverished children or to

impoverished elderly? If you were a political candidate running for national office, what social, economic, demographic, and political factors would you consider before taking your position on the issue? Use data to help explain the factors you find to be important and to justify your policy position.

chapter

9

CHILDREN

Teachers, politicians, and even musicians are fond of reminding us that "children are our future." While this statement may be a cliché, we can, to some extent, predict what the future of America may look like by observing the children of today. How have changes in household structure, gender roles, and employment opportunities affected children's lives? What impact will these changes have on society twenty or thirty years from now?

Over the last fifty years, attention to children's issues in public policy waxed and waned in relation to the relative size of the child population. During the late 1950s and early 1960s, public officials built new schools, hired more teachers, and provided more funding to educate the swelling ranks of the Baby Boomers. While changes in the educational system benefited children across the economic spectrum, other policies were directed specifically at children living in poverty. For example, Title I of the Elementary and Secondary Education Act (a part of the Johnson Administration's "War on Poverty") committed substantial amounts of federal aid to poor, underachieving children. Similarly, Head Start, Temporary Assistance to Needy Families (TANF) [Formerly Aid to Families with Dependent Children (AFDC)] and Women and Infant

Children (WIC) were designed to address child poverty. While each of these programs still exist, somewhat fewer initiatives designed for children have been implemented during the past twenty years; a fact partly explainable by the decreasing percentage of Americans under the age of eighteen. In other words, public policy was more focused on the needs and conditions of children when they represented a larger portion of the United States population. Conversely, as the size of the elderly population increases, issues like Social Security and health care are quickly becoming national priorities.

In the following sections, you will explore the current state of America's children. Who are they? How do they live? With whom do they live? Are some living in better conditions than others? Who are the advantages and disadvantages children, and why do these disparities exist? The chapter opens with a discussion of childhood trends since 1950 and provides a snapshot of the racial/ethnic distribution and immigration status of children in the present. Subsequent exercises examine critical changes in family structure, working mothers, and children living in poverty. The chapter concludes by taking a brief look at children and schooling in the current year. As you work through these exercises, pay particular attention to the differences among different groups of children and consider the effects that those differences may have on their future in addition to your own.

KEY

concepts

Child Population Persons 0-17 years old.

School Ages Population Persons 6-17 years old.

Public/Private Schools Persons attending school indicated that they were attending public school or private school:

> **Public school**—Any school or college controlled or supported by a local, county, state, or federal government.

> **Private school**—Schools supported and controlled primarily by religious organizations or other private groups.

OTHER concepts

Race/Ethnicity (Chapter Two)   **Poverty Status** (Chapter Eight)
Family Households (Chapter Seven)   **English Language Proficiency** (Chapter Three)
Immigration Status (Chapter Three)   **Income Relative to Poverty Cut-off** (Chapter Eight)
Education (Chapter Two)

A. Total Child Population

In addition to looking at the overall size of the child population, it is important to examine children as a percentage of the total U.S. population. As this percentage increases, the child dependency ratio—the number of children who need care, compared to the number of adults able to provide care—tends to increase as well. In practical terms, this often means that more kids have to share fewer resources. On the other hand, in policy and politics, a large cohort can sometimes wield more influence.

The line graph below shows the number of children (individuals ages 0-17) living in the U.S between 1950 and 2008. Notice how the size of the current child population compares to previous decades. What might account for the decline in the child population between 1970 and 1990, and the increase between 1990 and the present? Do you think attitudes toward children have changed since 1950? What are the social and economic implications of children constituting a large or small percentage of the total population? Do you think it is more advantageous to be born into a larger cohort or a small one? Why?

Number of Children in the U.S., 1950 to 2008

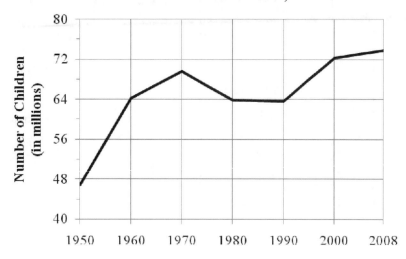

B. Race/Ethnicity, Immigration, and Children

The racial/ethnic composition of children has dramatically changed over the past few decades. Diversity is constantly increasing among the youngest Americans, a result of high birth rates among some racial/ethnic groups. Another significant factor is the increasing number of Hispanics and Asians immigrating to the United States since 1970. As you look at the racial/ethnic distribution of the child, note that some states have a more diverse population than others.

Exercise 1 Using current data, compare the racial/ethnic distribution of the child population (persons ages 0-17) with that of people ages 45-54. What differences do you see?

▸ *Dataset*: PovGeo.dat

▸ Create a stacked bar chart with two bars, one for 0-17 year-olds and one for 45-54 year-olds; stack by race/ethnicity. (Hint: Add or combine ages 0-5 with 6-17.)

Race/Ethnicity Distributions by Age, 20____

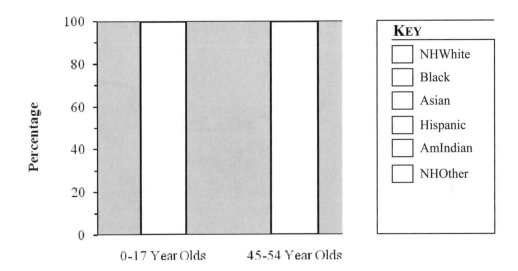

Exercise 2 Do some racial/ethnic groups have a larger child population than other racial/ethnic groups? Compare the percentages for each racial/ethnic group.

▸ *Dataset*: POVGEO.DAT

▸ Create a bar chart with bars for each major racial/ethnic group; show the percentage of each group's population made up of children (<18 years).

Percentage of Children by Race/Ethnicity, 20____

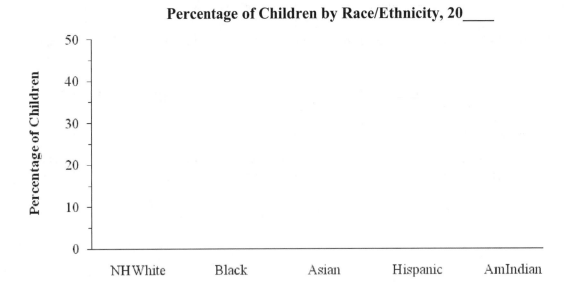

Exercise 3 On your own, repeat the previous exercise for each specific Hispanic and Asian group.

▸ *Datasets*: ENGASIAN.DAT, ENGHISP.DAT

Exercise 4 Does family size vary among racial/ethnic groups? Look at the family size distribution in each racial/ethnic group and describe any significant variation that you find among the groups.

▸ *Dataset*: CHILDPOV.DAT

▸ Stacking by family size, create a stacked bar chart with bars for each racial/ethnic group.

Family Size by Race/Ethnicity, 20____

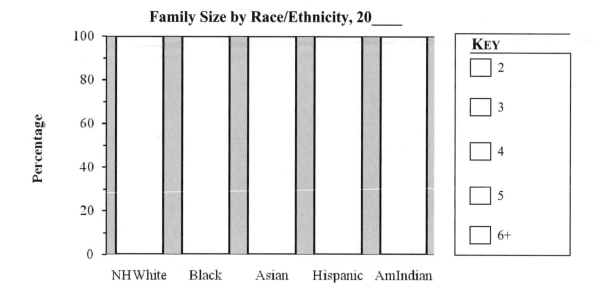

Exercise 5 According to the population projections based on the current data, what percentage of children will be Asian, Black, White, Hispanic, or American Indian in 2020?

▸ *Dataset*: POPPROJ.DAT

▸ Create a pie chart with divisions for your projected racial/ethnic distribution.

Projected Race/Ethnicity Distribution of the U.S. for 2020

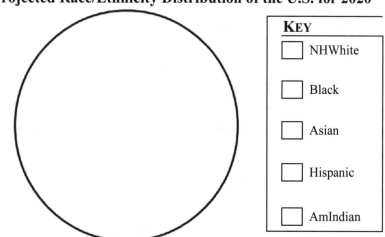

Exercise 6 What percentage of children living in the United States is foreign-born? What percentage of children in each racial/ethnic group is foreign-born? Describe your findings.

▸ *Dataset*: CHILDPOV.DAT

▸ Create a bar chart with a bar for the total child population and bars for each racial/ethnic group. For each group, indicate the percentage of children who are foreign-born.

Foreign-Born Children by Race/Ethnicity, 20____

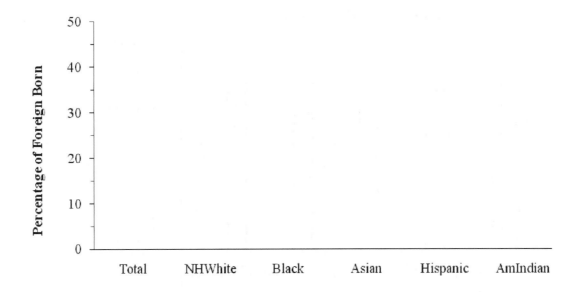

Exercise 7 On your own, repeat the previous exercise for each specific Hispanic and Asian group.

 ▸ *Datasets*: ENGHISP.DAT, ENGASIAN.DAT

Exercise 8 It is important to remember that Exercise 6 refers to the U.S. as a whole. As you can probably guess, in some states like California, the racial/ethnic distribution of children is very different from the distribution of the country as a whole. What racial/ethnic groups account for the largest proportion of Californian children? Compare the racial/ethnic distribution of Californian children with that of the entire nation.

 ▸ *Dataset*: POPPROJ.DAT

 ▸ Create two pie charts, one for the United States and one for California. In each pie chart, make divisions for racial/ethnic groups.

Race/Ethnicity Distributions in California and the United States, 20_____

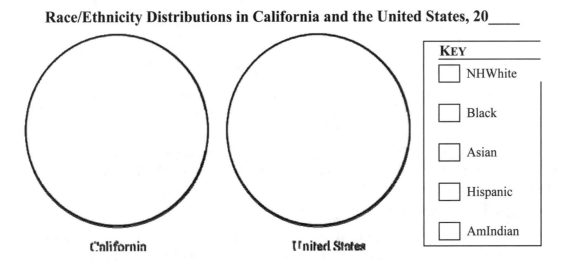

Exercise 9 Focusing on children living in California, examine the percentage of children in each specific Hispanic and Asian group. Which specific groups account for the greatest percentage of Asian and Hispanic children living in California?

Investigating Change in American Society | **188**

▶ *Datasets*: ENGHISP.DAT, ENGASIAN.DAT

▶ Create two pie charts, one for Asian children living in California and one for Hispanic children living in California. In each chart, make divisions for the specific groups.

Distribution of Asian and Hispanic Children Living in California, 20____

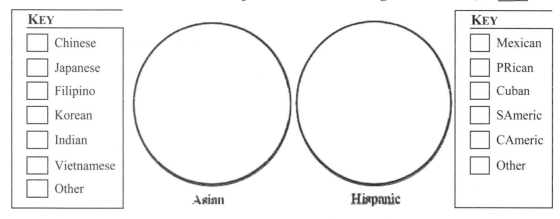

KEY	
☐	Chinese
☐	Japanese
☐	Filipino
☐	Korean
☐	Indian
☐	Vietnamese
☐	Other

KEY	
☐	Mexican
☐	PRican
☐	Cuban
☐	SAmeric
☐	CAmeric
☐	Other

Asian   Hispanic

Discussion Questions

1. What historical and economic factors may have influenced racial/ethnic distribution over the past few decades?

2. Why do some states have child populations that are more racially/ethnically diverse than others? Why aren't racial/ethnic groups distributed evenly across the country?

C. Family Structure

Previous chapters have addressed how changes in family structure affect household composition, socio-economic status, and labor force participation, but this demographic shift is particularly important for children. Families are the primary providers of nurture, aid, and other resources that children need for healthy physical, mental, and emotional development. Any changes in family structure can impact the ability of the family unit to provide these things for the child. Because children have always been, and will continue to be, dependent on their families for support, it is important to look at how family structure is changing over time.

Exercise 10 Keeping in mind the family type distribution discussed in Chapter 7, look at the percentage of children living in married-couple families, in female-headed families, and in male-headed families in the present. Describe your findings.

▶ *Dataset*: CHILDPOV.DAT

▶ Create a pie chart for all children with divisions by each family type.

Family Type Distribution for Children in the U.S, 20____

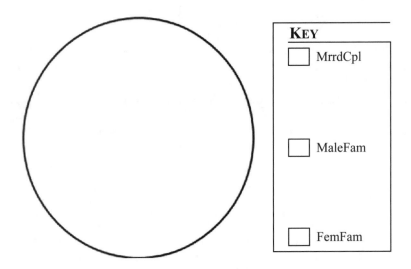

KEY

☐ MrrdCpl

☐ MaleFam

☐ FemFam

Exercise 11 Using current data, determine the percentage of children in each racial/ethnic group living in married-couple, female-headed, and male-headed families. For example, what percentage of white children live in single-mother families?

▶ *Dataset*: CHILDPOV.DAT

▸ Create a stacked bar chart with bars for each racial/ethnic group and stack by family type.

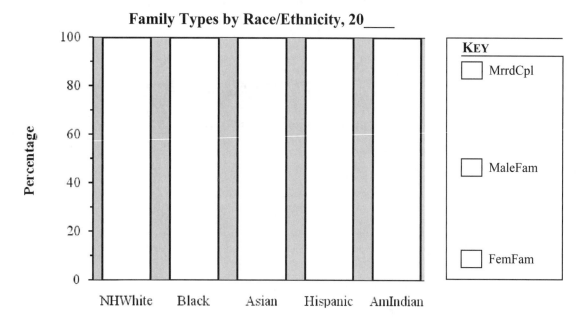

Exercise 12 As children get older, are they more likely to live in different types of families?

▸ *Dataset*: CHILDPOV.DAT

▸ On your own, create three pie charts, one for each family type. In each pie chart, make divisions for young children (ages 0-5) and older children (ages 6-17).

Discussion Questions

1. Based on what you have learned in other chapters, do you think there has been an increase in the number of children living in single-parent families over the past few decades? On what facts do you base your conclusions?

2. Do you think divorce is detrimental to children? Why or why not?

3. What makes single-motherhood such a contentious issue in American politics?

4. What might be the social implications of more children living in single-mother families?

D. Economic Well-Being of Children

Despite ongoing efforts to alleviate child poverty, it remains a problem in America today, particularly for children in predominantly urban and rural areas. Compared to the elderly, children are almost twice as likely to be poor. Moreover, poor children are very likely to remain poor in adulthood. Although it is clear that poverty negatively affects a child's health, career aspirations, and academic achievement, it is not clear how to resolve this seemingly intractable problem.

Exercise 13 What percentage of U.S. children live in poverty? How has this percentage changed since 1970?

▸ *Dataset*: POPPOV.TREND

▸ Create a line graph showing the percentage of children in poverty for each year.

Children in Poverty, 1970 to 20____

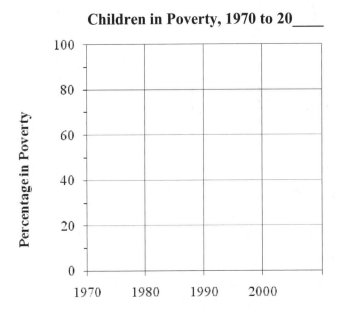

Exercise 14 In the present, what percentage of children live in families with "comfortable" incomes? (Note: See "Key Concepts" in Chapter 8 for a definition of comfortable incomes.)

▸ *Dataset*: POVGEO.DAT

▸ Create a bar chart with two bars: one for children and one for the overall population (all ages). In each bar, indicate the percentage living in families with "comfortable" incomes.

Comfortable Incomes—Children and Total Population, 20____

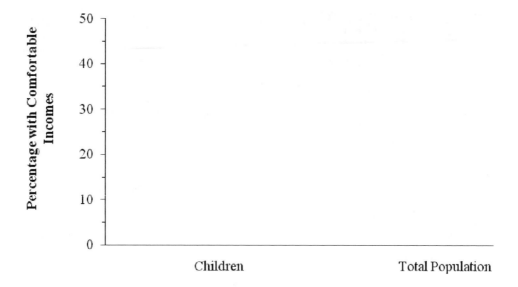

Exercise 15 Using current data, determine the percentage of those who live in poverty within each racial/ethnic group and the percentage of those who live in families with "comfortable" incomes. For example, how many black children live in families with "comfortable" incomes?

▸ *Dataset*: CHILDPOV.DAT

▸ Create a bar chart with side-by-side bars for poverty and "comfortable" incomes. For each racial/ethnic group, indicate the percentage of children who are living in families that are "poor" or "comfortable."

Children in Poor or Comfortable Income Families by Race/Ethnicity, 20____

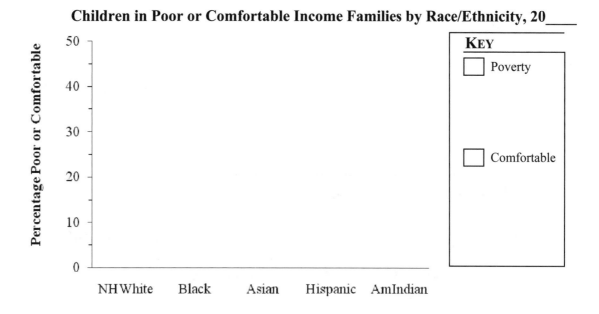

Exercise 16 According to current data, is there a substantial difference between the percentage of young children (ages 0-5) in poverty and the percentage of older children (ages 6-17) in poverty? Does the percentage of young and older children in poverty vary by race/ethnicity?

▸ *Dataset*: CHILDPOV.DAT

▶ Create two pie charts, one for young children and one for older children. In each chart, make divisions for "poverty" and "non-poverty".

Poverty Distribution of Young and Older Children, 20____

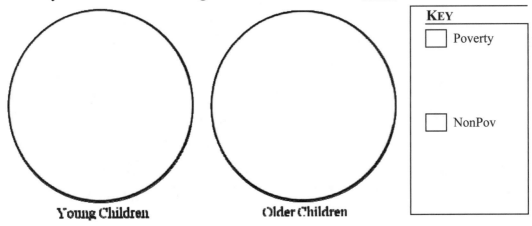

▶ Create a bar chart with side-by-side bars for young children and older children. For each racial/ethnic group, indicate the percentage of young and older children living in poverty.

Young and Older Children in Poverty by Race/Ethnicity, 20____

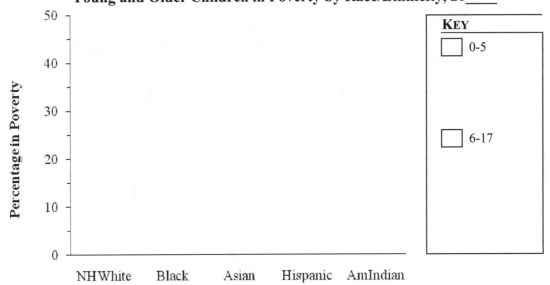

Exercise 17 Are children in poverty more prevalent in certain types of families? Focusing on the present, determine what percentage of all children in poverty live in each family type. For example, what percentage of children in poverty live in married-couple families?

▶ *Dataset*: CHILDPOV.DAT

▶ Create two pie charts: one for children in poverty and one for children not in poverty. In each chart, make divisions for family types.

Family Type Distribution for Children by Poverty Status, 20____

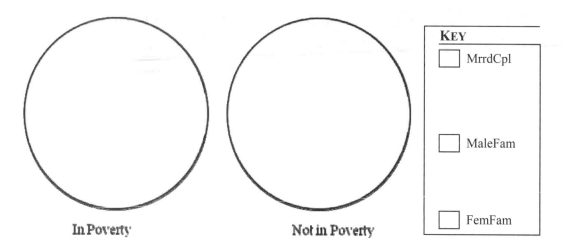

In Poverty   Not in Poverty

KEY

☐ MrrdCpl

☐ MaleFam

☐ FemFam

Exercise 18 Do your findings from the previous exercise vary for different races/ethnicities? For example, is the family type distribution for white children in poverty different than the family type distribution for Asian children in poverty? Compare the family type distribution of children in poverty and not in poverty for each racial/ethnic group.

▸ *Dataset*: CHILDPOV.DAT

▸ Create a stacked bar chart with side-by-side bars for children in poverty and not in poverty. For each racial/ethnic group, stack by the family type distribution.

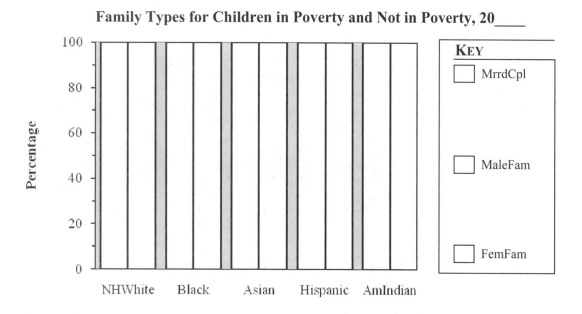

Family Types for Children in Poverty and Not in Poverty, 20____

KEY

☐ MrrdCpl

☐ MaleFam

☐ FemFam

Exercise 19 Are children with access to "comfortable" incomes more likely to live in certain types of families? Focusing on the present, determine what percentage of children with "comfortable" incomes live in each family type. How does this distribution vary from your results in Exercise 17?

▸ *Dataset*: CHILDPOV.DAT

▸ Create a pie chart for "comfortable" income children and make divisions for family types.

Distribution of Family Types for Comfortable Income Children, 20____

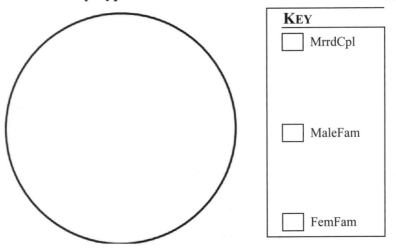

KEY

☐ MrrdCpl

☐ MaleFam

☐ FemFam

Exercise 20 Do your findings from the previous exercise vary among different racial/ethnic groups? For example, is the family type distribution of "comfortable" income black children different than the family type distribution for "comfortable" income Hispanic children? Using current data compare the family type distribution of "comfortable" income children for each racial/ethnic group. Compare your findings with your results for Exercise 19.

▶ *Dataset*: CHILDPOV.DAT

▶ On your own, create a stacked bar chart with bars for each racial/ethnic group and stack by the family type distribution for "comfortable" income children.

Discussion Questions

1. What are some recent economic and social events that may have influenced the percentage of children living in poverty?

2. Some critics suggest that child poverty, primarily, results of changes in family structure. Would you agree with this claim? If not, what other social and economic factors might contribute to child poverty?

E. Children in School

America's children spend a significant portion of their lives in school. Due to the vulnerability of children, policy-makers have historically attempted to use schools to advance and resolve critical social issues such as child poverty, race relations, gender inequality, and economic competitiveness. It is necessary to have a basic understanding of the population attending school in order to understand the success or failure of schools' involvement with larger social issues. Who are America's students? Are there differences between students who attend public and private schools? The census provides some valuable insight into the educational experience of America's children.

Exercise 21 Focusing on the present, determine what percentage of school-age children (ages 6-17) are enrolled in public schools. What percentage is enrolled in private schools?

▶ C *Dataset*: CHILDSCH.DAT

▶ Create a pie chart for children ages 6-17; make divisions for those enrolled in public and private schools, and those not enrolled in school.

School Type Distribution for Children, Ages 6-17, 20____

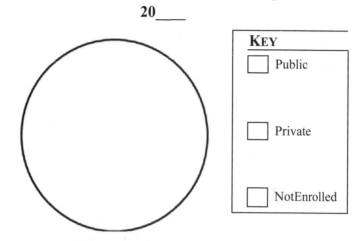

Exercise 22 According to current data, what percentage of school-age children (ages 6-17) in each racial/ethnic group are enrolled in public schools? In private schools? Why might some racial/ethnic groups have more students in private schools than others?

▶ *Dataset*: CHILDSCH.DAT

▶ Create a stacked bar chart with bars for each racial/ethnic group; stack by "public", "private", and "not in school".

School Type by Race/Ethnicity, 20____

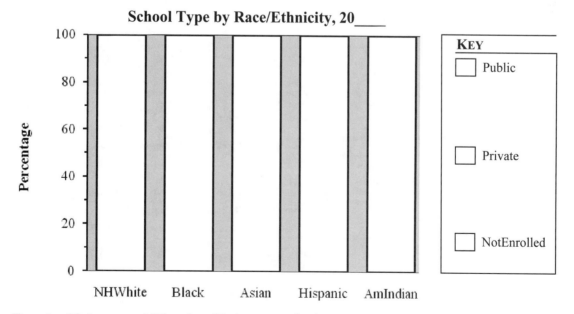

Exercise 23 Are poor children less likely to attend private schools? Using current data, examine what percentage of children living at or below the poverty line attend private schools. How does

this compare with the educational opportunities of children from families with "comfortable" incomes?

▶ *Dataset*: CHILDSCH.DAT

▶ Create two pie charts: one for children in poverty and one for "comfortable" income children. In each chart, make divisions for those in public and private schools, and those who are not enrolled in school

School Type Distribution of Poor and Comfortable Income Children, 20____

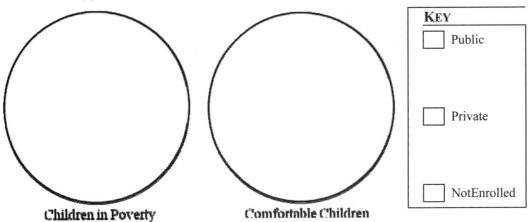

Exercise 24 Using current data, look at the percentage of 18, 21, and 24 year-olds in the U.S. with at least a high school diploma or the equivalent by race/ethnicity. Describe your findings.

▶ *Dataset*: CHILDSCH.DAT

▶ Create a bar chart with side-by-side bars for ages 18, 21, and 24. For each racial/ethnic group, indicate the percentage of high school graduates in each category.

High School Graduates at Ages 18, 21, and 24, 20____

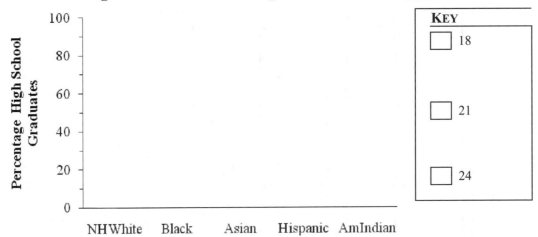

Discussion Questions

1. As the school-aged population becomes more racially/ethnically diverse, many people see an increasing need for multicultural education that takes into account the varied backgrounds of students. Unfortunately, there is little consensus about what such an education would actually look like in practice. Do you agree that primary and secondary education needs to be more multicultural? Why or why not?

2. Some legislators want to make English the official language of the United States. What pros and cons do you see in this type of policy as it relates to education?

THINK
tank

1. Over concern about high school drop-outs, the U.S. Department of Education funds a number of programs that attempt to make sure vulnerable students receive the resources necessary to graduate. If you were in charge of dispersing those limited resources, to which groups of students would you allocate the most funding? Which students appear to have the greatest risk of not completing high school? Identify as specifically as possible the demographic characteristics of a "typical" high school dropout.

2. According to the most recent census, what percentage of all older children (6-17) are proficient in English? Is English proficiency connected with whether or not the child attends school—or the type of school they attend? Is the ability to speak English correlated with race/ethnicity? Immigrant status? Analyze the relationship between immigration, schooling, poverty, and race/ethnicity. Describe your findings.

10 THE OLDER POPULATION

Before looking at trends in the elderly population, we need to define what we mean by "elderly." In this book, three categories are used to distinguish between the different age groups in the older population. People between the ages of 65 and 74 are the "young-old," those between the ages of 75 and 84 are the "old-old," and those age 85 or older are referred to as the "oldest-old."

This categorization of the elderly population attempts to recognize the changes in lifestyle and habits that occur with increasing age, even after retirement. While both are considered members of the elderly population, a 65-year-old and an 85-year-old likely lead very different lives. While the 85-year-old has probably experienced most of the social and physical changes that come with old age, the 65-year-old may only just beginning to undergo this transition.

Diversity in the elderly population is not limited solely to differences among age groups, though historical events experienced by one cohort but not by another do continue to play a role as populations age. Gender, race/ethnicity, marital status, and socioeconomic factors all play a strong role in shaping the existence of the older population. All of these variables must be taken into account when considering the elderly population and the issues that concern them.

Today, more Americans fall into "elderly" age groups than ever before. Due in part to medical and technological advances that have lead to increased life expectancies for both men and women, the elderly have been transformed, in one of the most significant demographic shifts in American history, from a relatively small component into a significant portion of the U.S. population. As the Baby Boomers born between 1946 and 1964 continue to age, this trend will become even more pronounced.

The Older Population, 1950 to 2050

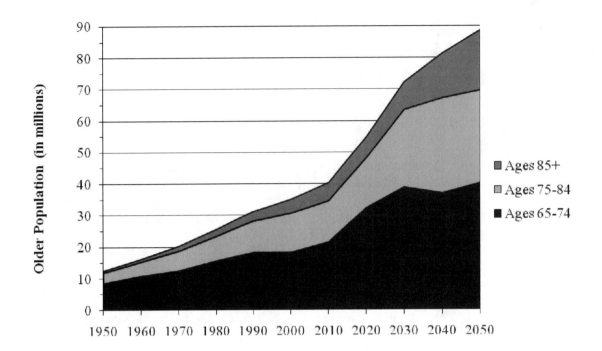

KEY

concepts

Older Population
Persons ages 65 and above who can be further classified as:

       Young-old—Population ages 65-74

       Old-old—Population ages 75-84

       Oldest-old—Population ages 85 and older

These categories are consistent with recognized stages of changing lifestyles and health.

Self-Care Limitation
Persons with this limitation report a physical, mental, or emotional condition which makes it difficult to take care of personal needs such as dressing or bathing.

Independent Living Limitation
Persons with this limitation report a physical, mental, or emotional which makes going outside the home alone (for example, to shop or visit a doctor) difficult.

OTHER concepts

Race/Ethnicity (Chapter Two)   **Education** (Chapter Two)
Labor Force Status (Chapter Four)   **Marital Status** (Chapter Five)
Household Type (Chapter Seven)   **Poverty Status** (Chapter Eight)
Income Relative to Poverty Cut-off (Chapter Eight)

Due to the significant size of the elderly population, few corners of American life have been untouched by the needs, demands, and contributions of the elderly. A significant proportion of all consumers, voters, workers, and homeowners are elderly, and policy-makers dealing with any of those groups must take the special concerns of the elderly into account.

In this chapter, we will take a look into the lives of the elderly. We will examine it in general terms of population shifts and trends, as well as explore more personal factors like family, economic situation, and health. In the end, you will gain a broader understanding of the elderly and their role in society.

A. Getting Older

Due to increases in life expectancy, both the "old-old" and "oldest-old" populations have grown remarkably in recent years. Today, the United States hosts one of the oldest elderly populations in the world and ages that were once considered virtually unattainable are now commonplace in American society.

However, not all groups have benefited equally from an overall increased life expectancy. For example, though the gender gap has narrowed somewhat, women still tend to live longer than men, and their average life expectancy is rising at a faster rate than men's. While the feminization of aging may seem attractive to some women, it can also leave elderly women vulnerable to certain problems associated with aging, such as poverty, widowhood, and institutionalization. Furthermore, widening gaps in life expectancy exist among different races/ethnicities. Blacks have a life expectancy approximately six to eight years shorter than their white counterparts, a discrepancy that is due in large part to high mortality rates among younger blacks.

Exercise 1 How has the elderly population changed over time? Look at men and women separately. What trends do you notice? Are they the same for men and women?

▶ *Dataset*: POP.TREND

▶ Create a line graph with two lines: one for men and one for women. For each year, indicate the percentage of elderly people.

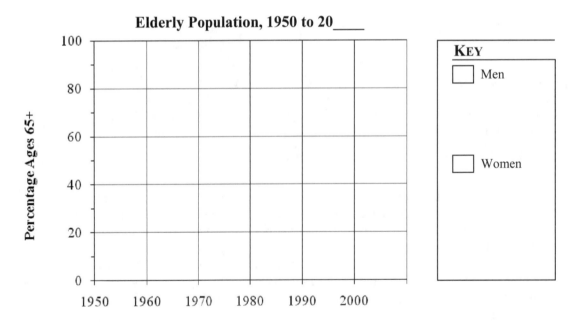

Exercise 2 How has life expectancy changed over time? Examine the age distribution of the elderly population and how it has changed over time. Do your findings surprise you? Why or why not?

▶ *Dataset*: ELDERLY.TREND

▶ Create a stacked bar chart with bars for each year, stacking by the three elderly age groups.

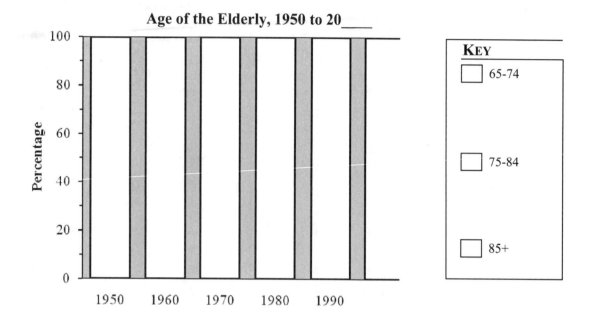

Age of the Elderly, 1950 to 20____

KEY
☐ 65-74
☐ 75-84
☐ 85+

Exercise 3 While keeping the gender gap in mind, look at the number of elderly men and women in each elderly age group. Are women living longer than men? Is this consistent for each age group or does it change with age?

▸ *Dataset*: ELDERLY.TREND

▸ Create a bar chart with side-by-side bars for men and women. For each age group, indicate the number of men and women in that group.

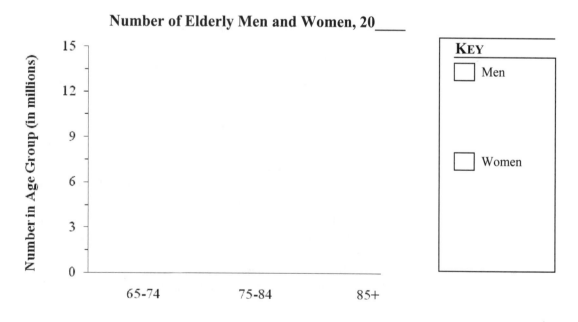

Number of Elderly Men and Women, 20____

KEY
☐ Men

☐ Women

Exercise 4 Now examine how the age distribution of the elderly population differs among racial/ethnic groups. In which groups is the greatest percentage of the population elderly?

▸ *Dataset*: ELDRPOV.DAT

▸ Create a stacked bar chart showing the elderly population by race/ethnicity. For each racial/ethnic group, stack by elderly age groups.

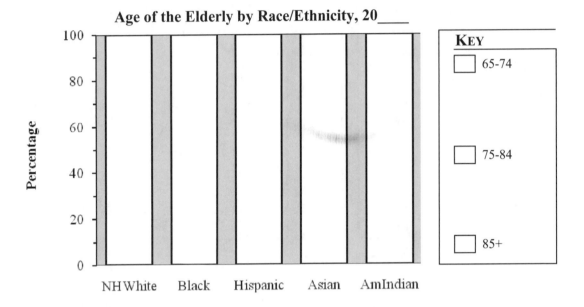

Age of the Elderly by Race/Ethnicity, 20____

Discussion Questions

1. We currently have a growing number of elderly citizens in America. What are the possible effects of this transition on society? Cite examples of aspects of American life that you feel have been affected by the aging population.

2. Considering gender and race/ethnicity, who has the best chances of living to old age? Why? What factors do you think contribute to the gender and race/ethnicity gaps discussed earlier? Are these gaps inevitable? If not, how could they be narrowed?

B. Marital and Household Changes

As married couples grow older, more marriages end with a spouse's death than divorce. Due to the gender gap in life expectancy and trend of women marrying older men, there are more female widows. Female widows are less likely than their male counterparts to remarry and more likely to rely on the support of grown children and nursing homes. Additionally, whereas most men have pensions to support themselves in retirement, elderly women who have not worked outside the home often find themselves slipping into poverty.

Race/ethnicity also plays a significant role in an elderly person's marital status. Generally speaking, older black women are less likely to be married than older white women. They are more likely to be divorced, never married or widowed due to high mortality rates for younger black men.

Elderly married couples are also impacted by changing marital trends. As American divorce rates increased in the 1970s, the elderly were not left untouched. While still a relatively small population, those who do divorce at an old age must often forego the lifestyles they enjoyed while married. Just like their younger cohorts, elderly divorced women are more likely to encounter financial difficulties after divorce and turn to their grown children for support and care.

Exercise 5 Begin by looking at the marital status of the elderly among different age groups. Look separately at men and women. What trends emerge as the elderly grow older? Are these trends the same for men and women?

- ▸ *Dataset*: ELDRPOV.DAT

- ▸ Create a stacked bar chart with side-by-side bars for men and women. Within each age group, stack by marital status.

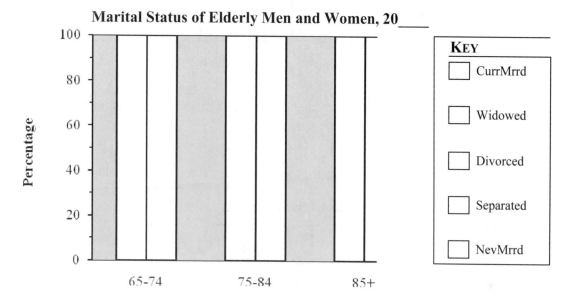

Marital Status of Elderly Men and Women, 20____

Exercise 6 Now compare the marital status of the elderly across racial/ethnic groups. What differences do you notice among racial/ethnic groups?

- ▸ *Dataset*: ELDRPOV.DAT

- ▸ Create a stacked bar chart with side-by-side bars for men and women. For each racial/ethnic group, stack by marital status.

Marital Status of Elderly Men and Women by Race/Ethnicity, 20____

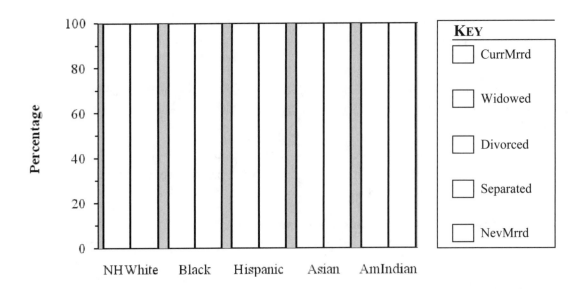

Exercise 7 How do household arrangements change as the elderly grow older? Does household type tend to vary among age groups?

▶ *Dataset*: ELDRHH.DAT

▶ Create a stacked bar chart with bars for each age group; stack by household type.

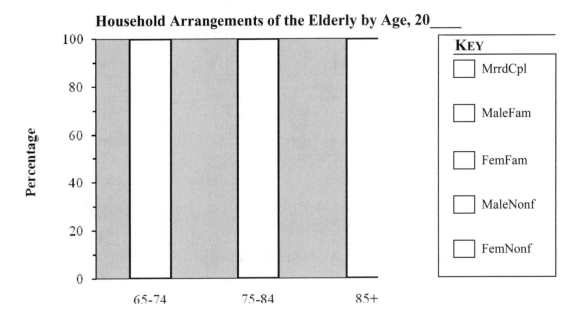

Household Arrangements of the Elderly by Age, 20____

Exercise 8 How do the household arrangements of the elderly differ among racial/ethnic groups?

▶ *Dataset*: ELDRHH.DAT

▶ On your own, create five pie charts, one for each major racial/ethnic group. In each pie, indicate the distribution of household types among the elderly.

C. Economic Situation

Mandatory retirement was eradicated during the late 1970s and first half of the 80s, but that had little impact on the retirement plans of most employees. Generally speaking, in the 1990s, workers chose to retire sooner than later. Today, with the support of Social Security, private pensions, and savings, many people nearing the end of their careers look forward to filling their days with activities other than those done at the office.

However, retirement is not always a voluntary release from the work force. Health problems sometimes restrict individuals' abilities to fulfill their work responsibilities, forcing them to leave their jobs. Other times, employees must accept retirement due to downsizing. These workers, should they seek new employment, often have difficulty finding a new job and may wind up leaving the labor force permanently. Even when they are able to find part-time work, these jobs often do not pay well or offer the benefits that the elderly need as they transition into retirement. Not surprisingly, a significant portion of the elderly unexpectedly face retirement are left vulnerable to financial distress.

The economic status of the elderly can be assessed using the "Income Relative to Poverty Cut-off" measure (introduced in Chapter Eight). While most of the elderly fall in the middle-income category, a significant number are categorized as poor or near-poor. Though the near-poor are not technically in poverty, any minor setback puts them in danger of falling below the poverty line. Due to the reasons previously discussed, elderly women are particularly vulnerable to poverty. Education and race also affect one's chances of staying above the poverty line. While a majority of those who are poor are white, racial minorities are greatly over-represented among the elderly poor.

Exercise 9 Begin by looking at the labor force participation of the elderly in the present. Look at men and women separately. How does labor force participation change as age increases? Is this the same for men as for women?

▸ *Dataset*: ELDREMP.DAT

▸ Create two bar charts, one for men and one for women. In each chart, indicate the percentage of each group in the labor force. (Hint: to determine the size of the total labor force, combine or add "unemployed", "full-time employed" and "part-time employed". For more explanation of these categories, see the "Key Concepts" section in Chapter 4.)

Elderly Men in the Labor Force by Age, 20____   **Elderly Women in the Labor Force by Age, 20____**

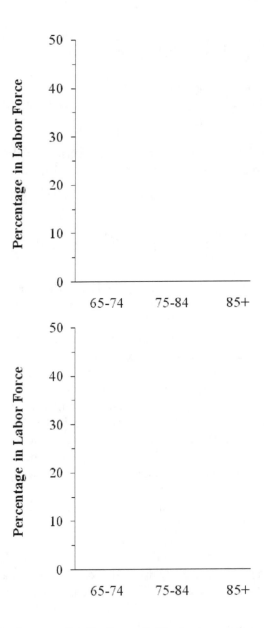

Exercise 10 Compare the income distributions of elderly men and women (use the "Income Relative to Poverty Cut-off" measure discussed in Chapter 8). How do elderly men and women differ in terms of poverty? In terms of "comfortable" income?

▸ *Dataset*: ELDRPOV.DAT

▸ Create two pie charts, one for elderly men and one for elderly women. In each chart, show the income distribution.

Income Distribution of Men and Women Ages 65+, 20____

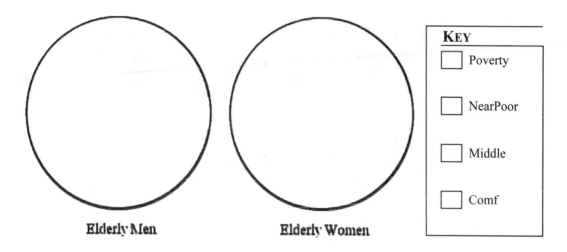

Elderly Men   Elderly Women

Exercise 11 Does poverty among the elderly vary by race/ethnicity? Which groups have the highest poverty levels? The lowest? Why do you think that this is so?

▶ *Dataset*: ELDRPOV.DAT

▶ Create a stacked bar chart. For each racial/ethnic group, stack by income status.

Income Status of Elderly by Race/Ethnicity, 20____

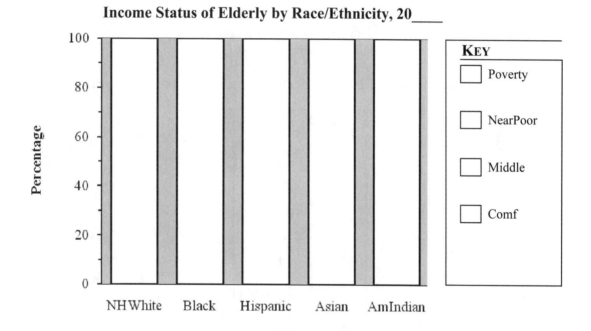

Exercise 12 Consider the relationship between marital status and poverty. Does the relationship differ between men and women? If so, how?

▶ *Dataset*: ELDRPOV.DAT

▶ Create a stacked bar chart with side-by-side bars for elderly men and elderly women. For each marital category, stack by income status.

Income Status of Elderly Men and Women by Marital Status, 20____

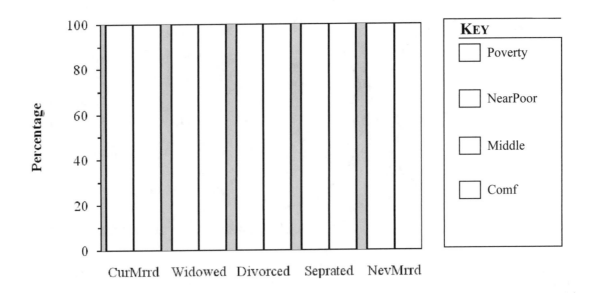

Exercise 13 Examine the educational attainment of the elderly over time. How has it changed? What do you think caused the changes that you observe?

▶ *Dataset*: EDUC.TREND

▶ Create a stacked bar chart with side-by-side bars for elderly men and elderly women. For each year, stack by educational attainment.

Educational Attainment of Elderly Men and Women, 1950 to 20____

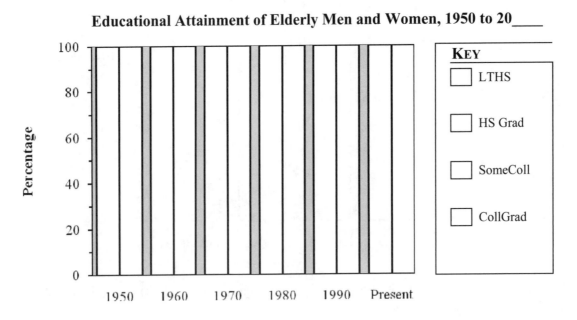

Exercise 14 Now look at poverty rates for the elderly across different educational attainment categories. Are those with higher education levels less likely to be in poverty? If so, why?

▶ *Dataset*: ELDREMP.DAT

▶ Create a stacked bar chart with side-by-side bars for men and women. For each educational category, stack by income status.

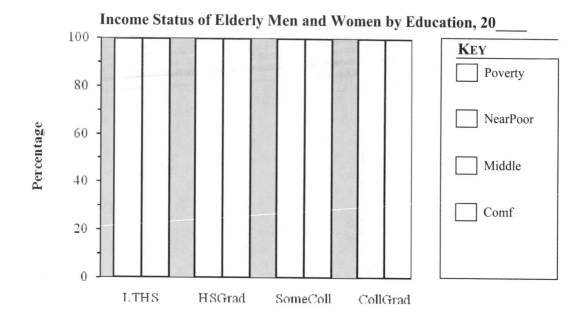

Income Status of Elderly Men and Women by Education, 20____

KEY
- Poverty
- NearPoor
- Middle
- Comf

(x-axis: LTHS, HSGrad, SomeColl, CollGrad; y-axis: Percentage, 0 to 100)

D. Health and Disability

The greater part of the elderly population report having at least one recurring health ailment. Because some conditions, like heart disease, can be life threatening, the elderly are often in need of extensive medical care. Even less serious health problems like arthritis still pose a threat to quality of life and independent living among the elderly, and those with the conditions often require assistance in daily living. Besides physical disorders, many elderly people live with mental health problems. Alzheimer's disease, a disease that affects only older people, is one of the major reasons why elderly Americans are institutionalized.

Those who need assistance, but are not institutionalized, often turn to their spouses, family members, and friends for supports. Other times, special services and agencies might be called upon to provide additional help when needed. Unfortunately, services are expensive and not available in all communities, making it difficult for those living near the poverty level to afford the professional assistance they need.

Exercise 15 Consider self-care limitations among the elderly. How do men and women differ in respect to self-care limitations? What differences exist among different elderly age groups?

▶ *Dataset*: ELDRDISAB.DAT

▸ Create a stacked bar chart with side-by-side bars for men and women. For each age group, stack by those who have self-care limitations and those who do not.

Self-Care Limitations of Elderly Men and Women by Age, 20____

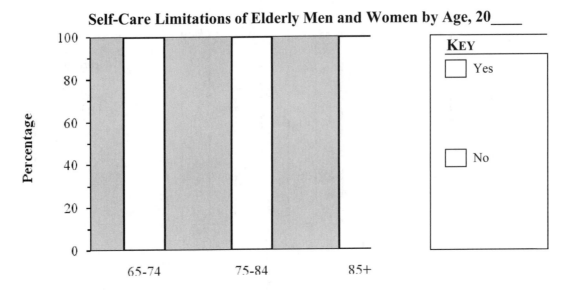

Exercise 16 Do the self-care limitations of the elderly vary by race/ethnicity? What differences do you notice among racial/ethnic groups? What might account for these differences?

▸ *Dataset*: ELDRDISAB.DAT

▸ Create five pie charts, one for each major racial/ethnic group. For each chart, indicate the percentage of those who have self-care limitations and those who do not.

Self-Care Limitations of Elderly by Race/Ethnicity, 20____

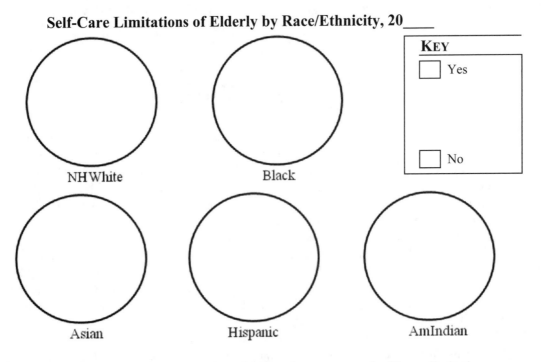

Exercise 17 Does income level seem to be related to the presence of self-care limitations among the elderly? How? Why do you think this is so?

- ► *Dataset*: ELDRDISAB.DAT

- ► On your own, create four pie charts, one for each income status category. In each chart, indicate the percentage of those who have self-care limitations and those who do not.

Exercise 18 Now consider independent living limitations among the elderly. How do men and women differ with respect to independent living difficulties? What differences do you notice among age groups?

- ► *Dataset*: ELDRDISAB.DAT

- ► Create a stacked bar chart with side-by-side bars for men and women. For each age group, stack by independent living limitation status.

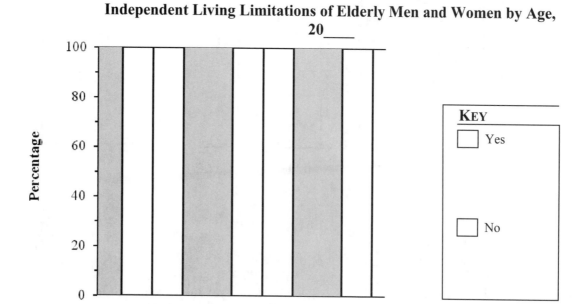

Independent Living Limitations of Elderly Men and Women by Age, 20____

Exercise 19 How do independent living limitations among the elderly correlate to income status?

▸ *Dataset*: ELDRDISAB.DAT

▸ Create a stacked bar chart, with bars for each poverty category; stack by independent living limitation status.

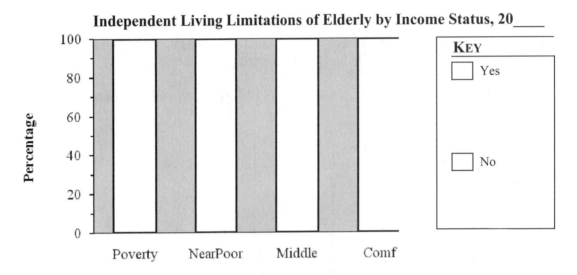

Independent Living Limitations of Elderly by Income Status, 20____

KEY
☐ Yes
☐ No

Discussion Questions

1. If we had examined the limitations of the elderly since 1950, do you think you would have noticed a change over time? What kind of change? Provide one or more explanations that support your hypothesis. Do you think the proportion of the elderly with one or more of the limitations discussed will continue to change over time?

2. Looking at the distribution of limitations among different income groups and different racial/ethnic groups, do you feel any parallels exist? If so, how? What, in your opinion, do you think this says about the health policies of the United States?

THINK
tank

1. Describe where you think you would most likely find elderly Hispanics. Would you be just as likely to find older Asians and Blacks in the same setting? Does the location of any of these groups seem to vary by region? Given that the elderly population is growing, and that the elderly are more inclined to use health care services than most other age

groups, what implications do the geographical location of the elderly have for health care providers?

2. The elderly are living longer than ever before, but are they also working longer? What percentage of the elderly was employed in 1950? How does this compare with the most recent data? Were elderly women as likely to be employed between 1950 and present as elderly men? Considering employment in recent years, were employed elderly women as likely to work as many hours as elderly men? Does race/ethnicity appear to be a factor? Do these employment characteristics seem consistent with elderly mobility limitations? Given that the elderly are living longer, do you think the official retirement age should be pushed back as well? How might such a change affect Social Security, Medicare, or other programs designed to assist older Americans?

SECTION III

References and Resources

THE CENSUS AND THE AMERICAN COMMUNITY SURVEY

The data in this work book draws from both the US Census of Population which is taken every ten years, and the most recently available wave of the Census Bureau's American Community Survey. The Census statistics provided the full array of information on the many topics in this book for the periods 1950 to 2000. After that time most of this information was shifted to the American Community Survey. Discussed below are further details of each of these sources.

US Census

Unlike most surveys or studies that sample only a small portion of the total population, the U.S. Constitution mandates that the Census count every resident of the United States. The first census was taken in 1790; the 2010 Census was the nation's 23rd.

The 2010 Census counted over 300 million people and 115 million housing units. Information on most of these people and places was collected via census forms received by the Bureau within two weeks of Census Day, April 1, 2010. In 2010, the Census Bureau advertising campaign included a Superbowl ad and the sponsorship of a NASCAR race car to increase awareness and response rates (below are two posters from the marketing campaign). Despite the efforts, nearly a third of households still failed to return their forms. Door-to-door enumerators, working through the spring and summer of 2010, collected information about those who did not respond using the form.

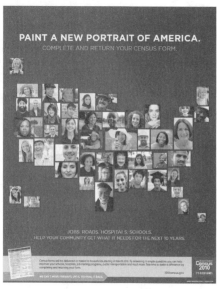

The official purpose of the census is to determine the size of population for use in congressional district apportionment, but the significance of the data it collects extends far beyond a simple head count. It provides a ten-year "benchmark" for the nation's population. Through the 2000 Census, a certain share of households (about 1-in-6 for the 2000 Census) received a longer form that included a larger battery of questions about the respondents' social characteristics (e.g. education and English language proficiency), economic circumstances (e.g. occupation and labor force status), and housing situations. Although the "long-form" items were only asked to a portion of the total population, the sample was substantial enough to yield accurate estimates for population subgroups and smaller geographic areas. Starting with the 2010 Census, the "long form" is no longer used to collect this detailed information; instead, the annual American Community Survey (ACS), separate from the decennial census, has taken its place. The 2010 Census contained only a short, ten-question form. Thus data for the most recent year after 2000 is drawn from a recent American Community Survey (discussed below).

This book takes advantage of the suitability of census data for trend analysis by providing a number of exercises that look at change in the United States from 1950 to 2000. Several of the questions asked in the 2010 Census have comparable questions in each of the censuses administered over this period, making it possible to investigate ongoing change in the areas of age, race, population, household arrangements, and beyond. Although successive censuses ask questions about the same subjects, it is important to remember that the particulars of the question will often change with time. Still, it is possible to do as the authors of this book have done and re-allocate these responses into broader categories that make analysis over time possible. Other questions, such as those relating to age or racial status, have appeared in almost the same form on many earlier census questionnaires. A question on racial status, for example, has been asked on every census since the first one in 1790.

The census distributes its results in the form of tables and computerized data files that are available in many formats. Published volumes are available for all U.S. censuses and can be found, for the most recent censuses, at most college, university and large public libraries. In the mid-1990s, the Census Bureau began an effort to make census tables and other information available electronically over the Internet. Today, almost all current census data are available for download at http://www.census.gov. The Census Bureau's homepage includes a wealth of technical and historical information on the U.S. Census, as well as detailed reports on specific topics. From the main page, you can easily access the American FactFinder tool, which lets users download tables from the recent US Censuses using geographies ranging from the entire nation to counties to zip codes to census blocks. Finally, although the data are readily available in computerized format, many important resources are not. A good way to learn about the variety of census publications and other data products from the census would be to explore what is available at your college or university library. The best way to learn about the Census Bureau and the wide variety of products and services it offers, however, is to visit the Census Bureau website itself.

The census data used in the datasets that accompany this book were compiled by the author from the Public Use Microdata Samples (PUMS) from the 1950 to 2000 Censuses and the American Community Survey. While prepared from "samples" of census responses, the numbers in your data sets are statistically weighted up so that they actually represent the total U.S. population in each of the census years.

American Community Survey

Due to rapidly changing American demographics, the decennial census did not sufficiently capture the most current data. Thus, in 2005, the Census Bureau officially began an effort to replace the "long form" with the American Community Survey (ACS), which is mailed to about 250,000 American households each month. This ongoing survey with annual data releases is used by the government to inform decisions on everything except taxation and representation (for which the government still uses the decennial census). The ACS offers similar information to the long-form but now includes yearly social and economic information, revised questions about disabilities, food stamps and more detailed poverty-related information. The government requires such information in order to analyze the best ways to tailor programs for community development, aid to needy families, bilingual services, veterans support, and other important programs. The ACS has largely replaced the Census as the primary source of information for social scientists, journalists, and even advertisers who rely on public demographic data.

ACS data, like Census data, are distributed publically by the Census Bureau with new data released each year. There are some differences between the US Census and the ACS data in how they are collected, which have small effects on their comparability. Further details about this can be obtained from the ACS website at http://www.census.gov/acs/www/index.html.

While the datasets in this book were generated using microdata, further investigation can also be done on the aggregated data available on the Census Bureau's FactFinder website. Due to the small sample size relative to the decennial long form, the summarized data are released in one-year, three-year, and five-year products that cover a varying degree of geographies. That is, the three year and five year data are "pooled" multiyear estimates that are combined to provide something like an average value for the years involved. Because of its larger sample size than single year data, the datasets used with this publication come from the 3-year pooled data (e.g. 2006-8) which will be updated in subsequent years. Just as with the old census "long form", the ACS provides a wealth of data on various social, demographic, and economic characteristics of our population.

INTERNET
resources

The Web can be an excellent source of demographic information, both qualitative and quantitative. Listed below are some sites that deal directly with the issues discussed in this book.

Textbook Companion Website—http://www.cengage.com/sociology/frey
The *Investigating Change in American Society* website includes access to all the datasets needed to complete the exercises in this workbook. Each dataset can be loaded instantly with WebCHIP or downloaded for use with the desktop version of StudentCHIP. The website includes tutorials in graphing and using StudentCHIP, background information on the Census, updated information on datasets, and other resources designed to help students learn from this book. Also includes a special section for instructors in courses using this text.

SSDAN: Social Science Data Analysis Network—http://www.ssdan.net
The Social Science Data Analysis Network (SSDAN) is a university-based organization that creates demographic media, such as user guides, web sites, and hands-on classroom computer materials that make U.S. Census data accessible to policy-makers, educators, the media, and informed citizens.

DataCounts!—http://www.ssdan.net/datacounts/
This SSDAN product provides access to learning modules developed by faculty around the country. Visitors can also find a variety of WebCHIP-type datasets or submit their own learning modules for inclusion in the catalog.

CensusScope—http://www.censusscope.org
Another SSDAN product, this award-winning website takes the most relevant Census data, with trend data back to 1960 in some cases, and presents it to the public using simple and straightforward charts, graphs, and maps for the national, state, county, and metropolitan level. In addition to a detailed section on racial segregation, CensusScope provides information on population, race, family, and household structure, income and poverty, age, migration, occupation and more.

Teaching with Data—http://www.TeachingWithData.org/
A joint venture with the Inter-university Consortium for Political and Social Research (ICPSR) at the University of Michigan, which aims to provide a centralized search for materials that encourage the integration of data into the classroom.

William Frey's Homepage—http://www.frey-demographer.org
The author's page provides tools for analysis of race and migration data. Dr. Frey's publications and research reports on U.S. demographics can be downloaded or ordered via the website.

U.S. Census Bureau—http://www.census.gov
The Census Bureau's homepage includes a wealth of technical and historical information on the U.S. Census, as well as detailed reports on specific topics. The site's American FactFinder tool lets users download tables from the 2000 and 2010 Censuses (as well as the American Community Survey) using geographies ranging from the entire nation to counties to zip codes to census blocks.

INDEX
key concepts

The concepts used in this book's exercises are defined in the Key Concepts sections of the chapters in which they are introduced or featured. For easy reference, each of these concepts is listed below along with the investigation topic and page number where it is defined.

Hispanic Groups	Two	42
Marital Status	Five	100
Mobility Limitations	Ten	178
Occupation	Two	43
Older Population	Ten	178
Origin Country	Three	62
Ownership	Seven	127
Part-time Workers	Four	84
Percent Unemployed	Four	84
Percent in Labor Force	Four	84
Poverty Status of a Family	Eight	146
Poverty Status of a Person	Eight	146
Presence of Children Under 18	Seven	126
Private Schools	Nine	162
Public Schools	Nine	162
Race/Ethnicity	Two	42
Region	One	22
Rentership	Seven	127
School-Aged Population	Nine	162
Self-Care Limitations	Ten	178
State	One	22
Unemployment Rate	Four	84
Unmarried Partner	Five	100
Year	One	22
Year-round Full-time Worker	Four	84

DATASET GUIDE

The following pages provide a comprehensive guide to the datasets needed to complete the exercises in this book. They are divided into two parts. The first part lists the datasets that contain trend data from 1950 to the present. These have the extension ".TREND". The second section includes datasets created using only data from the most recent American Community Survey. These have the extension ".DAT." The datasets in this list are all available at the companion website (http://www.cengage.com/sociology/frey) for use with WebCHIP or for download for use with the desktop version of StudentCHIP. The "Accessing Data and Making Tables" section in the front of this book provides additional information on accessing and using the datasets.

For a variety of reasons, you may choose to look up the dataset you will be working with using this list. When you are doing an exercise that pertains to an over-time analysis, that dataset end with ".TREND". When you are doing an exercise that pertains only to the current year, that dataset will end with ".DAT" list. Datasets with names that have suffixes: "-35" or "-W" designate datasets specific to a specific group; -35 pertains to the 35-45 age group, and -W pertains to women, etc.)

These lists can be useful to you because they indicate the variable names that appear in each dataset, and the names of the categories associated with each variable. Especially if you are expanding your investigations beyond the exercises, this guide will help you determine what datasets include the information you are looking for.

Below is an explanation of the information that appears on each dataset listing.

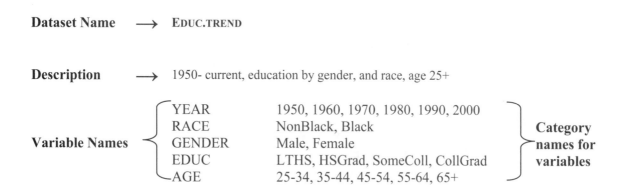

Dataset Name ⟶	EDUC.TREND	
Description ⟶	1950- current, education by gender, and race, age 25+	
Variable Names	YEAR	1950, 1960, 1970, 1980, 1990, 2000
	RACE	NonBlack, Black
	GENDER	Male, Female
	EDUC	LTHS, HSGrad, SomeColl, CollGrad
	AGE	25-34, 35-44, 45-54, 55-64, 65+

Category names for variables

Trend Datasets

EDUC.TREND

1950-current, Education by gender, and race, age 25+
YEARTREND: 1950, 1960, 1970, 1980, 1990, 2000, current
RACE: NonBlack, Black
GENDER: Male, Female
AGEEDUC: 25-34, 35-44, 45-54, 55-64, 65+
EDUC: LTHS, HSGrad, SomeColl, CollGrad

EDUCOCCUP.TREND

1950-current, Education by occupation, race, and gender, age 16+
YEARTREND: 1950, 1960, 1970, 1980, 1990, 2000, current
RACE: NonBlack, Black
GENDER: Male, Female
AGEWORK: 16-24, 25-34, 35-44, 45-54, 55-64, 65+
OCCUP3: TopWC, OtherWC, Service, BC
EDUC: LTHS, HSGrad, SomeColl, CollGrad

ELDERLY.TREND

1950-current, Elderly by gender, marital status, age groups
AGEELDR: 65-74, 75-84, 85+
YEARTREND: 1950, 1960, 1970, 1980, 1990, 2000, current
GENDER: Male, Female
MARITAL: CurrMrrd, Widowed, Divorced, Separated, NevMrrd

EMPLOY.TREND

1950-current, Employment Status by race, marital status, and gender, age 16+
YEARTREND: 1950, 1960, 1970, 1980, 1990, 2000, current
RACE: NonBlack, Black
EMP: Empd, Unempd, NILF
AGEWORK: 16-24, 25-34, 35-44, 45-54, 55-64, 65+
MARITAL: CurrMrrd, Widowed, Divorced, Separated, NevMrrd
GENDER: Male, Female

FAMPOV.TREND

1970-current, Families by race, age, marital status, and poverty status, age 15+
YEARTREND2: 1970, 1980, 1990, 2000, current
RACE: Black, Nonblack
AGEMAR: 15-24, 25-34, 35-44, 45-54, 55-64, 65+
FAMTYPE: MrrdCpl, MaleFam, FemFam
POVLEVEL2: Poverty, NearPoor, Other

HOUSEHOLDS.TREND

1950-current, Households by household type, household size, race, age 15+
YEARTREND: 1950, 1960, 1970, 1980, 1990, 2000, current
HHTYPE: MrrdCpl, MaleFam, FemFam, MaleNonf, FemNonf
HHSIZE: 1, 2, 3, 4, 5+
RACE: NonBlack, Black
AGEMAR: 15-24, 25-34, 35-44, 45-54, 55-64, 65+

MARITAL.TREND

1950-current, Marital status by race, and gender, age 15+

YEARTREND: 1950, 1960, 1970, 1980, 1990, 2000, current
RACE: NonBlack, Black
GENDER: Male, Female
AGEMAR: 15-24, 25-34, 35-44, 45-54, 55-64, 65+
MARITAL: CurrMrrd, Widowed, Divorced, Separated, NevMrrd

POP.TREND

1950-current, U.S. Population by age and gender for blacks and non-blacks

YEARTREND: 1950, 1960, 1970, 1980, 1990, 2000, current
RACE: NonBlack, Black
GENDER: Male, Female
AGEALL: 0-4, 5-14, 15-24, 25-34, 35-44, 45-54, 55-64, 65+

POPPOV.TREND

1970-current, U.S. Population by age groups, race, age, gender, and poverty status

YEARTREND2: 1970, 1980, 1990, 2000, current
RACE: NonBlack, Black
AGEALL2: 0-5, 6-17, 18-24, 25-34, 35-44, 45-54, 55-64, 65+
GENDER: Male, Female
POV: Poverty, NonPov

POPSTRUC.TREND

1930-current, U.S. Population (in 1,000s) by age groups and gender

AGEALL: 0-4, 5-14, 15-24, 25-34, 35-44, 45-54, 55-64, 65+
GENDER: Male, Female
YEARPOP: 1930, 1940, 1950, 1960, 1970, 1980, 1990, 2000, current

Current Year Datasets

ASIANPOP.DAT

Asian Alone Population by Asian group, age, gender, and immigration status

ASIAN: Chinese, Japanese, Filipino, Korean, Indian, Vietnamese, Other
IMMENTRY: Native, FB<1980, FB80-89, FB90-99, FB00-current
GENDER: Male, Female
AGEALL: 0-4, 5-14, 15-24, 25-34, 35-44, 45-54, 55-64, 65+

CHILDGRAD.DAT

Education by race/ethnicity, poverty, gender and metro, age 18-24

EDUC: LTHS, HSGrad, SomeColl, CollGrad
RACEETH: NHWhite, Black, Hispanic, Asian, AmIndian, NHOther, NHMulti
GENDER: Male, Female
POV: Poverty, NonPov
GEO: City, Suburb, NonMetro
AGEYNG: 18, 19, 20, 21, 22, 23, 24

CHILDPOV.DAT

Children by race/ethnicity, poverty, household type, family size, and immigration status

AGEKIDS: 0-5, 6-17
RACEETH: NHWhite, Black, Hispanic, Asian, AmIndian, NHOther, NHMulti
POVLEVEL: Poverty, NearPoor, Middle, Comf
FAMTYPE: MrrdCpl, MaleFam, FemFam
FAMSIZ: 2, 3, 4, 5, 6+
IMM: Native, ForeignBorn

CHILDSCH.DAT

School-age children by school attendance, poverty, English proficiency, race/ethnicity, immigration status, and gender

SCHOOL: Public, Private, NotEnrolled
POVLEVEL: Poverty, NearPoor, Middle, Comf
ENGSPKG: EngOnly, Verywell, Well, Notwell, Notatall
RACEETH: NHWhite, Black, Hispanic, Asian, AmIndian, NHOther, NHMulti
IMM: Native, ForeignBorn
GENDER: Male, Female

COHAB-M.DAT

Men cohabitors not currently married, age 15+

AGEMAR: 15-24, 25-34, 35-44, 45-54, 55-64, 65+
MARITAL2: NevMrrd, Divorced, Separated, Widowed
EDUC: LTHS, HSGrad, SomeColl, CollGrad
RACEETH: NHWhite, Black, Hispanic, Asian, AmIndian, NHOther, NHMulti

COHAB-W.DAT

Women cohabitors not currently married, age 15+

AGEMAR: 15-24, 25-34, 35-44, 45-54, 55-64, 65+
MARITAL2: NevMrrd, Divorced, Separated, Widowed
EDUC: LTHS, HSGrad, SomeColl, CollGrad
RACEETH: NHWhite, Black, Hispanic, Asian, AmIndian, NHOther, NHMulti

DOCTORS.DAT

Physicians: full-time, year-round workers age 25-64 by race/ethnicity, gender and earnings

RACEETH: NHWhite, Black, Asian, Hispanic, AmIndian, NHOther, NHMulti
GENDER: Male, Female
AGEPRO: 25-34, 35-44, 45-54, 55-64

EARN2: <40K, 40-54K, 55-69K, 70-84K, 85-99K, 100-124K, 125-149K, 150-199K, 200K+

EARN.DAT

Full-time, year-round workers, age 16+

RACEETH: NHWhite, Black, Hispanic, Asian, AmIndian, NHOther, NHMulti
GENDER: Male, Female
AGEWORK: 16-24, 25-34, 35-44, 45-54, 55-64, 65+
EARN: <25K, 25-34K, 35-49K, 50-69K, 70-99K, 100K+

EARNASIAN.DAT

Asian Alone by Asian groups: full-time, year-round workers age 25-34

ASIAN: Chinese, Japanese, Filipino, Korean, Indian, Vietnamese, Other
GENDER: Male, Female
IMMENTRY: Native, FB<1980, FB80-89, FB90-99, FB00-current
EARN: <25K, 25-34K, 35-49K, 50-69K, 70-99K, 100K+

EARNASIANALL.DAT

Asian Alone by Asian groups: full-time, year-round workers age 16+

ASIAN: Chinese, Japanese, Filipino, Korean, Indian, Vietnamese, Other
GENDER: Male, Female
AGEWORK: 16-24, 25-34, 35-44, 45-54, 55-64, 65+
EARN: <25K, 25-34K, 35-49K, 50-69K, 70-99K, 100K+

EARNHISP.DAT

Hispanic groups: full-time, year-round workers age 25-34

HISPANIC: Mexican, PRican, Cuban, CAmeric, SAmeric, Other
GENDER: Male, Female
IMMENTRY: Native, FB<1980, FB80-89, FB90-99, FB00-current
EARN: <25K, 25-34K, 35-49K, 50-69K, 70-99K, 100K+

EARNHISPALL.DAT

Hispanic groups, full-time, year-round workers age 16+

HISPANIC: Mexican, PRican, Cuban, CAmeric, SAmeric, Other
GENDER: Male, Female
AGEWORK: 16-24, 25-34, 35-44, 45-54, 55-64, 65+
EARN: <25K, 25-34K, 35-49K, 50-69K, 70-99K, 100K+

EDUCASIAN.DAT

Education and immigration status for Asian Alone by Asian groups, age 25-34

ASIAN: Chinese, Japanese, Filipino, Korean, Indian, Vietnamese, Other
IMM: Native, ForeignBorn
GENDER: Male, Female
EDUCALL: 0-9Yrs, 10-12Yrs, HSGrad, SomeColl, CollGrad, Masters, PhD-Prof

EDUCASIANALL.DAT

Education for Asian Alone by Asian groups, age 25+

ASIAN: Chinese, Japanese, Filipino, Korean, Indian, Vietnamese, Other
AGEEDUC: 25-34, 35-44, 45-54, 55-64, 65+
GENDER: Male, Female
EDUCALL: 0-9Yrs, 10-12Yrs, HSGrad, SomeColl, CollGrad, Masters, PhD-Prof

EDUCHISP.DAT

Education and immigration status for Hispanics groups, age 25-34

HISPANIC: Mexican, PRican, Cuban, CAmeric, SAmeric, Other
IMMENTRY: Native, FB<1980, FB80-89, FB90-99, current
GENDER: Male, Female
EDUCALL: <9Yrs, 10-12Yrs, HSGrad, SomeColl, CollGrad, Masters, PhD-Prof

EDUCHISPALL.DAT

Education for Hispanic groups, age 25+

HISPANIC: Mexican, PRican, Cuban, CAmeric, SAmeric, Other
IMM: Native, ForeignBorn
AGEEDUC: 25-34, 35-44, 45-54, 55-64, 65+
GENDER: Male, Female
EDUCALL: 0-9Yrs, 10-12Yrs, HSGrad, SomeColl, CollGrad, Masters, PhD-Prof

EDUCIMM.DAT

Education by immigration status, race/ethnicity, gender, age 25+

EDUCALL: 0-9Yrs, 10-12Yrs, HSGrad, SomeColl, CollGrad, Masters, PhD-Prof
IMMENTRY: Native, FB<1980, FB80-89, FB90-99, FB00-current
RACEETH: NHWhite, Black, Hispanic, Asian, AmIndian, NHOther, NHMulti
GENDER: Male, Female
AGEEDUC: 25-34, 35-44, 45-54, 55-64, 65+

EDUCOCCUP.DAT

Education by occupation, race/ethnicity, and gender for age 25+

RACEETH: NHWhite, Black, Hispanic, Asian, AmIndian, NHOther, NHMulti
GENDER: Male, Female
EDUCALL: 0-9Yrs, 10-12Yrs, HSGrad, SomeColl, CollGrad, Masters, PhD-Prof
OCCUP: TopWC, OtherWC, Service, TopBC, OtherBC
AGEEDUC: 25-34, 35-44, 45-54, 55-64, 65+

ELDRDISAB.DAT

Elderly by disability, gender, race/ethnicity, and poverty

AGEELDR: 65-74, 75-84, 85+
GENDER: Male, Female
RACEETH: NHWhite, Black, Hispanic, Asian, AmIndian, NHOther, NHMulti
POVLEVEL: Poverty, NearPoor, Middle, Comf
INDLVLMT: Yes, No
SELFCARE: Yes, No

ELDREMP.DAT

Elderly by employment, education, poverty, and gender, age 65+

AGEELDR: 65-74, 75-84, 85+
GENDER: Male, Female
EMP2: EmpFull, EmpPart, Unempd, NILF
EDUC: LTHS, HSGrad, SomeColl, CollGrad
POVLEVEL: Poverty, NearPoor, Middle, Comf

ELDRHH.DAT

Elderly households by age groups, gender, household type, and race/ethnicity

AGEELDR: 65-74, 75-84, 85+
HHTYPE: MrrdCpl, MaleFam, FemFam, MaleNonf, FemNonf
GENDER: Male, Female
RACEETH: NHWhite, Black, Hispanic, Asian, AmIndian, NHOther, NHMulti

ELDRPOV.DAT

Elderly by poverty, marital status, race/ethnicity, and gender, age 65+

AGEELDR: 65-74, 75-84, 85+
GENDER: Male, Female
RACEETH: NHWhite, Black, Asian, Hispanic, AmIndian, NHOther, NHMulti
MARITAL: CurrMrrd, Widowed, Divorced, Separated, NevMrrd
POVLEVEL: Poverty, NearPoor, Middle, Comf

EMPASIAN.DAT

Employment status by immigration status for Asian Alone by Asian groups, age 16-34

ASIAN: Chinese, Japanese, Filipino, Korean, Indian, Vietnamese, Other
GENDER: Male, Female
AGEWORK2: 16-24, 25-34
IMMENTRY: Native, FB<1980, FB80-89, FB90-99, FB00-current
EMP: Empd, Unempd, NILF

EMPASIANALL.DAT

Employment status for Asian Alone by Asian groups, age 16+

ASIAN: Chinese, Japanese, Filipino, Korean, Indian, Vietnamese, Other
GENDER: Male, Female
AGEWORK: 16-24, 25-34, 35-44, 45-54, 55-64, 65+
EMP: Empd, Unempd, NILF

EMPEDUC.DAT

Employment status by race/ethnicity, education, and gender, age 16+

RACEETH: NHWhite, Black, Hispanic, Asian, AmIndian, NHOther, NHMulti
EMP: Empd, Unempd, NILF
AGEWORK: 16-24, 25-34, 35-44, 45-54, 55-64, 65+
EDUC: LTHS, HSGrad, SomeColl, CollGrad
GENDER: Male, Female

EMPHISP.DAT

Employment status by immigration status for Hispanic groups, age 16-34

HISPANIC: Mexican, PRican, Cuban, CAmeric, SAmeric, Other
GENDER: Male, Female
AGEWORK2: 16-24, 25-34
IMMENTRY: Native, FB<1980, FB80-89, FB90-99, FB00-current
EMP: Empd, Unempd, NILF

EMPHISPALL.DAT

Employment status for Hispanic groups, age 16+

HISPANIC: Mexican, PRican, Cuban, CAmeric, SAmeric, Other
GENDER: Male, Female
AGEWORK: 16-24, 25-34, 35-44, 45-54, 55-64, 65+
EMP: Empd, Unempd, NILF

EMPLOY.DAT

Employment status for age 16+

RACEETH: NHWhite, Black, Hispanic, Asian, AmIndian, NHOther, NHMulti
GENDER: Male, Female
AGEWORK: 16-24, 25-34, 35-44, 45-54, 55-64, 65+
EMP: Empd, Unempd, NILF

EMP-W.DAT

Employment status by number of children, education for currently married women, age 25-34

RACEETH: NHWhite, Black, Asian, Hispanic, AmIndian, NHOther, NHMulti
EDUC: LTHS, HSGrad, SomeColl, CollGrad
KIDS: None, Kids<6, KidsOther
EMP2: EmpFull, EmpPart, Unempd, NILF

ENGASIAN.DAT

Asian Alone by Asian groups by immigration status, English proficiency, gender, state, and age

IMMENTRY: Native, FB<1980, FB80-89, FB90-99, FB00-current
ENGSPKG: EngOnly, Verywell, Well, Notwell, Notatall
ASIAN: Chinese, Japanese, Filipino, Korean, Indian, Vietnamese, Other
GENDER: Male, Female
AGEALL3: 0-17, 18-64, 65+
STATECAL: CA, RestofUS

ENGHISP.DAT

Hispanic groups by immigration status, English proficiency, gender, state, and age

IMMENTRY: Native, FB<1980, FB80-89, FB90-99, FB00-current
ENGSPKG: EngOnly, Verywell, Well, Notwell, Notatall
HISPANIC: Mexican, Cuban, PRican, CAmeric, SAmeric, Other
GENDER: Male, Female
AGEALL3: 0-17, 18-64, 65+
STATECAL: CA, RestofUS

FAMEARN.DAT

Married-couple families by earners age 16+, race/ethnicity, and poverty

EARNTYPE: 2ErnrFam, 1ErnrML, 1ErnrFML, None
RACEETH: NHWhite, Black, Hispanic, Asian, AmIndian, NHOther, NHMulti
POVLEVEL: Poverty, NearPoor, Middle, Comf
AGEALL4: <25, 25-34, 35-44, 45-54, 55-64, 65+

FAMILY.DAT

Families by family type, gender, poverty, and race/ethnicity, age 15+

FAMTYPE: MrrdCpl, MaleFam, FemFam
RACEETH: NHWhite, Black, Hispanic, Asian, AmIndian, NHOther, NHMulti
KID: None, Kids<6, KidsOther
POVLEVEL: Poverty, NearPoor, Middle, Comf
AGEALL4: <25, 25-34, 35-44, 45-54, 55-64, 65+

FAMPOV.DAT

Families by family type and poverty status

RACEETH: NHWhite, Black, Asian, Hispanic, AmIndian, NHOther, NHMulti
AGEALL4: <25, 25-34, 35-44, 45-54, 55-64, 65+
FAMTYPE: MrrdCpl, MaleFam, FemFam
POV: Poverty, NonPov

FAMPOVGEO.DAT

Families by family type, race/ethnicity, poverty, and metro, age 15+

RACEETH: NHWhite, Black, Hispanic, Asian, AmIndian, NHOther, NHMulti
POVLEVEL: Poverty, NearPoor, Middle, Comf
FAMTYPE: MrrdCpl, MaleFam, FemFam
GEO: City, Suburb, NonMetro
AGEALL4: <25, 25-34, 35-44, 45-54, 55-64, 65+

FAMPOVHISP.DAT

Family type by poverty status for Hispanic groups, all ages

HISPANIC: Mexican, PRican, Cuban, CAmeric, SAmeric, Other
AGEALL4: <25, 25-34, 35-44, 45-54, 55-64, 65+
FAMTYPE: MrrdCpl, MaleFam, FemFam
POV: Poverty, NonPov

HISPPOP.DAT

Hispanic population by Hispanic group, age, gender and immigration status

HISPANIC: Mexican, PRican, Cuban, CAmeric, SAmeric, Other
IMMENTRY: Native, FB<1980, FB80-89, FB90-99, FB00-current
GENDER: Male, Female
AGEALL: 0-4, 5-14, 15-24, 25-34, 35-44, 45-54, 55-64, 65+

HOUSEHOLDS.DAT

Households by household type, poverty, and race/ethnicity, age 15+

AGEMAR: 15-24, 25-34, 35-44, 45-54, 55-64, 65+
HHTYPE: MrrdCpl, MaleFam, FemFam, MaleNonf, FemNonf
POVLEVEL: Poverty, NearPoor, Middle, Comf
RACEETH: NHWhite, Black, Hispanic, Asian, AmIndian, NHOther, NHMulti

HOUSING.DAT

Households by household type, housing, race/ethnicity, and homeownership, age 15+

HOUSING: House, Apt2-9, Apt10+, MobHome, Other
RACEETH: NHWhite, Black, Hispanic, Asian, AmIndian, NHOther, NHMulti
HHTYPE: MrrdCpl, MaleFam, FemFam, MaleNonf, FemNonf
AGEMAR: 15-24, 25-34, 35-44, 45-54, 55-64, 65+
HOMEOWNER: Homeowner, Renter

IMMPOP.DAT

U.S. Population by race/ethnicity, gender, poverty, immigration status, and state

STATEUSA: CA, FL, IL, NJ, NY, TX, VT, RestofUS
IMMENTRY: Native, FB<1980, FB80-89, FB90-99, FB00-current
RACEETH: NHWhite, Black, Hispanic, Asian, AmIndian, NHOther, NHMulti
GENDER: Male, Female
POVLEVEL: Poverty, NearPoor, Middle, Comf

LAWYERS.DAT

Lawyers: full time, year round workers, race/ethnicity, gender, and earnings, age 25-64

RACEETH: NHWhite, Black, Asian, Hispanic, AmIndian, NHOther, NHMulti
GENDER: Male, Female
AGEPRO: 25-34, 35-44, 45-54, 55-64
EARN2: <40K, 40-54K, 55-69K, 70-84K, 85-99K, 100-124K, 125-149K, 150-199K, 200K+

MAR-M.DAT

Marital/cohab status for young men age 23-28

AGEYNG2: 23, 24, 25, 26, 27, 28
MARITAL3: NevMrrd, LivingTg, CurrMrrd, DivSepWid
EDUC: LTHS, HSGrad, SomeColl, CollGrad
RACEETH: NHWhite, Black, Hispanic, Asian, AmIndian, NHOther, NHMulti

MAR-W.DAT

Marital/cohab status for young women age 23-28

AGEYNG2: 23, 24, 25, 26, 27, 28
MARITAL3: NevMrrd, LivingTg, CurrMrrd, DivSepWid
EDUC: LTHS, HSGrad, SomeColl, CollGrad
RACEETH: NHWhite, Black, Hispanic, Asian, AmIndian, NHOther, NHMulti

MARASIAN.DAT

Marital status for Asian Alone by Asian groups, age 15+

ASIAN: Chinese, Japanese, Filipino, Korean, Indian, Vietnamese, Other
GENDER: Male, Female
AGEMAR: 15-24, 25-34, 35-44, 45-54, 55-64, 65+
MARITAL: CurrMrrd, Widowed, Divorced, Separated, NevMrrd

MAREDUC.DAT

Marital status by education, gender, and race/ethnicity, age 15+

AGEMAR: 15-24, 25-34, 35-44, 45-54, 55-64, 65+
GENDER: Male, Female
RACEETH: NHWhite, Black, Hispanic, Asian, AmIndian, NHOther, NHMulti
EDUC: LTHS, HSGrad, SomeColl, CollGrad

MARITAL: CurrMrrd, Widowed, Divorced, Separated, NevMrrd

MarEmp-W.dat
Marital/cohab status by Employment status for women age 25-34
RACEETH: NHWhite, Black, Hispanic, Asian, AmIndian, NHOther, NHMulti
EDUC: LTHS, HSGrad, SomeColl, CollGrad
MARITAL4: NevMrrd, LivingTg, CurrMrrd, Divorced, Separated, Widowed
EMP2: EmpFull, EmpPart, Unempd, NILF

Marital.dat
Marital status for age 15+
RACEETH: NHWhite, Black, Asian, Hispanic, AmIndian, NHOther, NHMulti
GENDER: Male, Female
AGEMAR: 15-24, 25-34, 35-44, 45-54, 55-64, 65+
MARITAL: CurrMrrd, Widowed, Divorced, Separated, NevMrrd

MarHisp.dat
Marital status for Hispanic groups, age 15+
HISPANIC: Mexican, PRican, Cuban, CAmeric, SAmeric, Other
GENDER: Male, Female
AGEMAR: 15-24, 25-34, 35-44, 45-54, 55-64, 65+
MARITAL: CurrMrrd, Widowed, Divorced, Separated, NevMrrd

MarPov-W.dat
Females by marital status, employment, and poverty, race/ethnicity, age 16+
AGEWORK: 16-24, 25-34, 35-44, 45-54, 55-64, 65+
MARITAL: CurrMrrd, Widowed, Divorced, Separated, NevMrrd
EMP2: EmpFull, EmpPart, Unempd, NILF
POV: Poverty, NonPov
RACEETH: NHWhite, Black, Hispanic, Asian, AmIndian, NHOther, NHMulti

Occup.dat
Occupations, age 16+
RACEETH: NHWhite, Black, Asian, Hispanic, AmIndian, NHOther, NHMulti
GENDER: Male, Female
AGEWORK: 16-24, 25-34, 35-44, 45-54, 55-64, 65+
OCCUP2: TopWC, OtherWC, Service, TopBC, OtherBC, Farm

OccupAsian.dat
Occupation and immigration status for Asian Alone by Asian groups, age 25-34
ASIAN: Chinese, Japanese, Filipino, Korean, Indian, Vietnamese, Other
GENDER: Male, Female
IMMENTRY: Native, FB<1980, FB80-89, FB90-99, FB00-current
OCCUP2: TopWC, OtherWC, Service, TopBC, OtherBC, Farm

OccupAsianAll.dat
Occupations for Asian Alone by Asian groups, age 16+
ASIAN: Chinese, Japanese, Filipino, Korean, Indian, Vietnamese, Other
GENDER: Male, Female
AGEWORK: 16-24, 25-34, 35-44, 45-54, 55-64, 65+
OCCUP2: TopWC, OtherWC, Service, TopBC, OtherBC, Farm

OccupHisp.dat

Occupation and immigration status for Hispanic groups, age 25-34

HISPANIC: Mexican, PRican, Cuban, CAmeric, SAmeric, Other
GENDER: Male, Female
IMMENTRY: Native, FB<1980, FB80-89, FB90-99, FB00-current
OCCUP2: TopWC, OtherWC, Service, TopBC, OtherBC, Farm

OccupHispALL.dat

Occupations for Hispanic groups, age 16+

HISPANIC: Mexican, PRican, Cuban, CAmeric, SAmeric, Other
GENDER: Male, Female
AGEWORK: 16-24, 25-34, 35-44, 45-54, 55-64, 65+
OCCUP2: TopWC, OtherWC, Service, TopBC, OtherBC, Farm

OccupImm-25.dat

Full-time year round workers by occupation, gender, immigration status, race/ethnicity, and education age 25-34

OCCUP: TopWC, OtherWC, Service, TopBC, OtherBC
GENDER: Male, Female
IMMENTRY: Native, FB<1980, FB80-89, FB90-99, FB00-current
RACEETH: NHWhite, Black, Hispanic, Asian, AmIndian, NHOther, NHMulti
EDUCALL: 0-9Yrs, 10-12Yrs, HSGrad, SomeColl CollGrad, Masters, PhD-Prof

OccupImm-35.dat

Full-time year round workers by occupation, gender, immigration status, race/ethnicity, and education age 35-44

OCCUP: TopWC, OtherWC, Service TopBC, OtherBC
GENDER: Male, Female
IMMENTRY: Native, FB<1980, FB80-89, FB90-99, FB00-current
RACEETH: NHWhite, Black, Hispanic, Asian, AmIndian, NHOther, NHMulti
EDUC: LTHS, HSGrad, SomeColl, CollGrad.

PopCA.dat

California population by age, gender, race/ethnicity and immigration status

RACEETH: NHWhite, Black, Asian, Hispanic, AmIndian, NHOther, NHMulti
IMMENTRY: Native, FB<1980, FB80-89, FB90-99, FB00-current
GENDER: Male, Female
AGEALL: 0-4, 5-14, 15-24, 25-34, 35-44, 45-54, 55-64, 65+

PopGA.dat

Georgia population by age, gender, race/ethnicity and immigration status

RACEETH: NHWhite, Black, Asian, Hispanic, AmIndian, NHOther, NHMulti
IMMENTRY: Native, FB<1980, FB80-89, FB90-99, FB00-current
GENDER: Male, Female
AGEALL: 0-4, 5-14, 15-24, 25-34, 35-44, 45-54, 55-64, 65+

PopGeo.dat

U.S. Population by age groups, metro, regions, and race/ethnicity
AGEALL: 0-4, 5-14, 15-24, 25-34, 35-44, 45-54, 55-64, 65+
GEO: City, Suburb, NonMetro
REGION: Northeast, Midwest, South, West
RACEETH: NHWhite, Black, Hispanic, Asian, AmIndian, NHOther, NHMulti

PopLacnty.dat

L.A. County population, age, gender, race/ethnicity and immigration status
RACEETH: NHWhite, Black, Asian, Hispanic, AmIndian, NHOther, NHMulti
IMMENTRY: Native, FB<1980, FB80-89, FB90-99, FB00-current
GENDER: Male, Female
AGEALL: 0-4, 5-14, 15-24, 25-34, 35-44, 45-54, 55-64, 65+

PopMI.dat

Michigan population by age, gender, race/ethnicity and immigration status
RACEETH: NHWhite, Black, Asian, Hispanic, AmIndian, NHOther, NHMulti
IMMENTRY: Native, FB<1980, FB80-89, FB90-99, FB00-current
GENDER: Male, Female
AGEALL: 0-4, 5-14, 15-24, 25-34, 35-44, 45-54, 55-64, 65+

PopProj.dat

Projected population by race/ethnicity, state, and age
AGEALL3: 0-17, 18-64, 65+
RACEETH3: NHWhite, Black, Hispanic, Asian, AmIndian
PROJYEAR: 1995, 2000, 2005, 2010, 2015, 2020
STATEUSA: CA, FL, IL, NJ, NY, TX, VT, RestofUS

PopUSA.dat

US population by age, gender, race/ethnicity and immigration status
RACEETH: NHWhite, Black, Asian, Hispanic, AmIndian, NHOther, NHMulti
IMMENTRY: Native, FB<1980, FB80-89, FB90-99, FB00-current
GENDER: Male, Female
AGEALL: 0-4, 5-14, 15-24, 25-34, 35-44, 45-54, 55-64, 65+

PovEduc.dat

U.S. Population by race/ethnicity, poverty, gender, and education, age 25+
RACEETH: NHWhite, Black, Hispanic, Asian, AmIndian, NHOther, NHMulti
POVLEVEL: Poverty, NearPoor, Middle, Comf
GENDER: Male, Female
AGEEDUC: 25-34, 35-44, 45-54, 55-64, 65+
EDUCALL: 0-9Yrs, 10-12Yrs, HSGrad, SomeColl, CollGrad, Masters, PhD-Prof

PovGeo.dat

U.S. Population by age groups, race/ethnicity, poverty, metro, and gender
RACEETH: NHWhite, Black, Hispanic, Asian, AmIndian, NHOther, NHMulti
POVLEVEL: Poverty, NearPoor, Middle, Comf
GENDER: Male, Female
AGEALL2: 0-5, 6-17, 18-24, 25-34, 35-44, 45-54, 55-64, 65+
GEO: City, Suburb, NonMetro

SPOAGE-M.DAT

Spouses: married men age 25 by education and wife's age 15-29+

H-RACEETH: NHWhite, Black, Hispanic, Asian, AmIndian, NHOther, NHMulti

H-EDUC: LTHS, HSGrad, SomeColl, CollGrad

W-AGE: <23, 23, 24, 25, 26, 27, 28, 29+

SPOAGE-W.DAT

Spouses: married women age 25 by education and husband's age 15-29+

W-RACEETH: NHWhite, Black, Hispanic, Asian, AmIndian, NHOther, NHMulti

W-EDUC: LTHS, HSGrad, SomeColl, CollGrad

H-AGE: <23, 23, 24, 25, 26, 27, 28, 29+

SPOEDUC.DAT

Spouses: husband and wife's education and race/ethnicity

H-RACEETH: NHWhite, Black, Hispanic, Asian, AmIndian, NHOther, NHMulti

W-RACEETH: NHWhite, Black, Hispanic, Asian, AmIndian, NHOther, NHMulti

H-EDUC: LTHS, HSGrad, SomeColl, CollGrad

W-EDUC: LTHS, HSGrad, SomeColl, CollGrad

SPOEDUC-M.DAT

Spouses: married men age 15+, by race/ethnicity and education, by wife's education

H-AGE3: 15-24, 25-34, 35-44, 45-54, 55-64, 65+

H-RACEETH: NHWhite, Black, Hispanic, Asian, AmIndian, NHOther, NHMulti

H-EDUC: LTHS, HSGrad, SomeColl, CollGrad

W-EDUC: LTHS, HSGrad, SomeColl, CollGrad

SPOEDUC-W.DAT

Spouses: married women age 15+, by race /ethnicity and education, by husband's education

W-AGE3: 15-24, 25-34, 35-44, 45-54, 55-64, 65+

W-RACEETH: NHWhite, Black, Hispanic, Asian, AmIndian, NHOther, NHMulti

W-EDUC: LTHS, HSGrad, SomeColl, CollGrad

H-EDUC: LTHS, HSGrad, SomeColl, CollGrad

SPORACE.DAT

Spouses: husband's and wife's age 15-45+ and husband's and wife's race/ethnicity

H-RACEETH: NHWhite, Black, Hispanic, Asian, AmIndian, NHOther, NHMulti

W-RACEETH: NHWhite, Black, Hispanic, Asian, AmIndian, NHOther, NHMulti

H-AGE2: 15-24, 25-34, 35-44, 45+

W-AGE2: 15-24, 25-34, 35-44, 45+

SPORACE-M.DAT

Spouses: married men age 15+, by education and race/ethnicity, by wife's race/ethnicity

H-AGE4: 15-24, 25-34, 35-44, 45-54, 55+

H-EDUC: LTHS, HSGrad, SomeColl, CollGrad

H-RACEETH: NHWhite, Black, Hispanic, Asian, AmIndian, NHOther, NHMulti

W-RACEETH: NHWhite, Black, Hispanic, Asian, AmIndian, NHOther, NHMulti

SPORACE-W.DAT

Spouses: married women age 15+, by education and race/ethnicity, by husband's race/ethnicity

W-AGE4: 15-24, 25-34, 35-44, 45-54, 55+
W-EDUC: LTHS, HSGrad, SomeColl, CollGrad
W-RACEETH: NHWhite, Black, Hispanic, Asian, AmIndian, NHOther, NHMulti
H-RACEETH: NHWhite, Black, Hispanic, Asian, AmIndian, NHOther, NHMulti

WORK.DAT

Work hours for workers, age 16+

RACEETH: NHWhite, Black, Hispanic, Asian, AmIndian, NHOther, NHMulti
GENDER: Male, Female
AGEWORK: 16-24, 25-34, 35-44, 45-54, 55-64, 65+
WORKHRS: Full35, 20-34, 10-19, <10

WORK-25.DAT

Full time, year round workers by education, occupation, and earnings, age 25-34

RACEETH2: NHWhite, Black, AllOther
GENDER: Male, Female
EDUC: LTHS, HSGrad, SomeColl, CollGrad
OCCUP3: TopWC, OtherWC, Service, BC
EARN: <25K, 25-34K, 35-49K, 50-69K, 70-99K, 100K+

WORK-35.DAT

Full time, year round workers by education, occupation, and earnings, age 35-44

RACEETH2: NHWhite, Black, AllOther
GENDER: Male, Female
EDUC: LTHS, HSGrad, SomeColl, CollGrad
OCCUP3: TopWC, OtherWC, Service, BC
EARN: <25K, 25-34K, 35-49K, 50-69K, 70-99K, 100K+

WORK-45.DAT

Full time, year round workers by education, occupation, and earnings, age 45-54

RACEETH2: NHWhite, Black, AllOther
GENDER: Male, Female
EDUC: LTHS, HSGrad, SomeColl, CollGrad
OCCUP3: TopWC, OtherWC, Service, BC
EARN: <25K, 25-34K, 35-49K, 50-69K, 70-99K, 100K+

WORKASIAN.DAT

Work hours by immigration status for Asian Alone by Asian groups, age 16-34

ASIAN: Chinese, Japanese, Filipino, Korean, Indian, Vietnamese, Other
GENDER: Male, Female
AGEWORK2: 16-24, 25-34
IMMENTRY: Native, FB<1980, FB80-89, FB90-99, FB00-current
WORKHRS: Full35, 20-34, 10-19, <10

WORKASIAN-25.DAT

Full-time year round Asian Alone by Asian workers by earnings, immigration status, education, occupation, and gender, age 25-34

EARN: <25K, 25-34K, 35-49K, 50-69K, 70-99K, 100K+
IMMENTRY: Native, FB<1980, FB80-89, FB90-99, FB00-current
EDUC: LTHS, HSGrad, SomeColl, CollGrad
OCCUP: TopWC, OtherWC, Service, TopBC, OtherBC
GENDER: Male, Female

WORKASIAN-35.DAT

Full-time year round Asian Alone by Asian workers by earnings, immigration status, education, occupation, and gender, age 35-44

EARN: <25K, 25-34K, 35-49K, 50-69K, 70-99K, 100K+
IMMENTRY: Native, FB<1980, FB80-89, FB90-99, FB00-current
EDUC: LTHS, HSGrad, SomeColl, CollGrad
OCCUP: TopWC, OtherWC, Service, TopBC, OtherBC

WORKASIANALL.DAT

Work hours for Asian Alone by Asian groups, age 16+

ASIAN: Chinese, Japanese, Filipino, Korean, Indian, Vietnamese, Other
GENDER: Male, Female
AGEWORK: 16-24, 25-34, 35-44, 45-54, 55-64, 65+
WORKHRS: Full35, 20-34, 10-19, <10

WORKEDUC.DAT

Work hours by race/ethnicity, gender, education, age 16+

RACEETH: NHWhite, Black, Hispanic, Asian, AmIndian, NHOther, NHMulti
GENDER: Male, Female
AGEWORK: 16-24, 25-34, 35-44, 45-54, 55-64, 65+
EDUC: LTHS, HSGrad, SomeColl, CollGrad
WORKHRS: Full35, 20-34, 10-19, <10

WORKHISP.DAT

Work hours by immigration status for Hispanic groups, age 16-34

HISPANIC: Mexican, PRican, Cuban, CAmeric, SAmeric, Other
GENDER: Male, Female
AGEWORK2: 16-24, 25-34
IMMENTRY: Native, FB<1980, FB80-89, FB90-99, FB00-current
WORKHRS: Full35, 20-34, 10-19, <10

WORKHISP-25.DAT

Full-time year round Hispanic workers by earnings, immigration status, education, occupation, and gender, age 25-34

EARN: <25K, 25-34K, 35-49K, 50-69K, 70-99K, 100K+
IMMENTRY: Native, FB<1980, FB80-89, FB90-99, FB00-current
EDUC: LTHS, HSGrad, SomeColl, CollGrad
OCCUP: TopWC, OtherWC, Service, TopBC, OtherBC
GENDER: Male, Female

WORKHISP-35.DAT

Full-time year round Hispanic workers by earnings, immigration status, education, occupation, and gender, age 35-44

EARN: <25K, 25-34K, 35-49K, 50-69K, 70-99K, 100K+
IMMENTRY: Native, FB<1980, FB80-89, FB90-99, FB00-current
EDUC: LTHS, HSGrad, SomeColl, CollGrad
OCCUP: TopWC, OtherWC, Service, TopBC, OtherBC
GENDER: Male, Female

WORKHISPALL.DAT

Work hours for Hispanic groups, age 16+

HISPANIC: Mexican, PRican, Cuban, CAmeric, SAmeric, Other
GENDER: Male, Female
AGEWORK: 16-24, 25-34, 35-44, 45-54, 55-64, 65+
WORKHRS: Full35, 20-34, 10-19, <10

WORKIMM-25.DAT

Full-time year round workers by earnings, immigration status, education, occupation, and gender, age 25-34

EARN: <25K, 25-34K, 35-49K, 50-69K, 70-99K, 100K+
IMMENTRY: Native, FB<1980, FB80-89, FB90-99, FB00-current
EDUC: LTHS, HSGrad, SomeColl, CollGrad
OCCUP: TopWC, OtherWC, Service, TopBC, OtherBC
GENDER: Male, Female

WORKIMM-35.DAT

Full-time year round workers by earnings, immigration status, education , occupation, and gender, age 35-44

EARN: <25K, 25-34K, 35-49K, 50-69K, 70-99K, 100K+
IMMENTRY: Native, FB<1980, FB80-89, FB90-99, FB00-current
EDUC: LTHS, HSGrad, SomeColl, CollGrad
OCCUP: TopWC, OtherWC, Service, TopBC, OtherBC
GENDER: Male, Female